THE HIDDEN HISTORY OF LIBRARY MUSIC

THE HIDDEN HISTORY OF LIBRARY MUSIC

BY DAVID HOLLANDER

Edited by Mark Iosifescu and Dominic Masi, Jr.
Additional texts by Mark Iosifescu

ANTHOLOGY EDITIONS
NEW YORK

TABLE OF CONTENTS

PREFACE 7
David Hollander

FOREWORD 8
George A. Romero

INTRODUCTION 17
David Hollander

BRITISH LIBRARIES 31

- KPM 33
- Robin Phillips 55
- Peter Cox 57
- Adrian Kerridge 58
- Bruton Music 61
- Keith Mansfield 67
- Johnny Pearson 76
- Alan Hawkshaw 78
- John Cameron 86
- Brian Bennett 93
- Ron Geesin 94
- Les Baxter 99
- Delia Derbyshire 100
- Themes International 103
- Alan Parker 107
- Madeline Bell 109
- Alan Tew 110
- Music De Wolfe 112
- Amphonic Music 119
- Sven Libaek 121
- Peer / Southern 122
- Josef Weinberger / Impress 124
- Tod Dockstader 126
- Conroy Recorded Music Library 133

GERMAN LIBRARIES 135

- Sonoton 137
- Gerhard Narholz 149
- Coloursound 156
- Joel Vandroogenbroeck 159
- Klaus Weiss 163
- Selected Sound 165

FRENCH LIBRARIES 171

- Montparnasse 2000 173
- Janko Nilović 182
- Jean-Jacques Perrey / Pat Prilly 190
- Les Structures Sonores Lasry-Baschet / Teddy Lasry 192
- Yan Tregger (Ted Scotto) 196
- L'Illustration Musicale 202
- Tele Music 204
- Musique pour l'Image 206
- Bernard Parmegiani 208

ITALIAN LIBRARIES 211

- Romano di Bari 213
- Flipper 220
- CAM 222
- Stelvio Cipriani 228
- Fabio Frizzi 230
- Stefano Torossi 231
- Giampiero Boneschi 232
- Ennio Morricone 233
- Alessandro Alessandroni 234
- Piero Umiliani 237
- Omicron 239
- Fonit: Serie Usignolo 249
- Gemelli 250
- Jump 251
- Leonardi 257
- Daniela Casa 263

NORTH AMERICAN LIBRARIES 275

- Parry Music Library 277
- Emil Ascher Library 278
- Jean-Michel Jarre 281
- Ebonite 282

FILM & TELEVISION 287

ACKNOWLEDGMENTS 313

INDEX 315

PREFACE

—

DAVID HOLLANDER

My strange journey through the world of library music began more than twenty years ago in the bins of Record Supply in West Los Angeles. While browsing the soundtrack section, I came across a stack of LPs in generic sleeves, all with the same logo on the label. They were from the Major Records Production Music Library, and the music on them was sublime. Some of the composers' names were vaguely familiar, like Italian film composer Mario Nascimbene, but others—Roger Roger, Sam Spence, and Piero Umiliani—were less so. My interest piqued, I started searching for more. And so began a long slide into my becoming singularly obsessed with and totally consumed by this peculiar brand of utilitarian music, created for films that did not yet exist, and listened to carefully only by those who select and edit music into films, television, and radio. As I delved deeper, I began to put a face on this otherwise faceless, obscure music.

As my collection of library music grew to thousands of LPs, I became interested in reissuing some of the music contained therein. I reached out to Thomas and Frank Valentino, the jovial brothers in New Jersey whose father had created the Major Records library, and found them amenable to the project. That resulted in *Cinemaphonic: Electro Soul*, a collection of tracks from the Major Library which was received in the US and UK with great enthusiasm. Prior to *Electro Soul*, there had been some excellent reissues of European library music; some of the libraries in the UK, France, Italy, and Germany are well-known to collectors there. But *Cinemaphonic* marked the first time US-originated library records had reached a large international audience. From that point, it was not long before I was working as a music supervisor / music editor, exclusively using vintage library music on shows for Cartoon Network and feature films like *Black Dynamite*.

As a library music collector, I wondered how rare library records really were—did the various library companies still have dead stock of their LPs? And as a music supervisor working with vintage library, I wanted to know if the libraries had archived their master tapes, and if any of the music had been digitized. In the summer of 2002, I made my first pilgrimage to Europe to visit some of the major library music archives in Europe, hoping to discover more music. That first trip took to me to EMI (then headquartered at Charing Cross in London), EMI Hamburg, and Sonoton in Munich; two years later, I went to Rome as well. It was an inspiring voyage that included meeting some of the great, now elderly composers and producers of the library world. The trip also afforded me a glimpse into the dusty archives housing endless shelves of reel-to-reel tapes, and the studios where the music was made back in the day.

A small group of music lovers, DJs, and producers have turned on to vintage library music samples in a big way, making the extant LPs some of the most sought-after artifacts in the record collecting universe. Although they were never commercially released, many library LPs have found new life in the hands of a dedicated legion of hardcore collectors. Still, much remains opaque about these eccentric records. This book is meant to serve as an introduction to this extraordinarily ordinary category of music for everyone outside of the hermetic world of record collectors.

FOREWORD

—

GEORGE A. ROMERO

OPPOSITE

Romero on the set of 1985's *Day of the Dead*. Image courtesy Everett Collection.

I have always loved movie music. As a boy, I remember seeing a film called *Captain from Castile* (1947). Beautiful Technicolor cinematography (Arling and Clarke), beautiful people (Tyrone Power, Jean Peters, Cesar Romero), and beautiful music; *sensational* music (Alfred Newman).

This film isn't remembered in cinema studies classes. It was a pulpy, sexy bit of revisionism in which Cortez is portrayed as a hero instead of the marauding fortune hunter that history more accurately describes him as having been. So why do I have such affection for this piece of commercial fluff?

Well, it was my father who first took me to see the film, at the RKO Castle Hill in the Bronx. (He was quick to point out that Cesar Romero shared our family name.) Born a Castilian himself, raised in Cuba from age two, my dad longed to return to Spain even though he had no recollection of the place. He had come to New York City to attend college. He was a talented artist, but there were few jobs. He was an amazing tennis player—could have become a pro—but there was no money in tennis in those days. He hired on as an usher in a Times Square movie theater. The lady at the box office was named Anne Dvorsky, a Lithuanian. In typical "melting pot" fashion, Anne and my dad got married.

I remember my dad proudly telling a story about Basil Rathbone coming to the theater where he and my mom worked. Rathbone had come to see *The Adventures of Robin Hood* (1938—score by Korngold), presumably to bask in his own glory. (As my dad told it, Basil was hoping to be recognized.) My mom was a real "looker" and, apparently, Mr. Rathbone put some serious moves on her. My mom told Hollywood's Supreme Villain that she was already committed to a "fella." My dad hoped that he was that fella. As it turned out, he was. (Icing on the cake: Mr. Rathbone brought two Russian wolfhounds to the theater that evening, fully expecting that they would be granted admittance. My dad got to deliver the manager's message: "*No dogs are allowed!*")

My dad held down three jobs for as long as I can remember: he worked at the New York post office, sorting mail (he didn't get home on weekdays until nearly midnight); he was a radio man in the Naval Reserve (when I was in college, he was flying into Vietnam); and he was a "layout man" at the National Flag Company. He designed and built those cloth banners that used to announce that a building was "AIR-CONDITIONED" or that a store was currently having a "LABOR DAY SALE!" (My dad designed and built the largest American flag ever manufactured at that time. It covered the entire front wall of Macy's, on 34th. It made headlines when it was torn apart by high winds.)

Many of the banners my dad designed were done for New York movie theaters. But occasionally a request came in for a banner that was meant to hype a specific film. (I specifically remember my dad objecting to the grammar in the ads for one film. The ads said, "*The Birds* Is Coming." My dad felt that it should have read "*The Birds* ARE Coming.")

NIGHT OF THE LIVING DEAD
VHS

NIGHT OF THE LIVING DEAD
NIGHT OF THE LIVING DEAD
Starring JUDITH O'DEA • DUANE JONES
• MARYLYN EASTMAN •
KARL HARDMAN • JUDITH RIDLEY • KEITH WAYNE
Produced by Russel W. Streiner and Karl Hardman • Directed by
George A. Romero • Screenplay by John A. Russo
MEDIA
MEDIA HOME ENTERTAINMENT, INC.

NIGHT OF THE LIVING DEAD
★ Duanne Jones ★ Judith O'Dea
★ Russel Streiner

NIGHT OF THE LIVING DEAD
STARRING
Duanne Jones
Judith O'Dea
Russel Streiner
VHS

OPPOSITE

Four home video copies of *Night of the Living Dead* (dir. George A. Romero, 1968). *Clockwise from top left*: Good Times Video, 1984. Media Home Entertainment, Inc., 1982. Memory Lane Video, 1984. Video Treasures, no date.

The stark, black-and-white graphics designed by Saul Bass (*Exodus*, *Anatomy of a Murder*, *Bunny Lake Is Missing*) lent themselves to reproduction in cloth. My dad got to meet Otto Preminger when the maestro came to approve the banners for *The Man with the Golden Arm.* My dad used to bring home stills—8 x 10, 11 x 14 promo pieces that he could cull for images he might be able to use. I coveted those photos, brought them to school, became a "show-off" (hey, it kept me from gettin' my ass kicked).

When I look back, as I am doing now, I realize that in my youth... shit, even before I was *born*... I was connected, in a distant way, to movies. In the early days—the *way* early days—of television, my dad went out and rented a receiver for a week. It was an unwieldy contraption with no cabinet, wires exposed, and tubes mounted in a metal chassis. The largest of those tubes was the "picture tube," of course. Circular, not rectangular, it dominated the device, Cyclops-like, as if demanding attention. (Little did anyone realize, back then, that a descendant of that "video contraption" would still be demanding attention today... and getting all too much of it.)

Back in the day, there was basically nothing on that tube that warranted attention. Daily newspapers would post not *what* was on TV, but *when* there was *anything* on at *all*! The night after my dad brought home that "newfangled gizmo," the *New York Journal-American*, on one of its back pages, indicated that, that evening, something—I can't remember exactly how it was characterized; I believe it read something like "A Special Programming Event"—was to be. I remember my dad telling me, in the Spanish accent to which he clung for the rest of his days: "*Summthin' is comin' at sevin-on-the-clock*."

That "summthin'" turned out to be a film directed, in part, by Michael Powell. It was *The Thief of Bagdad*, a fantasy borrowed from the *Arabian Nights* tales, complete with giant spiders, flying carpets, genies, and Sabu, "the Elephant Boy." Wow! I ate it *up*! I was able to watch a real *movie* in my *living room*... and it was a *cool* movie! There was this silly little ditty that Sabu sang. It has replayed in my head ever since: "*I want to be a sailor sailing on the sea*." Music. That film is chock-full of marvelous visual images, but what I remember *most* is the music.

Back to *Captain from Castile.* Though my dad was disappointed with its representation of Cortez, of the Spanish Inquisition, of the way Spain itself was portrayed as evil, the kid sitting beside him (me) was utterly engrossed. As I've mentioned, it's a handsome film, worthy of admiration for its pulchritude alone, but what captivated me most was the *music*! In fact, *Captain from Castile* won acknowledgment from the Academy in only one category. It was Oscar-nominated for best "Music Score of a Dramatic or Comedy Picture." (Miklos Rozsa won for *A Double Life.* I could go on about Rozsa, but this foreword is already too long.)

Imagine my joy and amazement when my mother took me to a record store, one of those where customers could step into sound-

OPPOSITE

Production still from *Night of the Living Dead*.

proof booths and use a private turntable to sample records. While Mom was in one of those booths sampling the flipside of "(How Much Is) That Doggie in the Window," I was wandering the aisles. Something caught my eye: a photo of Tyrone Power, sword in hand, leather gloves with cuffs the size of elephant ears. It was an image I instantly recognized: the poster image for *Captain from Castile.* Right there, in my local record store, they were selling the musical score from the film... a score that I'd naively believed myself to be the only one ever to have noticed. (I wasn't getting the Academy newsletters back then). I wanted to buy it. My allowance was fifty cents. Not enough. My mom suggested that I could sample it. She bought that Patti Paige flipside just so I would be allowed access to the sampling booth.

There were three records. Not "LPs"; regular 78-rpm discs, ten-inchers. I dropped a needle on the "Overture." I skipped carefully to "A Warning." Then to "Prison Escape." Every passage, every note, brought a moment from the film into mind.

Informed by that experience, I have since deduced that if music from a film can evoke such vivid recollections of the film itself—such equivalent emotions—then the composers of that music are almost as important as the scriptwriters and filmmakers.

Many filmmakers argue that they don't need music to support their messages. True. Another "guilty pleasure" from my youth was *King Solomon's Mines* (1950): no score at all. And then there was *Fail Safe* (1964), which generated Hitchcock-like suspense without a single note of music. But when there *is* music and when that music *works*, it helps define the personality of a film—even, in some cases, to describe its purpose. (*The Bridge on the River Kwai*, for example. And how can we forget *Jaws*?)

When I first encountered that album of music from *Captain from Castile*, I never realized that its appearance on the shelf was one of the earliest acknowledgments of film music's value. Today, there are entire sections in the aisles of music shops that are labeled "Film Music" or simply "Soundtracks." I can list the ones that move me (*The Best Years of Our Lives*, *King's Row*, *Green Dolphin Street*), the ones that stir me (*The Guns of Navarone*, *The Great Escape*, *The Magnificent Seven*), the ones that never fail to make me cry (*To Kill a Mockingbird*, *Spartacus*, *The Quiet Man*—whenever I play the original score from *The Quiet Man*, somewhere between the first and fourth notes I begin to weep; it's such a wonderful film and the music makes my long forgotten Catholicism tug at my heart, seeming to say, "This is the way the world was meant to be!").

Music is the perfect art form. When we hear it, we rarely recognize that it has a purpose, unless it is some sort of anthem. We hear a melody and we instantly develop an affinity or a dislike, both completely personal. We interpret music through the filter of our own life experiences. But, for the composer, there is an elusive ingredient in the recipe, like Mama's "*A little bit o' this, a little bit o' that*," which informs his or her talent and enables that composer

to find... to find... What is it? It's amorphous. A feeling, at best. A twitch of some ephemeral nerve that suddenly produces exactly the right notes.

When I made my first film, *Night of the Living Dead*, in 1968, I found myself with barely enough of a budget to complete the project, let alone hire a composer. The finished film played... *mmm*, pretty well, but something was missing. It needed music. Several friends of mine and myself had a small production company at the time, the Latent Image, which was surviving on beer commercials, industrial films, and the like. In order to make *Night of the Living Dead*, we partnered up with an audio production company, Hardman and Associates. (Karl Hardman ended up playing the despicable Harry Cooper in the film. Marilyn Eastman and Judith Ridley, both "Hardmanites," ended up playing Helen Cooper and Judy. This was truly a homegrown production.)

As it turned out, Karl's audio company had hundreds... I might say thousands (it *seemed* like thousands)... of records, vinyl discs that contained countless hours of music. None of it was specific to any film, but there were passages titled "Anticipation," "Suspense," "Sudden Shock."

The composers of all this music had conjured the needs of low-budget filmmakers and had provided scores that could be bought for a fraction of what it might cost to hire a composer and / or an orchestra. Each "needle drop" cost a prescribed amount of money that was easily affordable. (The collection that Karl had in house was the Capitol Hi-Q library.)

All of a sudden, *Night of the Living Dead* inherited a score. Karl and I spent days, weeks, months listening to tracks. I pulled out musical candidates and would bring them back to my editing room to audition them against scenes from the film. Informed, I suppose, by *Captain from Castile*, *Mockingbird*, and *The Quiet Man*, I constructed a score that I believed to be not only cohesive but supportive of the film's narrative. I like to think that I, with Karl's help, pulled passages from those library tracks that served our film almost as well as if we had been able to hire a composer.

I've since worked with composers on "original scores" (Donald Rubinstein on *Knightriders* and *Bruiser*, John Harrison on *Creepshow* and *Day of the Dead*—a score I consider to be nearly flawless), but let me tell you: As a filmmaker who grew up on Alfred Newman, Bernard Herrmann, Victor Young, it is difficult, almost *impossible*, to communicate an idea, *your* idea, which comes from deep inside you somewhere, to another artist. With Donald and John, there was a kind of magic. Maybe we knew each other well enough to make unspoken, visceral connections. But I remember culling through those library tracks and selecting exactly the music that I felt was right for each specific scene in the film. No communicating required. No translating. Karl and I made the picks.

When we made *Dawn of the Dead*, the wonderful Italian filmmaker Dario Argento was one of our partners. He brought in a group called Goblin to score the Italian version of the film. When I listened to the tracks, I thought some of their music was "hot," but some of it missed the mark, as far as I was concerned. For the US release of the film, I abandoned Goblin in many scenes and went with library tracks. One of them, "The Gonk," has become the theme song for the film.

When you're finishing a film, you normally use a "temp track," music that you lift from movies that you have admired over the years. When working with a composer, your first attempt to communicate usually involves showing him or her your movie with that temp track. You've lived with that music in some cases for *months*! You've come to *love* it! How can you express to a composer what it is that you love about it? It's all about emotion, isn't it? "*How do you hold a moonbeam in your hand?*" (That's a lyric that makes me cry.)

Some filmmakers have enough clout to insist that their temp tracks be used in the final product instead of music that has been composed and often already recorded at great expense. ("Zarathustra" in *2001: A Space Odyssey* and "Tubular Bells" in *The Exorcist* were temp tracks that survived to become iconic.) I like to believe that Friedkin and Kubrick were so aware of the effects of film music that they were not willing to compromise. They chose music that was not composed expressly for their films but seemed to be appropriate. In a way, that's no different from what I was doing when Karl Hardman and I listened to thousands of recordings and selected the few that we believed might enhance *Night of the Living Dead*.

As someone who knows, or *thinks* he knows, what film music is meant to do, I'm here to testify that the unknown, unsung artists who compose, conduct, and perform library tracks are heroes. Without a script, they imagine love and hate, enmity and friendliness, salvation and damnation, and are able to express them in the most abstract of mediums. The sounds that result—however abstract—strike something within us that is built-in, hardwired... an elusive, indefinable trigger that makes us laugh, makes us cry, makes us want to dance.

I made a film. It wasn't complete without music. We scored it with library tracks that greatly contributed to the film's success. There is actually a soundtrack album available on vinyl. It might be the only commercially distributed film score that is composed entirely of library music.

Thank you, guys... whoever you are. I think back to the first soundtrack album I ever saw, *Captain from Castile*, and I can hardly believe that I made a movie that appears in many of the same cinema journals... and I did it without Alfred Newman.

I owe a lot to a lot of people. A big part of what I owe must go to you: the composers, arrangers, and musicians who never even saw my first film, but who, drawing on their own imaginations, were able to conjure up musical passages that put meat on the bones of *Night of the Living Dead.* The film would be greatly diminished without their contributions. I don't know their names, nor did they ever know mine, but we made beautiful music together.

George A. Romero
Toronto, July 2016

A SHORT INTRODUCTION TO LIBRARY MUSIC

—

DAVID HOLLANDER

Library music is, simply defined, incidental film music ready-made for film, television, and radio production and used instead of, or in addition to, an original musical score. Also known as "production" or "cue" music, library music has been around since the dawn of commercial media—before television, library 78s were "spun in" to live radio broadcasts—and it continues to be made and widely used today. But library music really blossomed and branched out in the '60s and '70s, a golden age of television and genre filmmaking where increased production led to a need for more and more soundtrack music. Enterprising composers began churning out tunes to meet the demand, and producers eagerly exploited the new stream of cheap, ready-made scores that were available for a fraction of the cost of recording music themselves. Sleaze, drama, sports, educational films—legions of anonymous musicians set to work producing imagined soundtracks for every possible genre of filmed entertainment.

The basic business model was simple. Music libraries would set up recording sessions where everyone involved—composer, musician, producer, and engineer—was working "for hire." While deals were usually based on a revenue share between the library and the composer, production costs were kept way down, and the library would act as administrator, distributing the music to potential customers on LP, and generating all the necessary paperwork. This streamlined the licensing process, so production music libraries could offer music for film / television / radio synchronization at a much cheaper rate, one well below the cost of creating original music for a given project.

Library music was never made available to the average consumer. The music was available for preview only on LPs that were either loaned or sold exclusively to producers of film, television, and radio; at the time, the library music companies probably never dreamed that anyone else would be interested in it. When a track was selected for use, a dub of the master tape would be made and sent off to the client. After the LPs had outlived their usefulness, they were either thrown out or sent back to the library, relegated to becoming obsolete objects that would sit, neglected, in company archives for years until they were ultimately disposed of—or rescued by a collector.

Sometimes the use of library music was less clearly defined, serving as a temporary soundtrack for a film or television project in order to help shape the director's creative vision. Tracks would be selected and synchronized during editing just to create a specific mood, or to suggest to the composer what kind of original music might work for the sequence; some directors still use library music this way. It's also not unusual for the "temp mix" to be left in place and actually used in the final picture.

When making library music, composers were tasked with describing specific kinds of narrative action or creating a particular mood. They had to meet specific criteria pertaining to narrative: volume, tempo, instrumentation, and track length. They were given general notes about the potential usage for their music, like "drama"

OPPOSITE

Shelves of master tapes from the Conroy library, housed at EMI's Charing Cross offices in London until a recent move to deep storage.

or "industry." Often they were left to their own devices to spontaneously create. In essence, library musicians were required to invent films made of sound, and this demanded a high level of innovation and experimentation—not to mention technical expertise. Most of the artists working on library music were skilled session players working in total obscurity, but the high demand for material gave more visionary musicians the opportunity to break into composing—a dream that would have been much harder to achieve in the world of pop music.

Without the pressure to generate "hits," young library composers were free to play around and experiment, and they took full advantage. The need for speed in production contributed to the ethos of spontaneous creativity. Genres were spliced, conventions dispensed with, and oftentimes hybrid music of astonishing complexity was produced. Elements of rock, jazz, soul, even twentieth-century avant-garde composition were all utilized, and no stone was left unturned. As a result, some of the best library music defies all categorization, reflecting the individualistic quirks and artistry of the various musicians who made it.

On the other hand, originality was not exactly encouraged. One primary use for library music in film is as "source" music—i.e., music that happens within the diegetic universe of the film, coming from a car radio, or as muzak being piped in. Hence, libraries sought to create and contain every kind of music possible, from country western to classical to rock and roll. The producers mandated that if a certain kind of music existed, there had to be a library analog of it—they even ordered the creation of "sound-alikes" of popular tunes. Clever composers would then change a note or two to transform a song like "Hey Jude," which would have been prohibitively expensive for budget-conscious filmmakers to license, into an accessible and cheap copycat version. It was all business, but this was still the world of music; by all accounts it was a fast, fun, lucrative, and hard-drinking scene that enabled a good number of talented musicians to spend nearly all their waking hours making music.

While there is a wealth of oddball and completely original, indefinable library music out there, it was in the area of genre filmmaking that library music made an indelible imprint on popular culture. Sci-fi, horror, educational, and even porn films all used library music extensively. And it was in the genre of crime films—the *policier*, the Italian gangster film, and the blaxploitation film—where certain library music (like Alan Tew's music for *The Hanged Man*) rises to the level of being unique and memorable. Composers and performers from the UK, Italy, France, and Germany all created iconic crime jazz that wound up in use as library music in film, television, and radio all over the world.

Adult films from the '70s also leaned heavily on library music; hearing a well-known library track during a classic porno film adds to the charm of the genre. One of my favorite uses of library music in erotic film is Madeline Bell's "You Got What It Takes," which plays during a lesbian seduction in a discotheque between Annette Haven

115A LONDONS UNDERGROUND 11
116A SWINGING BAROQUE
116B SWINGING BAROQUE
117A KLAUS WEISS SOUNDS
119A ROCKMAN MOOG
119B ROCKMAN MOOG
120A CHILDREN'S CORNER
121A BACKGROUND ACTION
122B MULTI-TRACKS
123A K. RAUTENBERG ELECTRONIC

and C.J. Laing in the 1977 classic *Barbara Broadcast*, directed by Henry Paris (aka Radley Metzger). My guess is that this particular track wound up in a lot of porno films. Another enjoyable instance of library in porn is the theme song from the film *Sex World*, which actually uses a track from the Selected Sound library ("Highway Patrol") but adds a kitschy masculine male vocal over the tune.

All known genres of music are represented in library music, but, curiously, there is an overabundance of electronic music. The increase in electronic library albums ran concurrent with the proliferation of low-cost analog electronic synthesizers in recording studios around the world. It also corresponds to the decline of the orchestral model for recording music, prefiguring the explosion of home-based music recording where a single individual in a small studio is capable of turning out a substantial body of work. Some of the most unique library LPs are solo and small-group electronic efforts: Cecil Leuter's *Pop Électronique* on Neuilly, and the countless all-electronic solo LPs of Giampiero Boneschi are some of the most distinctive electronic records ever made. Also worth checking out are the library LPs made by Klaus Weiss on Selected Sound, *Time Signals* and *Sound Inventions*—unbelievable solo drum / synth workouts by the great German jazz drummer of "Niagara" fame. For fans of electronic children's music and the melted Moog sound, there are five LPs on Montparnasse 2000 by Jean-Jacques Perrey and his daughter Pat Prilly that are superlative. Perrey was even able to work his magic on tracks that were meant not for cartoons but for more dramatic material. I wonder if these tracks were ever synchronized, and my guess is that, like a lot of the best library music, they were not, being too anachronistic for film or television use.

In my travels to the various library music archives in Europe, one surprising thing became clear: The majority of the best vintage library tracks have not been digitized, and most likely never will be. Much of the best material was never chosen for use in a soundtrack, so it was shelved. In the eyes of the massive corporations who hold the rights for these records, if the music hasn't yet been synchronized, it never will be. There is a thriving niche reissue market, but the returns are too small to motivate large companies to spend the time and money needed to create a digital archive of the material. And it *is* a daunting task; the KPM 1000 series, currently administered by EMI, was recently completely digitized (as were other KPM-related series, including the KPM Brownsleeves and Themes International), but this is the exception to the rule. Additional EMI-administered libraries, including the superlative German library Coloursound, as well as Selected Sound and Conroy, will soon be fully digitized under the careful stewardship of the UK-based EMI Production Music, but most of the obscure and interesting material from libraries across Europe will probably never be digitally archived—the publishing rights for these records are still acquired and absorbed by giants like EMI and Universal, but many companies just don't see the point of archiving "dead" assets. Instead, select cuts are digitized and repackaged on CD, in sometimes appalling forms (i.e., as kitschy muzak). In fact, because of changes in the laws surrounding music publishing, the publishing rights for much of this material have reverted back to the composers (or remain in a kind of limbo), and the task of recapturing those rights is expensive and time-consuming. As a result, new library music that is meant to mimic vintage library is made, and, without fail, always misses the mark. All the same, that newly created "vintage" library music is still widely used and accepted.

In talking to the various library owners and administrators, I was shocked to discover that many of the most synchronized and revenue-generating library tracks are not the ones of interest to the library collector of today. I truly wonder if a library masterpiece like the Peer library LP *Mind Bender* by Stringtronics was ever synchronized (it probably was), and I'd be willing to bet money that not one second of the massive output of sublime solo electronic music by Giampiero Boneschi was ever used in a film. Admittedly, most library music makes for difficult listening, and quite a bit of it is profoundly banal or just plain bad; the gems are few and far between. There are entire LPs of stings, links, and bridges (cuts just seconds long), and entire LPs of solo instruments producing a single note (useful in music- and sound editing). In reality, given that the library music user paid up front to use specific cues and that was the end of it, the library companies did not keep records of who used what tracks in which films. So the process of forensically determining what vintage library music was used where is painstaking and often impossible.

The vast majority of library music used during the explosion of genre films of the 1960s and '70s came from Europe. At that time, the musicians' unions in the United States were powerful, and they frowned upon musicians giving up the rights to their compositions in buyouts by the libraries. Consequently, it took many years for United States–based libraries to gain traction, while US administrators of European libraries such as Emil Ascher were doing a brisk business. Libraries in each European country tended to impart a regional style or twist to the American popular music they were imitating. For example, if an Italian library called for a James Brown–sounding cue, then somehow the Italian version will have a quirky, distinctly Italian take on the form. Italian library music, no matter what the particular type of music, is nuanced by regional style and borrows heavily from leitmotifs found in Italian classical and folk music.

Italy, France, Germany, and the UK were by far the biggest purveyors of library music in Europe. Italy had scores of libraries, but the largest were the RCA and Creazioni Artistiche Musicali (CAM). CAM is the music publisher and soundtrack label responsible for recording and releasing most of the classic Italian film soundtracks, including the Nino Rota scores for the films of Federico Fellini. At some point in the late '60s, CAM developed their production music library. Unlike the majority of libraries, which recorded music specifically for use as library music, CAM repurposed preexisting soundtracks to make up their two-hundred-plus LP library. The CAM library is without question the single best library from Italy, although there are countless amazing individual library LPs from

TOP

Bruno Nicolai, Claude Bolling, François de Roubaix, Paul Misraki. *Atmosphere Caracteristique*. CAM (Italy): CmL 078, 1974.

BOTTOM

Giampiero Boneschi. *A New Sensation in Sound Vol. 1.* CAM (Italy): CmL 043, 1973.

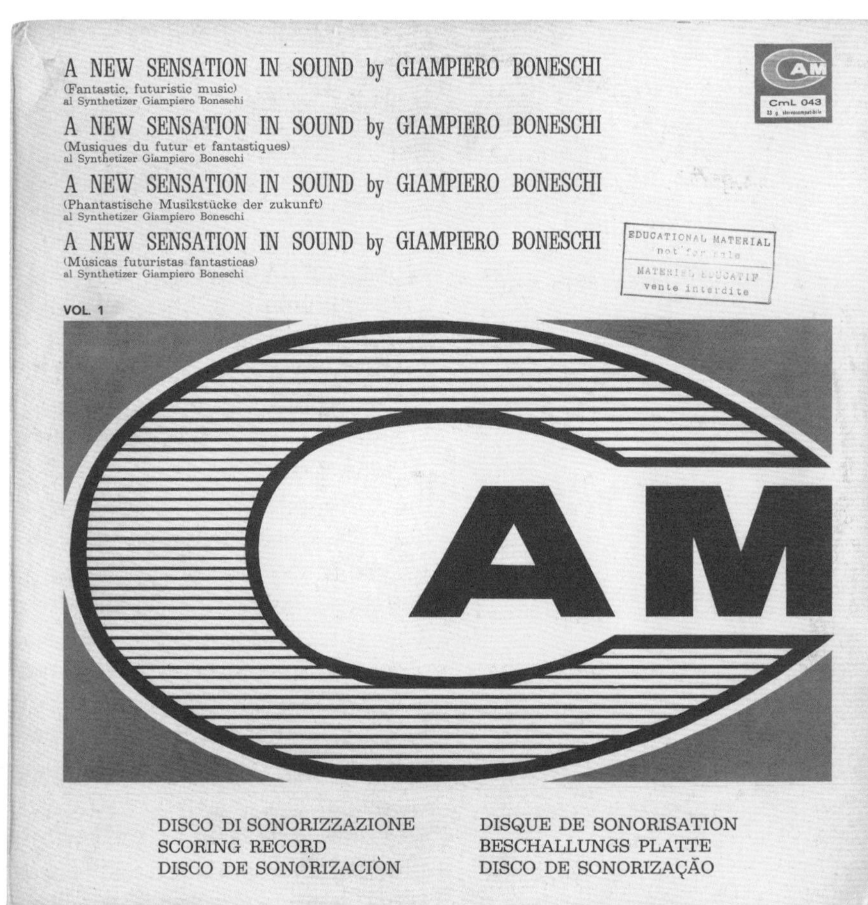

smaller publishers and labels, like Flipper, founded in 1972 by Romano di Bari. Both the RCA and CAM libraries have tracks by Italian soundtracks luminaries like Ennio Morricone, Bruno Nicolai, Stelvio Cipriani, Franco Micalizzi, and Carlo Rustichelli. Some of Micalizzi's work on the RCA library has found its way into contemporary American television—it was used to great effect in HBO's *Curb Your Enthusiasm*.

Montparnasse 2000 is probably the largest and most recognizable library from France, but there are a number of others worth noting. Eddie Warner's L'Illustration Musicale (IM) has a multitude of stunning releases, and labels like Musique pour l'Image (MPI), Neuilly, and Patchwork all contain various nuggets of true library genius. In addition to amazing work by Camille Sauvage, Jacky Giordano, and Teddy Lasry (to name a few), Montparnasse 2000 has some excellent library LPs made by Janko Nilović; standouts include *Rythmes Contemporains* and *Chorus*. Nilović was a Montenegrin-born composer whose output is made up largely of library releases, some of which were so popular that they were released commercially in France in the day, and have been reissued in whole LP form in recent years.

Some of the French and Italian labels were even able to convince well-known avant-garde musicians to produce library LPs, resulting in unusual and stellar library releases by Bernard Parmegiani, François de Roubaix, and Jacques Lasry. There was even some cultural cross-pollination, in the form of Montparnasse 2000's sub-label of Italian music, St Germain des Prés, which was actually Italian material on the Flipper label repurposed for use in France and beyond. Similarly, the Italian CAM library incorporated several LPs recorded in France by French musicians into their CmL series.

Germany, in particular Munich, was at the center of the explosion of library music in the late '60s and '70s. Much of the library music (German and otherwise) of the period was recorded in Munich, and in the case of the British library Conroy, recorded using German and British composers and session players. The single largest independent German library is Sonoton, but others worth noting are Selected Sound and Coloursound.

As might be expected of German libraries, all the master tapes at Sonoton in Munich and EMI in Hamburg were well archived, safely preserved, and shelved in meticulous order. The Coloursound catalog, administered by EMI, has been, for all intents and purposes, completely inactive up to this point. This intriguing library is housed in the basement of EMI Hamburg, and I went there to investigate the status of its master tapes. They were housed in a clean and well-organized archive, and were certainly being well looked after. The folks at EMI Hamburg generously shared their time with me, but I got the sense that they were a little puzzled as to why anyone would care about the material. Back in the day, the music enjoyed only limited success, and at this point the owners of a lot of this music simply do not care about it—they see it as a dead relic of the past, and view the current niche interest in vintage library as an anomaly. Nevertheless, Coloursound is one

OPPOSITE

Camille Sauvage. *Fantasmagories*. Montparnasse 2000 (France): MP 33, 1976.

of the most unusual '80s libraries, with scores of incredible LPs by Brainticket founder Joel Vandroogenbroeck working under the pseudonyms VDB Joel and Eric Vann. Vandroogenbroeck is one of the few artists who was able to translate his progressive rock sensibility into library tracks. Thankfully, some visionary leadership at EMI Production Music has finally seen to it that Coloursound will be digitized fully, and I am looking forward to Coloursound finding its way back into circulation through its use in new film and TV as well as commercial reissue.

The real money lies in music publishing, and British libraries like KPM, Southern, De Wolfe, Boosey & Hawkes, and Josef Weinberger all got their start as music publishing companies in the early twentieth century. With the advent of television in the 1950s, they began to produce music for synchronization. DeWolfe began operating as a production music library in 1927 and continues to this day. George A. Romero notably used DeWolfe both as temp and final music in his 1978 masterpiece *Dawn of the Dead*.

KPM began releasing its legendary 1000 series with its stock green covers (known as "greensleeves") in 1965, and it was an immediate success, with many UK and US TV themes being culled from its massive run of LPs and CDs (more than three hundred by 1989), including UK and US TV themes like *All Creatures Great and Small*, *Animal Magic*, and *Monday Night Football*, to name a few. Music from the 1000 series has been in constant use since its creation some fifty years ago—the Wimbledon theme, a cheery Keith Mansfield–penned track called "Light and Tuneful," has been used by the BBC for more than forty years.

The KPM 1000 series contains many essential library funk and electronic LPs, including *The Big Beat* volumes 1 and 2 and *Afro Rock*, and is largely understood as having set the standard for library music internationally. EMI Music Publishing eventually absorbed KPM and Themes International, and many other large music publishing companies have acquired the more lucrative library catalogs in recent years. The KPM 1000 series is one of the most successful libraries, and now that it has finally been completely digitized, KPM has recently brought together some of the original composers—Keith Mansfield, Alan Hawkshaw, John Cameron, Alan Parker, James Clarke, and Brian Bennett—to record a new LP of library music entitled *KPM 1000*. There have been concerts by some of the original composers touring as the "KPM All-Stars," and the original master tapes of the 1000 series are being donated to the British Library.

A few British library records were so popular that they were released commercially. Les Baxter has an LP of outstanding jazz samba on KPM called *Bugaloo in Brazil*, which was later released commercially as *African Blue*, and tracks from Madeline Bell's Themes vocal library LP *The Voice of Soul* were rerecorded and released as *This Is One Girl* on Pye Records in 1976. Brian Bennett's superb Bruton LP *Fantasia* was released commercially as *Voyage (A Journey into Discoid Funk)* in 1978.

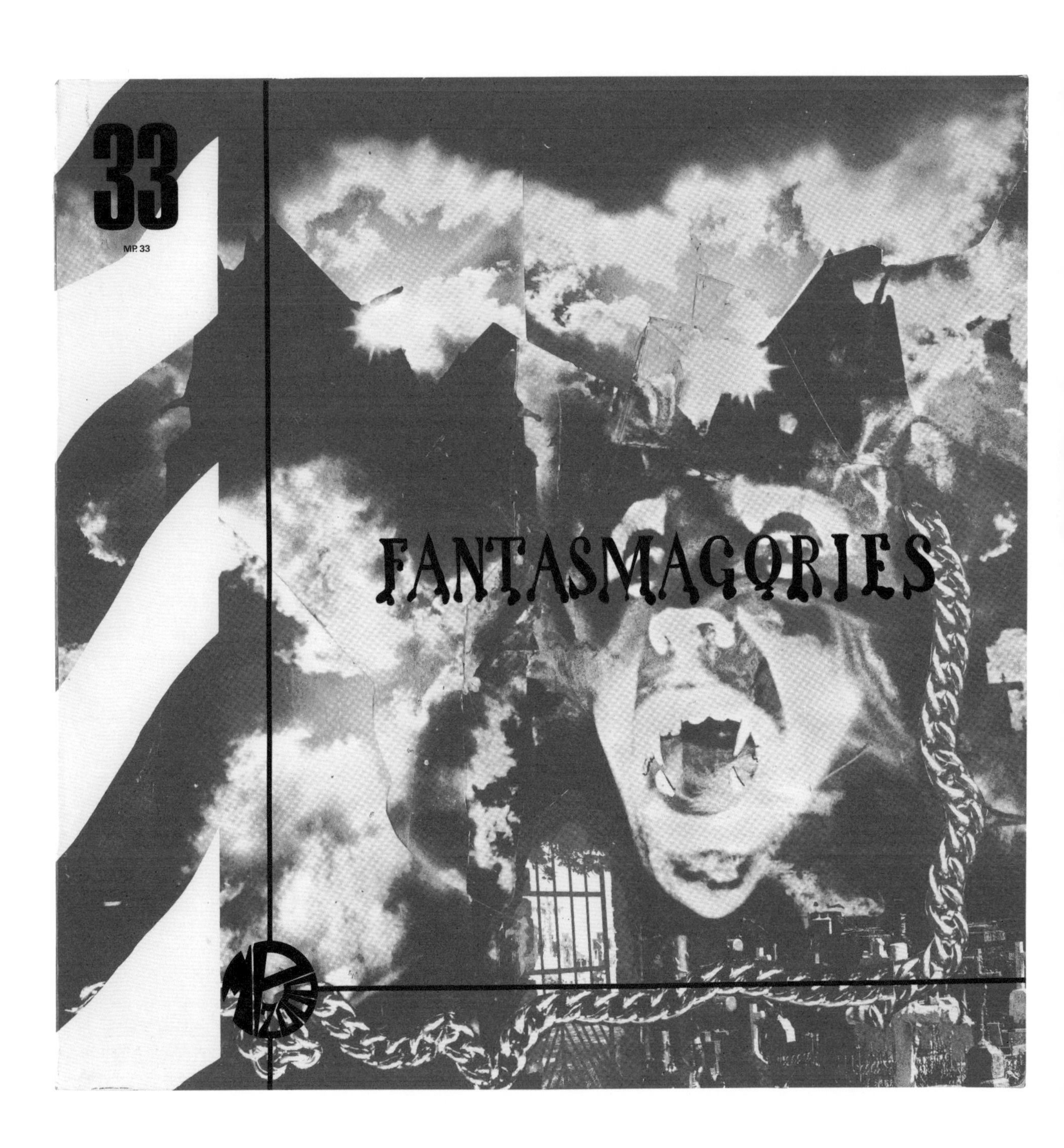
33
MP. 33
FANTASMAGORIES

Of the many great British library LPs produced, few are as superlative as Alan Tew's *Drama Suite* volumes 1 and 2 (Themes International TIM 1024 and 1025), truly the pinnacle of the British "cop funk" sound. The original LPs were issued in 1976 on the Themes International label, and consist of music that was originally commissioned for the Yorkshire TV cop drama *The Hanged Man*. Like much of the British (and German) library music of the period, they were recorded in Munich, at Studio M, using what was to become the standard Themes lineup: Mike Moran and Alan Hawkshaw (keyboards), Barry Morgan (drums), Les Hurdle (bass guitar), and Frank Ricotti (Latin and tuned percussion), plus the Max Gregor orchestra, with Tew composing, arranging, conducting, and producing all of the tracks. Permutations of the above lineup, sans Tew, appear on countless KPM, Themes, and Bruton releases. Tew is one of only a few library artists who did not perform any of his own compositions, but instead remained behind the mixing board, in complete control of the sessions. Needless to say, the recording techniques and analog studio gear used on these sessions was the stuff of legend, and cannot be matched or even emulated by today's digital standards.

The days in Studio M were filled with endless recording, and the *Hanged Man* sessions could have been just another day at the office for these seasoned musicians, but when working with Tew, things often got interesting. Graham Walker, head of Themes International at the time, remembers those sessions:

> On the evening prior to the commencement of the [*Hanged Man*] recording dates, we all went for a small and what turned out to be a very quick drink at the famous Bierkeller in the Schwabing district of Munich. It was a large underground vaulted cellar and it was full. It consisted of 2,000 thirsty drinkers, mostly in traditional Bavarian attire, sitting around big wooden tables singing German marching songs with great panache, accompanied by a typical Bavarian oompah band. Once we were seated, each with a two-liter stein of beer, Alan Tew went straight up to the band's conductor and asked in appalling German if he could conduct the band, to which the conductor quite rightly said, "Nein." Alan was a lovely and very talented guy, but he invited chaos or near disaster wherever he went. This was no exception; his reaction was to jump up onto our table and start singing "Rule Britannia" very loudly. The place went as silent as a morgue. We quickly shut him up and dragged him off the table, and backing out and waving, we made a very swift retreat with Alan asking why he couldn't finish his beer first! Thinking about it again, it's amazing we ever made [it to] the sessions alive!

Drama Suite volumes 1 and 2 went on to become memorable TV music in the UK on cop shows like *The Hanged Man*, *Van Der Valk*, *The Two Ronnies*, and *The Sweeney*, but the music became indelibly etched into the American collective consciousness in 1981, when it became the opening theme song for *The People's Court*. As the Alan Tew Orchestra, Tew commercially released a number of LPs, with him conducting and arranging big band covers of popular tunes of the 1970s.

The KPM 1000 series also contains one of the greatest collaborative teams in the annals of British library: Alan Hawkshaw and Brian Bennett. They worked together (and apart) on a huge number of KPM and Bruton releases, and in many ways were seminal in defining the British library sound. Alan Hawkshaw is universally recognized as one of the undisputed giants of library music, and has created a massive body of work (library and otherwise) of all kinds. Amongst funk collectors the world over, he is known as the man behind the Mohawks' *The Champ*, an LP collection of library organ funk tracks commercially released in 1968. As musical director, arranger, and performer, he has enjoyed fruitful collaborations with Serge Gainsbourg, Jane Birkin, and Catherine Deneuve, among many others. Brian Bennett was an in-demand percussionist in the late 1950s who started working with Cliff Richard and the Shadows in 1961, and became Richard's musical director in the 1970s. By the '80s, he was composing music for TV shows like *Dallas*, *Knot's Landing*, and *The Sweeney*. He continues to produce, arrange, and conduct music for film and television.

Library musicians routinely used pseudonyms, either instead of or in addition to their real names. There are certain individual artists in the world of library music who have authored literally tens of thousands of library compositions under a variety of assumed names. There is quite a bit of confusion as to the true identity of some of the pseudonymous artists, and oftentimes pseudonyms were used to bend rules; I have been told that certain British artists changed their names because there were specific BBC restrictions in place that kept them from working on library music—hence Pete Moore might have become Piet Van Meren. Many have surmised that library giants Nino Nardini and Cecil Leuter are one and the same person, or even related; I have not been able to confirm whether this is true or not. Gerhard Narholz, founder of Sonoton, has registered tens of thousands of compositions under a variety of pseudonyms (including Sammy Burdson and John Kingpop), making him a serious contender for most prolific library composer of all time. In addition to his wonderful work as a composer of every kind of music imaginable, he's always been a visionary in the field, creating one of the first stand-alone libraries devoted specifically to ethnic music of all kinds, the Sonoton Authentic Series (SAS). Although some of the music in that library is created by nonindigenous musicians recording in Munich, there are a number of fascinating releases on the label.

Without doubt, one of the most striking things about library LPs is the cover art and design. The graphic design is often starkly modern and standardized, and the uniformly red, orange, or green spines seen in a music library collection or archive communicate a seductive homogeny that belies their unique musical contents. Some library covers are so minimal and simple that they manage to achieve a truly generic look. Others, as in the case of the Sonoton SON series, feature eye-catching and iconic full-bleed color photographs that abstractly illustrate the contents of the

MONO-STEREO
MC 8005
POP ELECTRONIQUE
LES SONS ELECTRONIQUES DE CECIL LEUTER

OPPOSITE

Cecil Leuter. *Pop Électronique: Les sons électroniques de Cecil Leuter*. Neuilly (France): MC 8005, 1969.

record. In the case of the SON records, the multi-talented Gerhard Narholz not only founded the company and composed and performed much of the music—he also took many of those cover photographs. Other libraries' covers are profoundly bizarre, like the awesome Coloursound covers, which consist of crude, prison-art-style images that appear to have been rendered with crayons. Those drawings, I have been told, were made by the wife of the library owner. Also worth noting are the minimal but elegant British pop art style illustrations that grace the covers of the Themes International series. Like many of the musicians who played on the records, most of the artists who designed the covers are cloaked in anonymity. The pop art graphic sensibility is further expanded in the Montparnasse 2000 LP covers, which feature some of the wildest designs in the library universe.

Over the years, some libraries have themselves deleted and destroyed virtually their entire LP catalogs, but thankfully the records have found their way into the hands of DJs, collectors, and producers of sample-based music. Some of the rarest library LPs now fetch astronomical prices at auction, and library samples can be heard throughout the entire history of hip-hop, from the genesis of B-boy culture to the present. There have also been some excellent vintage library compilations released in past years, and a profound debt is owed to the many people in the reissue world who, by virtue of their determined efforts, have kept this music from slipping into complete obsolescence.

Not surprisingly, the master tapes for many important libraries have hit the dumpster. I still lose sleep over knowing that I missed, by a week, the chance to save the entire Southern / Peer library collection of master tapes and a full run of the LPs. I did find the case for the original master tape of Sven Libaek's classic *Solar Flares*, only to discover the tape inside was of country music. I have been offered some pretty good libraries for sale, including the complete ownership (masters, LPs, and publishing) of certain well-known libraries at bargain-basement prices. I have also seen libraries change hands for astonishingly low prices. Many years ago, I managed to acquire the only remaining set of master tapes and a full LP run of Montparnasse 2000. It was a library that was used extensively in French film and television, and while they were in business in the '70s and '80s, MP 2000 was wildly successful throughout Europe. It is still difficult to fathom how completely untethered the material is now, despite the fact that the catalog is owned and administered by a major music company, Universal. The reality is that it will languish on the shelf, occasionally resulting in some performance royalties, but otherwise gathering dust, until it disappears completely, never to be synchronized again.

All of the existing master tapes that I have seen are quarter-inch stereo masters, and many are pushing forty-five to fifty years old. No multitrack masters still exist. Hence, many are in terrible shape and would need to be baked in an oven before being put on a tape machine. Others, by virtue of the particular tape stock originally used or poor storage conditions, are already lost. Some just need to be restored with great care. There is a very finite lifespan for the tapes—they need to be digitized now or they will be lost completely. In the cases of many libraries, the surviving LPs are the only form in which the music still exists. Some important libraries are safe—the entire run of Themes International, owned by KPM and administered by EMI, has been digitized and is presently available for synchronization.

Romano and Fabio di Bari are seeking to bring new life to their archival library catalog by digitizing and rebranding their earlier labels into a new label called Canopo Vintage. I commend them for their commitment to preserve and bring new life to the excellent material that they control, but so much of the incredible trove of Italian library music will most certainly be lost because of lack of interest and foresight on the part of label owners, publishers, and estates to archive and maintain these precious assets.

In my research, I learned that the library companies, as well as the producers who used the LPs for preview, consistently threw out or destroyed the LPs when they finished with them. Library administrators still very occasionally receive returns of LPs no longer needed by customers, and those are universally destroyed. In the past, certain library administrators have gone as far as attempting to stifle sales of vintage library LPs on eBay (officially it is illegal to resell them), but that has proven to require way too much effort, so for the time being, it is allowed. All of which should go to show just how rare library LPs are, and that they will only get rarer in the coming years.

What does the future hold for this curious genre of music? At this very moment, some of the best vintage library music is still being synchronized in film and television every day, and the huge trove of library that remains extant might be the last sizeable tract of virgin timber left for sample-based music production. "Lost" library gems are being unearthed all the time—and it would appear that there is a seemingly endless supply of totally obscure Italian library music, including an extraordinary amount of unreleased material from some of Italy's greatest film composers. There is even library music I have not yet heard from places like Poland and Brazil. So in spite of the fact that some of this mysterious music will no doubt disappear completely in the rubble heap of culture, vintage library LPs will continue to manifest and astound and amaze in the years to come...

David Hollander
San Antonio, October 2017

BRITISH LIBRARIES

With origins stretching back to its 1780 founding in London, KPM is today one of the most storied and celebrated music libraries in the world. Initially a musical instrument shop named for its founder, Robert Keith, the company expanded to sheet music and theater ticket sales after Keith partnered with William Prowse, a music publisher, in 1830, forming Keith-Prowse Music. Once gramophones enabled home listening in the early twentieth century, the brand diversified into recordings, and in 1955 the music publishing wing was spun off into its own company, which itself was soon merged (in 1959) with Peter Maurice Publishing, forming the Keith-Prowse-Maurice library, or KPM. Under the stewardship of manager Patrick Howgill, KPM produced themes for film and television on 78-rpm discs, but it was the 1965 shift in direction under new manager Robin Phillips that set KPM on the path to its now-legendary status.

Phillips made the momentous decisions to release music on 12" LPs, and to hire and nurture forward-thinking, hugely talented composers such as Alan Hawkshaw, Keith Mansfield, and many other giants of the genre. The result was the seminal KPM 1000 series, considered by many fans to be the peak of the British library sound. Produced by Phillips and engineered by the versatile and talented Adrian Kerridge, the KPM 1000 LPs marked the first appearance of dozens if not hundreds of iconic recordings.

In 1969, KPM was acquired by the multinational EMI Music, and eight years later Robin Phillips left the company; the KPM library, however, continued to distinguish itself under new manager Peter Cox, who led the label until 2009. Currently a subsidiary of Sony / ATV Music Publishing, KPM remains a leader in library music, and its vaults contain some of the greatest recordings the industry ever produced.

Origins

Peter Cox: I applied for a job in the *Melody Maker*, and it said somebody with a thorough knowledge of music to join this company; it didn't say what it was. I went along to an interview with Robin Phillips at 21 Denmark Street, and it just caught me at that age—I must have been about twenty-eight, at the right moment. And that enthusiasm was what Robin picked up on.

Keith Mansfield: It was an exciting time to be there; there was so much happening in London. KPM, Denmark Street, which was where my office was, was the height of the music scene. So much energy and activity. The musicians—every day you were working with the best guys, all the young guys who were up and coming.

John Cameron: Oh, there was a lot of pub involved. There was no place you would rather be—I mean, meetings to discuss a project were usually in the pub. And you thought, *We better have some lunch in a minute, you know,* [laughs] *because otherwise I'm going to fall over*.

OPPOSITE

Denmark Street in London's West End, birthplace of the British music industry and site of KPM's offices.

Peter Cox: It was great, joining this new crew. It was just a small one: there was Joe Richardson, he was the secretary; Aaron Harry, I worked with; Robin; and myself. We were on the top floor of Denmark Street, and down below us were the other departments. There was the arranging department with Gordon Rees, there was the studio in the basement, Jimmy Phillips—Robin's dad, who was an old-time publisher, who was a legend actually, he had published things like "Stardust," and worked with Charlie Chaplin, people like that, extraordinary man—[Robin's] brother Peter, lovely Peter Phillips, who was the creative director... It was a lovely situation, it was vibey, and that time in the early '70s there was so much going on. There was the Sex Pistols, they were wandering out of the old Tin Pan Alley bar, and so on.

Recording

Adrian Kerridge: There was an issue in those days, problems with the musicians' union. Insomuch that, yes, you *could* record library music in the United Kingdom, but in order to do so, if it was used on another program, or sections of it, you had to pay the musicians again. So this was, you know, a typical union—made it impossible, economically, to record in the United Kingdom.

Peter Cox: We went abroad, because at that point, library music was banned by the musicians' union in this country. So everything, all the large sessions, had to be done abroad. Well, there was a certain amount of recording, of small ones, with consenting musicians, in the old studio in Denmark Street and others, but it had to be kept to a fairly small number.

Alan Hawkshaw: If we were recording it in London... the producers would always be coming up looking a bit nervous in case the musicians' union guy walked in. And there was a guy called, well, we called him "Doctor Death." He was from the union and he had a habit of turning up on recording sessions and probing and asking what the session was for. I remember one in particular: He turned up on a session at KPM. We were recording this thing and he said, "What is this session?" And the manager said, "It's for a movie." He said, "Well, what is the film?" And we hadn't recorded the jingle yet. It's a typical case of cart before the horse. And we managed to talk our way out of it that way. So you were a little bit nervous about unions turning up.

Adrian Kerridge: So we went to Germany. And that started in 1966, and I had a briefing from Robin. The original composers, both not alive now, with whom I worked were Johnny Pearson and Syd Dale. And that's where it started in '66, with those two guys. And then it went on for a number of years, until—I think it was 1975 when there was an agreement with the union that library music recording could come back, could be done in the country. Yes, it *could* be done in the country, but who the hell is going to pay all that money? When you could go abroad, you pay once—they were four-hour sessions, you pay the guys one fee, and you could get multiple uses out of the master tapes. It's a no-brainer.

DENMARK STREET WC2
TO LET
ENTIRE S/C
UPPER PART
All Enquiries
DUNLOP
HEYWOOD
LORENZ
020 7409 2121
INDIAN CUISINE
VINTAGE GUITARS
AT
ROSE-MORRIS
DENMARK
STREET WC2
Locktec

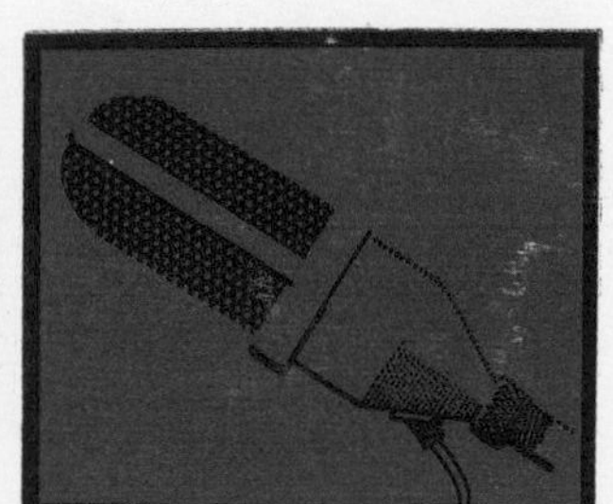

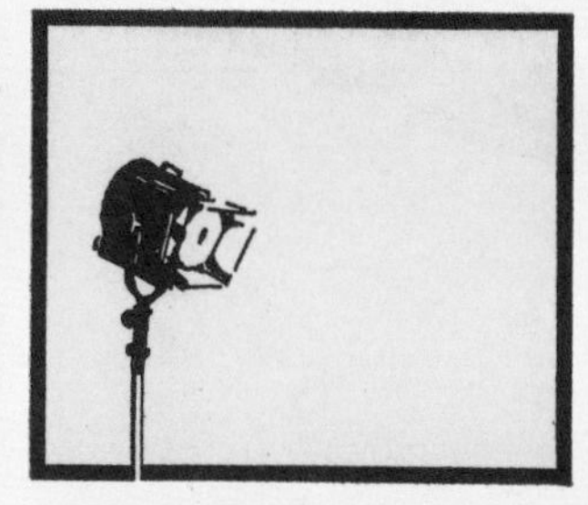
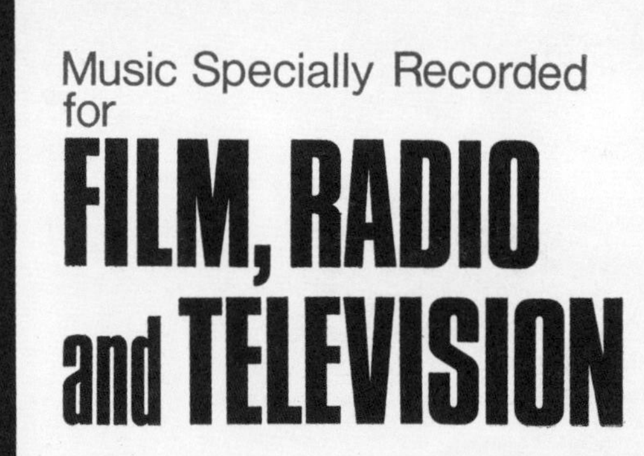
Music Specially Recorded
for
FILM, RADIO
and TELEVISION

3 ATV

VOL

KPM
MUSIC

SCENE
66
TAKE
1
SOUND
K.P.M.
PROD. FILM - T.V + RADIO
DIRECTOR
CAMERA JIM GOFF
DATE
EXT.
INT.

OPPOSITE

An example of the KPM 1000 series' alternate stock cover (used alongside the better-known "greensleeves").

Peter Cox: So the big stuff had to be done abroad, and at that point Adrian Kerridge was the engineer.

Adrian Kerridge: Yes, [I engineered] all of [the KPM 1000 series], to my knowledge.

Peter Cox: So we used to bunk off to—when I was there—to the Fonior Studios, the Decca studios in Brussels. And we did camp with a rhythm section, with a brass player, with the composers. And I think the rhythm section at that point, from memory, was Brian Bennett on drums, Dave Richmond with his Bison black bass, Clive Hicks, who died quite recently, he was on guitar, Steve Gray, who is no longer with us, he was on keyboards, and Derek Watkins as lead trumpet. And Derek was such a great player; he would inspire the other musicians, and actually raised the benchmark as the week went on. So as the week progressed, it got better and better and better.

Adrian Kerridge: Well, the first sessions were at Ariola Studios in Cologne. The studio was run by a company called Sonopress. Very well equipped, no problems. Good *Tontechnikers* [sound engineers], as they called them. And good console. They never heard anything like my recordings before—the Germans were very correct about recording. We went there every year until 1969, when the studio was going to be converted into a rock-and-roll studio. Then we went to Trixi Studios in Munich, [where] the players weren't very good, and another set of players was engaged, and that was with Neil Richardson. And then we did some recordings in another studio in Cologne.

Alan Hawkshaw: It was fun. When we went to Paris or Brussels, or Munich, they'd cram as much as they could into one session. I remember often doing ten songs. And that's one thing the union would eventually cotton on to, by the way; they wouldn't let you do more than three or four titles a session. So either way around, library was banned. So they used to do three sessions of music in one session, because you had a big orchestra; it got expensive.

John Cameron: There was something—the thing is, when you went in the studio in 1968, with three songs and a producer and your rhythm section, you could come to the end and your producer could say, "Oh, thanks guys, but never mind." Or you could come up with "Sunshine Superman." So basically, the pressure was on for it to happen in the three hours. You couldn't say, "Oh, look, we'll redo the bass later, and I'll lay down a drum track and we'll bring this in." You had to produce the performance there and then. It was dangerous. In fact I don't think we were allowed to overdub until the late '70s, early '80s, so it had to be–*whack!* You know. You had to put tracks in a three-hour session. You were allowed twenty minutes of music. So you were allowed ten two-minute pieces of music. Now, you're scrambling to get them in. A full orchestra, rhythm section, everything else—it takes you the first half hour to sound balance, and then it's go. It's a real scramble.

OPPOSITE

KPM employees including composer Keith Mansfield (*second from left*) and manager Peter Cox (*third from left*) in the control room.

Adrian Kerridge: Um... (*laughs*). Well, for me, it was a bit of a kick bollock and a scramble, because we had so much to do. But it was good. Robin Phillips was good to all the guys, you know, there were no issues, it was friendly, it was a laugh. We relaxed in the evenings. Well, some evenings, if we weren't working late. I mean, the first sessions, for me to get my head around the studio, we worked quite late, because the musicians weren't used to the English way of working. But they were very, very good musicians, excellent musicians. You know, some of the cream of the German guys, international musicians as well. We had great musicians in Germany.

Peter Cox: We did three four-hour sessions a day, basically recording the woodwind, brass, and rhythm section in the day. Scissor-editing the multitrack tape, and then the strings would come in in the evening, and overdub on complete masters.

Adrian Kerridge: I mean, in '68, there were a longer series of sessions in Ariola that we'd done. Gosh, I was exhausted at the end of it, you can imagine; it was a lot of work. Very, very much work...

Peter Cox: And we used to do five LPs roughly at a time, that's what it worked out as, a difference of categories, and then come back [from abroad] and title them and put them out. But normally it was about four to five a week, three four-hour sessions a day, so it was pretty productive, very full-on.

Keith Mansfield: KPM would be there for a week, and the composer [would] go in and out, arriving the day before their session or sessions, and then traveling a day later.

Peter Cox: And then when Robin took the musicians over, each one would just get up in turn like a rotor, whether it was Johnny Scott, or Keith Mansfield, or Johnny Pearson, or any of these people, and conduct the band doing those tracks. And out of that came some wonderful themes.

Keith Mansfield: I can remember one time in, I think it was Belgium, where both Johnny Scott and John Pearson had either already done their sessions, or I was in the middle of them and they were both there. Steve Gray was the keyboard player, and I think it might have been Alan Parker on guitar. Anyway, I'm doing this piece of music and Johnny Pearson and Johnny Scott rushed out and they said, "We'd like to play on this piece." Johnny Scott was a very good flautist, so he played flute along with the other flautist, and Johnny Pearson played second keyboard. I mean, things like that were great fun, just great fun.

Peter Cox: One time, I was the one doing the scissor-editing—you didn't have much time to do it; you literally had to jump into the breaks because we were pretty much flat on—and I forgot, or somehow omitted to add an end edit on one of Keith Mansfield's pieces. So when the strings came in in the evening, I had the frightening, embarrassing moment where the track just broke down: it didn't have an ending. Of course, it was entirely up to me. And I am being abjectly apologetic, going up to Keith's hotel room

OPPOSITE TOP

Musicians tackling a KPM composition during a recording session.

OPPOSITE BOTTOM

Composer Johnny Dankworth during a KPM recording session.

in the evening saying, "I'm so sorry about that." And actually Keith was very nice about it, and they actually managed to fake an end on this track. But it was a good learning curve because you really had to get it quick.

Keith Mansfield: Well, part of that is having grown up early on with the library. When we first did library tracks—it must be funny for people to listen to them now, because there're these gaps all the time. And you think, *Why didn't they put a drum fill or whatever?* Well, the gap was necessary, because back in the '50s and '60s, editors had to get into the tape with scissors, or with a knife. And you had to give them the opportunity to get in there, because you didn't have cross-fading. I mean nowadays, you can do this cross-fading and it sounds wonderful; then, you had to be able to get in and get out. So all our themes would last twenty-eight and a half seconds. Because at the end of twenty-eight and a half seconds, they may carry on using the music, under dialogue, but it had to have an end, so if the editor wanted to, he could get out of it. And if you didn't do this, the editor might love your music, but just doesn't got time to work out an ending, so he's going to go for something else.

Peter Cox: I learnt to play music, of course, because you had to follow a score, because when I was doing the editing, quite often when we brought the tracks back [to London], they'd be mixing it in the studio in the basement, I'd be upstairs editing the quarter-inch tapes as they brought them up, and I'd get instructions—"Bar 2 of the French horn break"—and I'd have to get my head around this, because I was the one doing the tape chopping. Of course, nowadays you can just hit "undo" and it all disappears, but in those days it was a bit more taxing than that. But it was a great way to learn the craft.

Keith Mansfield: [Using gaps for tape slicing] was one of the ways you make sure your music is getting used, in place of a writer who maybe didn't understand that. So I was already used to that. And I was also used to the idea that you've got to keep the vibe, the atmosphere of the piece, you've got to sustain it. Of course, as it got more and more digital, you're sustaining the atmosphere, but you also allow [editors] to cut or to bleed the thing across at different points. For whatever reason they've got—they may have a scene and it's merging with something else, and they can use that point to bring something else in, which might be a later part of the piece where the tonality is slightly different. That sort of change is really effective, and it sounds like—well, if you weren't composing, you'd think, *How the hell did they do that?*

Alan Hawkshaw: Everybody gave their best. And you can get great things out of it. Get energy out of it. You weren't restricted by a song, by a melody of somebody singing... everybody could *play*. And that probably comes out in those original recordings.

Adrian Kerridge: Huge! I can't say any more than it was huge. What saddened me really is that when you look at the greensleeve [KPM 1000 series] albums, it actually doesn't give the recording

OPPOSITE TOP

KPM recording featuring well-known British session players including percussionist Stan Barrett (*standing in background*) and violinist Sidney Sax (*right foreground*).

OPPOSITE BOTTOM

Keith Mansfield conducting an orchestral performance.

date; it gives the issue date... I mean, in later work that I did, in Germany for Syd Dale and others, I've got my diary notes, and I can tell you how much, how long we worked for, how many sessions there were and how many minutes of music. But with Keith-Prowse [KPM], god, it was huge!

Composing

Alan Hawkshaw: There was a hell of a lot of good library music written and nobody really knew what we were writing it for... In fact, it's harder to write library music than it is to write a commissioned score, because with a commissioned score you've got a picture to look at. With a library piece, you've only got a blank piece of paper. And possibly a title: "Wildlife," "Corporate," "Drama." You've got that, and you start from there. You've got nothing to get you started except your own mind. You're starting with a blank sheet of paper. You haven't got a picture to look at. If you've got a picture to look at, the picture tells you... it's like you're halfway done with the piece. You just write whatever the picture needs. It makes it a hell of a lot easier than writing a piece for a movie or something that doesn't even exist yet.

Ron Geesin: For the first album [*Electrosound*] I had no idea of pictures, and I didn't want to have an idea of pictures. I wanted to make a good pattern, a good structure. So that was my root drive to do a piece.

Keith Mansfield: The other side of the story was that when Robin started to approach—I'm sure he said it was Elmer Bernstein. He'd approached Elmer Bernstein, and Elmer was interested, because—look, he was a noted Hollywood composer, who at that stage couldn't have been doing very much, and he was half-interested in doing it. And then when it came down to it he said, "I don't know where to start without the film. Where do I start writing? I don't know where to start." So in other words, if you come up through the film ranks, where everything is done with the idea of the picture being there, then it's hard to imagine what you do with a library.

Peter Cox: When we went abroad, you had something in mind. Like *Grandstand*, for instance. You knew they were looking for a new theme.

Adrian Kerridge: Keith Mansfield wrote the *Grandstand* theme for the BBC weekly sports program.

Keith Mansfield: Themes, where you're writing something that's going to be used in the front of a program, or to finish a program, that's got to be catching the ear, it's got to be something that catches the mood of what the program is about. That's a different thing.

Peter Cox: What Keith actually earmarked for *Grandstand* wasn't what they actually picked; it was another one entirely. But that was what you had... Bear in mind that these themes were coming up all the time: You pitched, and there was no means that you were

A selection of the KPM 1000 series' "greensleeve" covers.

TOP

Ron Geesin. *Electrosound*. KPM (UK): KPM 1102, 1972.

MIDDLE LEFT

Various. *Scenesetters - Fanfares and Punctuations*. KPM (UK): KPM 1057, 1970.

MIDDLE RIGHT

Herbie Flowers / Barry Morgan. *Bass Guitar and Percussion - Volume 2*. KPM (UK): KPM 1089, 1971.

BOTTOM LEFT

Peter Sander / Derrick Mason. *Technical Standpoint / Spice of Life*. KPM (UK): KPM 1087, 1971.

BOTTOM RIGHT

W. Merrick Farran. *Cartoon Capers - Typical Cartoon and Animation Set*. KPM (UK): KPM 1081, 1970.

actually going to get it. But at least you gave yourself something to aim for.

Adrian Kerridge: There was ITV, another composition by Keith Mansfield. I don't know what it was originally called, it was issued as "The Big Match"; that was for ITV. Keith Mansfield composed Wimbledon, the theme for Wimbledon. Don Harper composed *The World of Sport*; Don wasn't on the session, so somebody else conducted his work. John Scott wrote "Gathering Clouds," and that was the theme for America's Major League Baseball coverage—I don't know whether it still goes on. But Johnny Pearson wrote "Heavy Action," which is the introduction to America's *Monday Night Football*, and that is still broadcast I think. And then there was another Keith Mansfield, "International Athletics," ITV's tune to athletics coverage. There was an original theme by Brian Bennett for the Channel Nine World Series Cricket in Australia; I think that was Australia. The US Open tennis, the long-running tune to the US Open tennis series by Keith Mansfield, that was called "US Open Tennis." And that's just an insight.

Peter Cox: The theme to—I think it was actually the previous one, the Wimbledon one, but certainly the *Monday Night Football* theme, now, obviously, very popular in the States, came out of [the European] sessions. *Grandstand*—another one that ran and ran and ran. Wimbledon, I think very much the same way, but I think it was recorded on a previous one, just before I came there. But things like *Mastermind*, they were all recorded [abroad], these long-running themes.

Clients and Briefs

Peter Cox: We were meeting people all the time, and you were certainly aware that people would come up to Robin all the time and say, "Look, we've got this new show coming up, if you happen to be doing something like that, give us a sports theme." There was no sort of collusion, it wasn't as if it was done to order, it wasn't like that. But it certainly was that obviously we would get composers to pitch, and say, "Look, even if it doesn't work, you've still got a great football or sports theme." But you'd get several of them going for it. So when you came back you could ring up television companies and say, "We've done these, what do you think?" And you could give them a limited amount of exclusivity, perhaps, you know, before you actually released it.

Alan Parker: [Clients] would go to Robin or whatever, and then Robin would have a chat with various composers, one being me sometimes, and then you'd be asked to do [something] specific, shall we say, but it would go through the library obviously. I mean, yeah, that would happen an awful lot.

Peter Cox: We used to get the people from Monty Python in, doing the Monty Python films and acting out all the scenes—Terry Gilliam and Terry Jones, and all these sorts of people. And so it was with the people who were doing *The Sweeney*, another big sort of cop series. There used to be four producers doing that; they used to

OPPOSITE

Printed KPM catalog, used by clients to select music for synchronization.

come in and choose their music every single week. So it was a vibey thing all the time—you were constantly dealing with those sort of creative people. It was exciting.

Alan Parker: Robin knew all—well, not all, but let's say 99 percent of the editors and the producers and directors. And they'd go to Robin and say, "Have you got this?" And he might say, "Well, we haven't got that, but if you want that sort of thing, leave it with me and we'll get something sorted for you." And then he'd approach a couple of the composers that he would use and get them to write something specific like that.

Keith Mansfield: We didn't use to have big briefs; the brief would be very straightforward when we were doing it. Maybe because it was all so new, I don't know whether that was the reason.

Peter Cox: In those days, television companies had no notion whatever of the value of publishing. So of course you would get, by today's standards, the ridiculous situation that these people come along with a new show, and say, "What music have you got for us for a new show?" And so Aaron [Harry] and I picked, for instance, the theme to *Mastermind*, which is still running now. This was in '73. And they had this new quiz show, and we played them all the usually quizzy music that we had; none of it was right. And then, gradually, in talking to them, it came to the point where of course there was this rather threatening black chair and everything else. And what they actually walked away with was Neil Richardson's "Approaching Menace," which he'd written as a war theme.

Keith Mansfield: When it was a cops thing, my problem was I found it easier to write American cop music than English cop music. So, yeah, it's a funny thing. The American [cop music] just allowed you to be more harmonically interesting. Once you got harmonically interesting, if it was English, it didn't sound English. Quite a funny thing—funky and poppy and more straightforward, would be the English sort of cop music. In America, in so many of the programs, the music for those shows was written by great composers. Quincy Jones, I remember he did one... You got some wonderful music. So Americans are used to hearing that kind of advanced harmony. And they're used to big brassy things, because Americans grow up with that. All their schools have these big marching bands who play high, and play these funky rhythms and whatever. And they play big band harmonies. So, yeah, I found it easier to go that route than the English cop music.

Ron Geesin: I mean, you're also working to fixed, stated limitations, one being, it's got to have a start and a finish, and it's got to be no more than two minutes and fifteen seconds. Because the music libraries had already worked out that the average length of a film sequence that required music was going to be less than two minutes fifteen seconds. So that's fine because fortunately I—along with any competent music library composer—knew how to work within those limitations and make something meaningful.

kpm
MUSIC RECORDED LIBRARY
21 Denmark Street London WC2H 8NE Tel: 01-836 6699

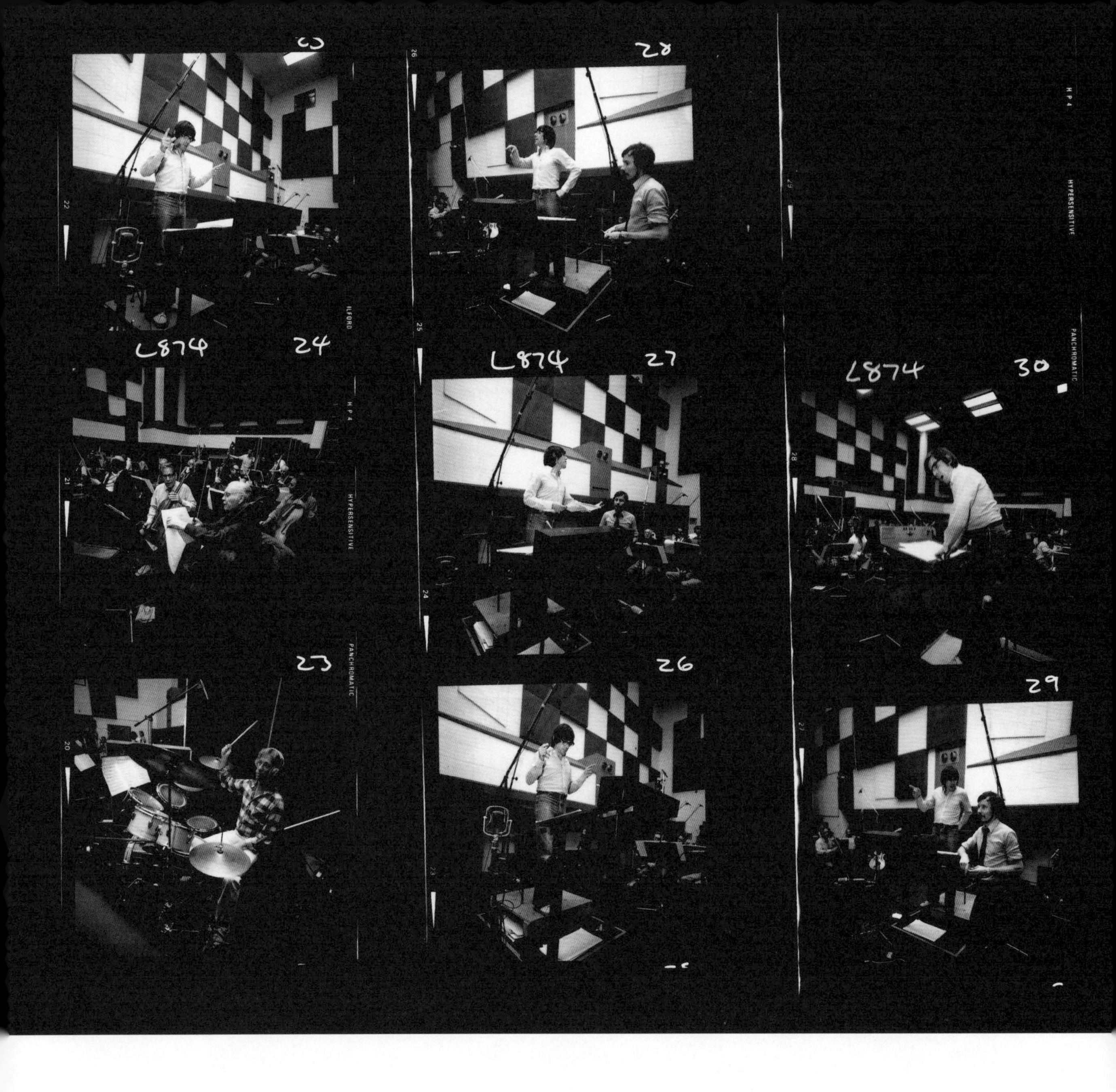
28
L874
24
L874
27
L874
30
23
26
29
ILFORD
HP4
HYPERSENSITIVE
PANCHROMATIC

OPPOSITE

Photos from a KPM recording session conducted by Keith Mansfield.

Keith Mansfield: With library music, one of the things you mustn't do is change the mood. You start there and however long it is, a three-minute, even if it is a five-minute composition, you have to sustain that mood for five minutes. If the editor wants to change the mood at twenty-nine seconds, he'll cut to another piece of music. You can never know when you write a piece of music when an editor is going to want you to be in a different mood, so you have to write the same mood. And somehow you have to make it interesting—or, when I say *interesting*, you can't just write the same thing. You've got to somehow—it's got to evolve without necessarily having too many climaxes, which you might do with a straight composition, a serious composition. You can't have too many climaxes. I'm not saying you can never do these things, but one of the things is to try and maintain a mood, but somehow make it interesting, without being too interesting, because it's if it's too interesting, suddenly you're aware of it. And what you're trying to do is for people not to be aware of it.

Alan Parker: If you're doing a commercial song, that's a different ball game. Or even TV dramas, of course, you're following the film again, whether it's a small screen or a big screen. So it's a different spectrum altogether. When you're composing for film to TV dramas or whatever... you're not *locked in*, that's the wrong way to put it, but you're locked in in the sense that you've got to follow that film, you know. And also there, you get a brief, generally speaking, or you used to; you get a brief from the producers and you follow their brief.

Keith Mansfield: There was one brief I remember which was a classic, because it was so easy to write for. It was called *Olympiad 2000*. So one brief would be "Empty Stadium" ["The Empty Arena"], so: before, like the lonely stadium feel. There'd be one balladic sequence, then "The Winner" ["World Champion"], you know, the sweaty side of it, you know, whatever—those sorts of things. Very easy to write that kind of music, you know. You've got descriptions.

Alan Parker: There was in essence—apart from the brief side of it, there was total freedom in library music because it was like, *Oh, help yourself*, in a way, as long as you've got the brief. And you can't really style it, because you've got to do what they want but, I mean, library music is much more liberal and it's much more open than if you're scoring a film... you've got much more freedom to experiment.

Keith Mansfield: I started doing this thing where you would do different versions, and you'd leave out the brass, but the brass would be on [its] own recording. And this editor came up one day—and I'd done this with *Olympiad 2000*, I'd done these edits on it. "Would you listen to it? I'm so proud of it." And I listened to what he'd done with it, where'd he'd taken the fanfares and put them into the music where they weren't originally there, and how it just sounded like the music had been written for the film. I mean that's when an editor is really able—he's given the music and the opportunity to make something special. And then you all feel good about it. The client has got to be happy, because it's costing a fraction of what it would cost to have it scored for him, the

OPPOSITE

(*From left*) Keith Mansfield, KPM manager Peter Cox, and engineer John Timperley during a recording session.

editor feels good because he's done something he is proud of, and it makes me feel good because the music is being used, and the music is being effective in the way that you hoped it would be.

Peter Cox: I think in those days... it was a much more cinematic market. And therefore the scale of the [library] compositions was proportionally larger. Whereas nowadays films are scored, and the use of library music in those is much more incidental. It's very infrequent that you would [use library music to] score a feature film, because the ownership of the score is potentially a money-making item, so it's not particularly economically attractive. So I think there's been a major shift of emphasis.

Alan Hawkshaw: Library music, per se, has kind of become an art form. Become a whole thing in itself. In other words, library music, at that time, was considered secondary to commissioned scores. Off the shelf music was really, in a sense, a second-class type of music. That's the way the attitude was, of a director. He wouldn't resort to using library music if he could afford to get the real thing, to get commissioned scores. That was an attitude that was around but, eventually, that's evaporated over the years. Thank goodness that it did.

Usages

Alan Parker: That's the only trouble with library music: unless it's something that's staring you in the face on the TV or something like that, you're very rarely aware of where it's been used. You might, if it's like a popular advert or a TV show. I remember a piece of guitar music I did for Robin was picked up by a TV series called... oh goodness, *Moody and Pegg* I think? I can't remember what the piece was called now, but it was picked up as the theme music. You know, it's like Johnny Pearson's stuff's picked up, Keith Mansfield's stuff's picked up, everybody's is. And sometimes you don't know until you hear it on the box, and it's as simple as that.

John Cameron: It's quite weird. I will say that library music is like children, you raise it to a certain thing, and then you don't know what it's going to do. I was rather shocked when "Half-Forgotten Daydreams" seemed to be all over the *Emmanuelle* soft porn things. And then the next minute I turn around and there's George Clooney with it, you know, so you kinda go, "OK" (*laughs*).

Keith Mansfield: Well, of course a lot of library music was used in porn. And sometimes you, as a composer, wouldn't know. And sometimes, guys would come say, "Oh, I saw that film you did." "Which one was that?" "The Swedish one." "What Swedish one?" "You know, the Swedish one..." And I'd have no clue what they were talking about. But you see, with porn, the sultry saxes, or those certain sort of chords, that all went with it. But to us, it's just music. It's music allowing you to do certain things, but it also has that vibe of seduction and whatever.

Alan Parker: Well, it's been used in a hell of a lot. And I'll tell you what library music is used for a lot—or it used to be, not so much

now—when you're doing a score, a movie score, the editors or whatever, the director, might want to what they call "temp score" it. You know, they put a temp score in there, so they can get the theme of the film and the music can be styled, and a lot of the temp music was library music. And I'll never forget, a couple of films that I scored, when I went along to do the spotting, I said, "Oh, that's my music." And the tech said, "What?" I said, "That's library music of mine." And it's weird when you get that situation, in other words, [being asked] "Can you do something like this?" It's bizarre sometimes.

Keith Mansfield: It's ironic, because some of the composers, some wonderful musicians, were very political. No problem with that. But usually if they were political, they were left-wing. And I remember one of these composers, in America his music was being used by the Republican Party, and he wanted to ban it. Well you can't do that; we have no, what we call, *moral right* over our music. Once it's in our library, anybody can use it for whatever they want. The person who has written it has no control at all. Nor does the publisher. So you've given away your moral right once you're writing for library music. So, no, I don't have those issues, I accepted that. If an editor would sometimes apologize—"Oh, I hope you don't mind, I've done this and that with your music." That's what I'm writing for. I'm glad that you can use my music that way, because that's what's meant to happen. I certainly didn't take it personally that they didn't think it was good enough to leave it as it was—it didn't even occur to me.

John Cameron: I did have a shock once. I didn't object to it being used, but when *Screen International* reviewed some rather dreadful piece of soft porn and credited myself and Duncan Lamont with the music—when it wasn't scored, it was all bought in. And I thought, *Well hold on; credit I don't really need, you know?*

Keith Mansfield: We had the same thing; particularly with porn films, they'd use your name. Even a western. I saw a western in a cinema magazine at KPM, and there: "Composed by Johnny Pearson and Keith Mansfield." And what they'd done was they'd just taken our music and cut it in the film, and it gives them a sort of prestige. It was a low-budget film, but they got proper composers there, it just gives it a sort of extra lift. Anyway, I'm very happy that they used our music, and I'm sure Johnny—speaking for Johnny—I'm sure Johnny was equally thrilled to have his music used in that same way...

Later KPM

Peter Cox: When Robin left, we were fed up with the idea that we had to record music abroad. And so we went, cap in hand, along to the Musicians' Union in 1977. And over the course of just over a year, we re-negotiated with the MU the right to record library music back in the UK. That's when that change happened, and we could subsequently record sessions in the UK, which we did a lot. And we went out, we were taken out by the MU to the most expensive restaurants in London they could possibly think of, and then they would never pick up the bill. So we ended up footing the bill, the whole bloody lot, but at the end of day we did negotiate a Musicians' Union deal. Which then freed up the fact that you could record great sessions in the UK. And at that point, it suddenly, I think, gave musicians in the UK a lot more work, and gave a lot of musicians like Derek Watkins and many others the chance to become writers as well as players, which was a nice benefit.

Adrian Kerridge: [After leaving KPM] Johnny Pearson became my partner. We owned recording studios from 1980 onwards, so he became my partner, and after the recordings in Germany he used the studios more often. Because he was an artist with Pye Studios—"Cast Your Fate to the Wind" was one of the big hits he had. So that's really what it's all about.

Peter Cox: When EMI took over [KPM], they already had a music publishing department. But what they didn't have at that point was the ability to—I mean, what was interesting about KPM was forefront library. And of course it dovetailed very well as a triangle: You happened to have a marvelous music catalog, library music, which was a dependable cash cow, and of course then the pop department. And in a way, there was a synergy between those. And the arranging department, which was people like Keith [Mansfield], Alan Moorehouse, people like that who could write pop arrangements, but they could easily cross into producing library music with Robin as well. So for them, it was a very creative company. And for EMI, a wonderful acquisition, there was no two ways about it. It made them a lot of money.

ROBIN PHILLIPS

The son of Jimmy Phillips—managing director of KPM and a legendary music publisher in his own right—Robin Phillips took on stewardship of the KPM library in 1965 and immediately began modernizing the firm's catalog, shifting the label's production focus from old-fashioned 78-rpm records to the increasingly popular LP form. Phillips also led the charge in commissioning compositions and recordings from forward-thinking young musicians, many of whom would go on to become legends in the field. Among Phillips' other innovations in the industry was his strategy of recording marathon sessions in continental Europe (thereby skirting a temporary British Musicians' Union ban on library recording), as well as his practice of writing up "briefs" for his composers (descriptions of suggested moods and themes for recordings). After KPM was sold to EMI in 1969, Phillips began looking toward starting his own homegrown library, and in 1977, he left to form Bruton Music, which would become another seminal publisher.

Keith Mansfield: With Robin Phillips, who was KPM, we formulated the new rules of the game.

Adrian Kerridge: Library music in the United Kingdom in that day was like orchestral, distant recordings: off-the-wall recordings, as I call them. Nothing wrong with that, but it was light music. It wasn't up-front with rhythm sections and the right composers being chosen. That's just the way it was. And Robin wanted to change it.

John Cameron: What Robin would do would be, he'd say, "Look I want an album with this specific theme to it, and I'd like you to do half and Alan Hawkshaw to do half." Or sometimes what would happen is Robin would go, "Those tracks go with those tracks and that would make a nice concept."

Adrian Kerridge: [Robin] would decide who he was going to use as a composer, and then he would brief them on the genre, the type of the music, and they would write accordingly... They would write to Robin's brief. And he was a very, very foresighted person in that way.

John Cameron: Robin was very sociable—smoked like a chimney. But he was a great man for kind of giving you your head, but then saying, "No, what I really need is for it to do *this* or it to do *that*," because he knew where his market was—he could help you just angle it towards that. I've been used to working to parameters on almost everything, so I don't mind if somebody says, "Look, just make it a little more that way." You're always thinking on your feet. So Robin was great for that positioning.

Adrian Kerridge: He knew what he wanted, and what he wanted he was given by the composers, because the brief was good. And we never had any issues on the sessions about bad briefs.

John Cameron: [The composers] were well briefed by Robin in what he wanted in the scoring, and the purpose of the music and for what it was going to be used. And everything met the brief that

Robin had given them. He'd give me a brief, he'd say, "I want it to be different, I want it to be more up-front than the old stuff." And that's precisely how we did it.

Alan Parker: [Robin] would give a brief and then you went away and hoped you did what they were looking for, let's put it that way. And I know it's happened to quite a few composers, you know—you got back on the floor and Robin would say, "Yeah OK, that will do for that one." Meaning he probably wasn't too impressed with that one, so he'd move on to the next one. But that's how it worked; you did your best to follow the brief that you were given.

Adrian Kerridge: You know, commercial television started in this country I think in 1955, and was beginning to expand. And of course there was the BBC, and the BBC used a lot of music; there was a lot of competition. So the other libraries, from my memory, were behind the curve in that sense. So Robin did this, and he was ahead of the curve at the time of the recordings. It was very foresighted of him.

John Cameron: Robin was kind of so similar in some ways to Mickie Most—the producer who looked after Donovan and Hot Chocolate and CCS—in that he was very good at putting the package together, in saying, I want *this* composed and *these* players, and *this* is the theme, *this* is where it's going to be targeted. And so you agreed with him, you maybe went in and said, "I'm going to write a spy series," and he'd go "OK, the way I want to work it is that I want it to be centered towards *that* kind of use, or *that* kind of use." So it took the kind of business side out of your hands; that was great. You could just get on with writing music.

PETER COX

Originally a 1960s folk singer under contract with the Beatles' Northern Songs label, Peter Cox worked the college circuit in the UK before chancing on an interview at KPM via a job listing in *Melody Maker*. He started at the library in 1972, and when KPM's manager Robin Phillips left the company in 1977, Cox took over. Over the next thirty years, he steered the KPM library through industry shifts and into the CD and digital era. He left the company in 2009 and became the creative director of his own library, the Scoring House.

Peter Cox: I came from a folk background. I was doing the university circuits, doing the all-nighters... and that was in the company of people who were crashing around in those days like Paul Simon, Art Garfunkel—I did number of concerts with him. It was a great time to be in the folk business—a lot of fun, some extraordinary players. I was under contract to Dick James at Northern Songs, and the reason they wanted me to be under contract to them was to sing; they'd signed a guy called Reg Dwight, who they thought was a good songwriter, but didn't have much personality as a pop star. So I ended up doing Elton John's demos at the old studio in New Oxford Street. And then Elton John took himself off to do a small tour, I think maybe his early events in the States, and it went very well. And at that point, Dick James revised his opinion that maybe he did have some talent after all.

And that's when I applied [to work at KPM]. I was not at all qualified to do it—I couldn't read music at all, and when I went for the first interview [Robin Phillips] had a great pile of scores on his desk, so I thought, "My god, he's going to ask me to sight-read these." But he didn't. I think probably he saw the hunger that I had at that time—I would have done anything to get in to some brand of the music business. And it was just a wonderful, exciting time.

ADRIAN KERRIDGE

OPPOSITE TOP

Kerridge, with Robin Phillips, behind the mixing board at KPM.

OPPOSITE BOTTOM

Kerridge during one of the KPM team's German recording trips.

Known for his decades of studio innovation and his seminal work with producer Joe Meek and the Dave Clark Five, Adrian Kerridge began working at KPM in 1962. He soon became the key engineer at the label, and during its heyday he masterminded the recording sessions in Munich and Cologne that would turn out many of the library's most lastingly popular pieces and result in the seminal KPM 1000 series. Kerridge passed away in October 2016, and his autobiography, *Tape's Rolling, Take One!*, was released in November of that year.

Adrian Kerridge: I was brought up musically, so I had a good understanding of scores and writing. I could look at the score, and interpret what the guys wanted. Because that's what you've got to do: You've got to get it out of the composer's head to know what they want, and then record it. Take that picture and set it up, with a lot of perspective... I'd work the brief that Robin [Phillips] gave me. And Robin's brief was, it had to be different.

My approach to recording was a lot different to the engineers then in those days... My recording techniques were very up-front, very hot; I recorded things pretty hot and pretty close, but with perspective. It sounds facetious to say this, but I painted pictures in sound. You know, it's like a painter: you get a palette, and you get a canvas, and the blank canvas in this instance is a score. You've got to look at it, you've got to choose the right microphones, you've got to have the right studio, you've got to have the right equipment, and then paint that canvas with the sound, with the depth and perspective. And of course it's much better doing it in stereo. And that was really Robin's brief to me, we wanted to be different. "Mr. K," as he called me, "we want to be different, and you're the right guy to do it."

BRUTON
MUSIC

BRUTON MUSIC

OPPOSITE

A printed Bruton Music catalog from the early 1980s, with musical offerings categorized and listed alphabetically according to possible use.

BELOW

Photo from a Bruton company party, featuring balloons branded with the library's distinctive wordmark. Robin Phillips is pictured at left.

Named for its offices at 12 Bruton Street in London, Bruton Music was the library Robin Phillips founded upon his departure from KPM in 1977. While making use of many of the same innovations he developed while directing KPM (and the hugely talented musicians he'd worked with there), Phillips also ensured that Bruton stood out from his former library through its eye-catching, often bizarre record sleeves, a far cry from the standardized "greensleeves" used for the KPM 1000 series.

A. FANFARES, LINKS, BRIDGES, STINGS

B. JINGLES

C. NEUTRAL, SOLO INSTRUMENTS, SADNESS

D. LEISURE, PASTORAL, NATURE, TENDERNESS, ROMANCE

E. CHILDREN, ANIMATION

F. COMEDY, PARODIES

G. HAPPY, BRIGHT, OPEN AIR, SPORT

H. CONTEMPORARY, POP, ROCK

I. FUTURISTIC, ELECTRONIC

J. THEME SETS, DOCUMENTARY & DRAMA SUITES

K. ACTION, PACE, DANGER, FORCE OF ELEMENTS

L. INDUSTRY

M. SUSPENSE, TENSION

N. GRANDIOSE, IMPRESSIVE, PANORAMIC

O. HISTORICAL, PERIOD

P. CLASSICAL, SEMI-CLASSICAL, RELIGIOUS, SERIOUS VEIN

Q. MILITARY, MARCHES

R. FOLK, NATIONALISTIC, KNOWN WORKS

S. JAZZ, DANCE

Selected pages from the Bruton catalog binder.

OPPOSITE

The library's alphabetized musical categories.

BELOW

Track breakdown for John Cameron and Paul Martin's *Little Creatures*. Bruton Music (UK): BRD 3, 1978.

BRD 3

LITTLE CREATURES

The frailty, tenderness and fear of nature.

SIDE A

1. Papillon	John Cameron	2:57	Gentle Flute and Harp.
2. Picture Book	,,	2:26	Reflective Clarinet and Harp.
3. Little Girl Lost	,,	2:47	Gentle, emotional.
4. Watermill	,,	2:16	Placid Oboe and Harp.
5. Pastures Green 1.	,,	1:09	Idyllic, nature or rest.
6. Pastures Green 2.	,,	1:01	More contemporary feel.
7. Drifting	,,	2:26	Suspended, timorous.
8. Lonely Oboe	,,	1:25	Plantive.
9. Lonely Clarinet	,,	0:57	Neutral.
10. Lonely Bass Flute	,,	1:07	Lonely, worried.
11. Peasants Pasture	Paul Martin	3:08	Quaint, peaceful.

SIDE B

12. Little Dance	Paul Martin	2:20	Petite, innocent.
13. Pastures	,,	2:22	Inquisitive, picturesque.
14. Castles In The Air	,,	1:48	Restful, pretty.
15. Moment Of Warmth	,,	3:03	Tranquility.
16. Innocence	,,	1:58	Placid beauty.
17. Birdclusters	,,	2:12	Bare fearsome underscore.
18. Thaw	,,	2:00	Darkness to light.
19. Warning	,,	1:15	Fearful to sudden startle.
20. Warning Tag	,,	0:21	Editable to tail.
21. Preface 1.	,,	0:55	Neutral rustic scenesetter.
22. Preface 2.	,,	0:08	Rustic link.
23. Preface 3.	,,	0:10	Longer rustic link.
24. Postlude 1.	,,	0:55	Restful resolve.
25. Postlude 2.	,,	0:18	Restful link.

TOP

John Cameron. *Hot Doughnuts*. Bruton Music (UK): BRG 32, 1985.

BOTTOM

James Asher. *Flash Music*. Bruton Music (UK): BRH 21, 1984.

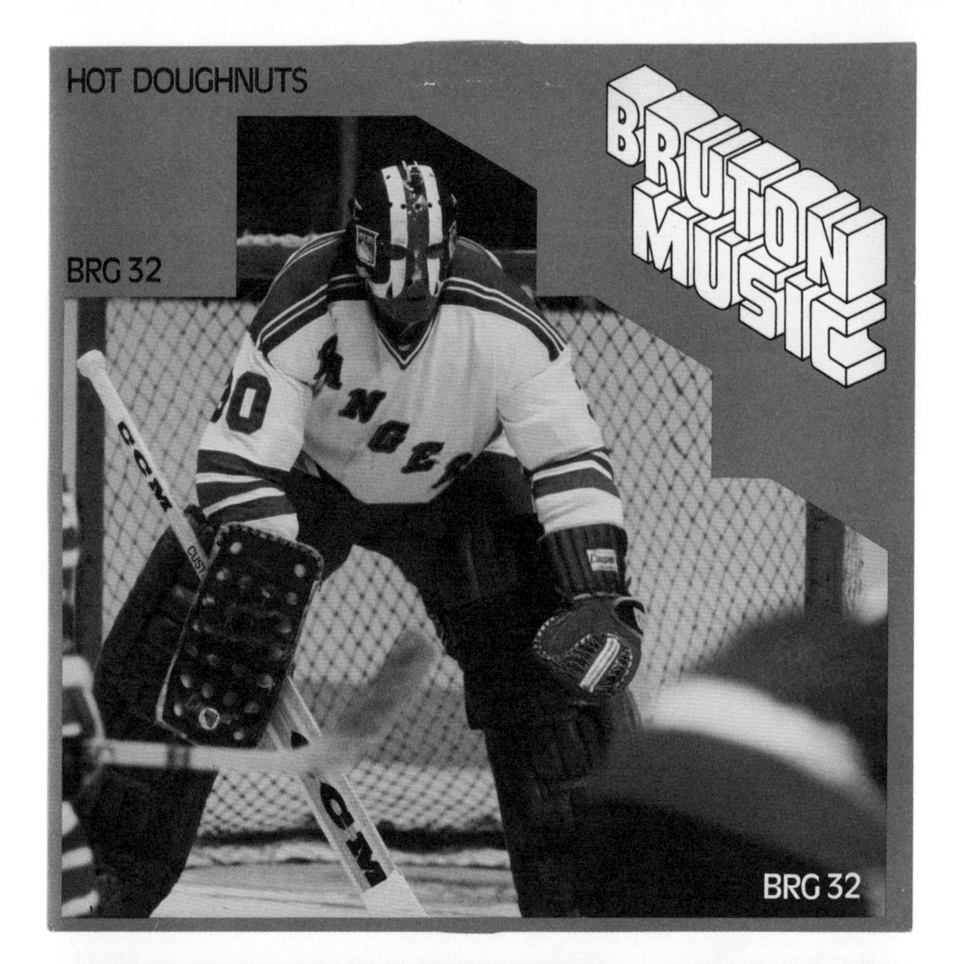

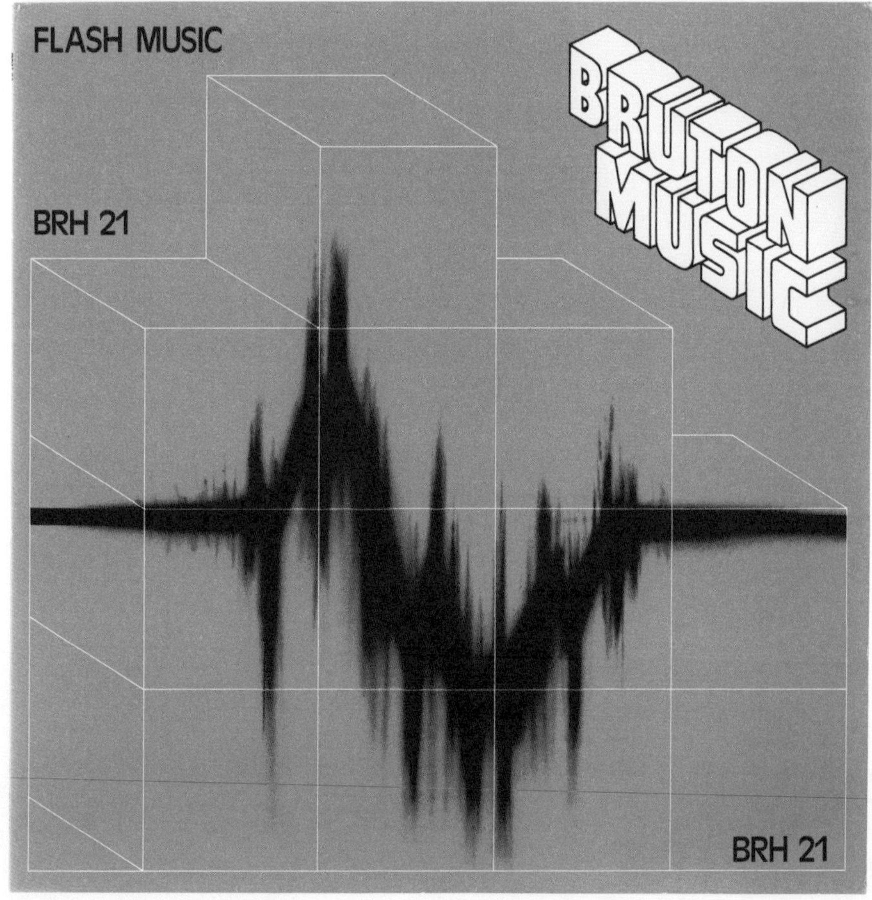

TOP

Simon Benson / Eugenio Grandi / David Snell. *String Tension*. Bruton Music (UK): BRM 13, 1985.

BOTTOM

Various. *Have a Nice Day*. Bruton Music (UK): BRG 34, 1985.

KEITH MANSFIELD

A stalwart KPM composer known for his funky, mod-tinged brass arrangements, Keith Mansfield started at KPM as a copyist before eventually becoming perhaps the most celebrated library composer of all time. Among his hundreds if not thousands of pieces, Mansfield wrote and recorded the seminal library recordings that have triumphantly soundtracked British sports presentations from the 1960s to the present day—themes for *Grandstand*, *The Big Match*, the Wimbledon tennis tournament, and more, firmly cementing his work in the minds of every UK television viewer of the last half century. Mansfield's music has also been sampled by hip-hop producers including Madlib and Danger Mouse, and remains ubiquitous on film and television around the world.

Peter Cox: Keith was always the absolute doyen of library music. Extremely commercial. A great producer. A great arranger... and was absolutely top of his craft. And kept top of his craft.

Keith Mansfield: I was certainly a bridge between the old world and the new world.

When I first came to KPM, I was moving away from being a traditional musician. I was a saxophone player—I played five or six instruments, but I was essentially a saxophone player. When I turned pro at eighteen, I wanted to become a writer. Well, at eighteen, nobody is going to arrest you and let you become a writer. So I worked in various brass bands, but I also had no more money because I got married very young and had my first son when I was twenty-two years old; if I wasn't making it by the age of twenty-five, I was going to have to find another job, because I couldn't see how just sitting in bands for the rest of my life would be satisfactory to bring up a family. So I moved to KPM when I was twenty-four, which was fantastic.

First of all, just going into Denmark Street, that was the key—because Denmark Street *was* the music business. As a musician, you're blinkered; with the greatest respect in the world, you're blinkered. It was the hub of the pop scene in England. Half the music going on in London, particularly pop sessions, would come through our office.

It was a team of four copyists and two arrangers, who sat in the office every day, my staff, and others who would come and go—they'd work from home and they would come in to finish off scores and give the ones they'd finish to the copyist to copy. But I had my own space in this office that was my own little room with a piano. I was there every day, and I would arrange there and compose there. My starting time was regularly six o'clock in the morning, and I'd break up the day, but I regularly wouldn't leave until nearly midnight. It was a killing life. A real killing. I couldn't have lasted into my thirties for too long.

Arranging

Peter Cox: [Keith] was one of those people who had wonderful rapport with brass players. I think because they respected the arrangements that he was doing. He was always capable of producing something with real fire behind it.

Keith Mansfield: When I got into KPM, it was all kinds of music. Every day: orchestral, brass band, pop music, whatever. You were doing all of it. I can remember the first day a pop score came in for me to copy. I'm not kidding, I was nearly *ill* by how basic it was—it sort of knocked the wind out of my sails. I listened to the record, and the record was fine, but the arrangement was cut down to the bone. It was just a bit of a pattern that the lead guitar played, a bit of a pattern that the acoustic guitar played, a bit of a pattern that the bass guitar played... copy the guitar part on the right hand of the piano, copy the bass guitar on the left hand of the piano, the drums—one beat, one bar of rhythm, and then it went on and on for sixteen bars, the same thing. I thought, *This is insulting*. But what it did—when the musicians got there, they almost didn't need to read it. They had all the information they needed.

See, as an arranger, when I first started out, I used to give the drummer every bloody thing he had to play, with his feet as well. It was a nightmare! You needed a contortionist to play the part. It was hard as an arranger to learn how to give them the simplest part, but to give them the information so that they could give you what you wanted. You had to learn how to not write too much. On the other hand, the brass and the strings, and all those others, you had to write exactly what you wanted, because that's what you were going to get back.

Orchestrating

Keith Mansfield: To be honest, it's really easy to write tunes; it's even really easy to write good tunes. Writing non-tunes is difficult. Then when you're writing tunes without a rhythm section, then when you're writing sets without any chords... You know—*How do you write it without melody? And then how do you sustain interest?*—just almost like with intervals or with rhythmic things. Space. They were things that were really interesting to me, to find something new.

To [write for a larger band], you've got to be a composer and an orchestrator... I remember one editor would come in and he would be bitching, "You bloody writers, you're always saying everything based around the rhythm section." And truly, in the late '60s, that's what was happening: everybody wanted funky rhythms and a cute line or whatever on top. And that's where the musicians came into their element. Because they were used to getting all these great tracks together rhythmically. And all they had to do was come up with a tune on top of it and they had winning titles. Well, I decided not to go that route. I decided to take the hard woods, all the orchestral music and things like that. Because as a composer, I didn't come in just to write a rhythm section with a cute top line. I thought I was supposed to do more than that.

So even though it was hard work, I did a lot of those bigger things. As a consequence, I have very little funky music to show for those

Mansfield conducting a KPM recording session.

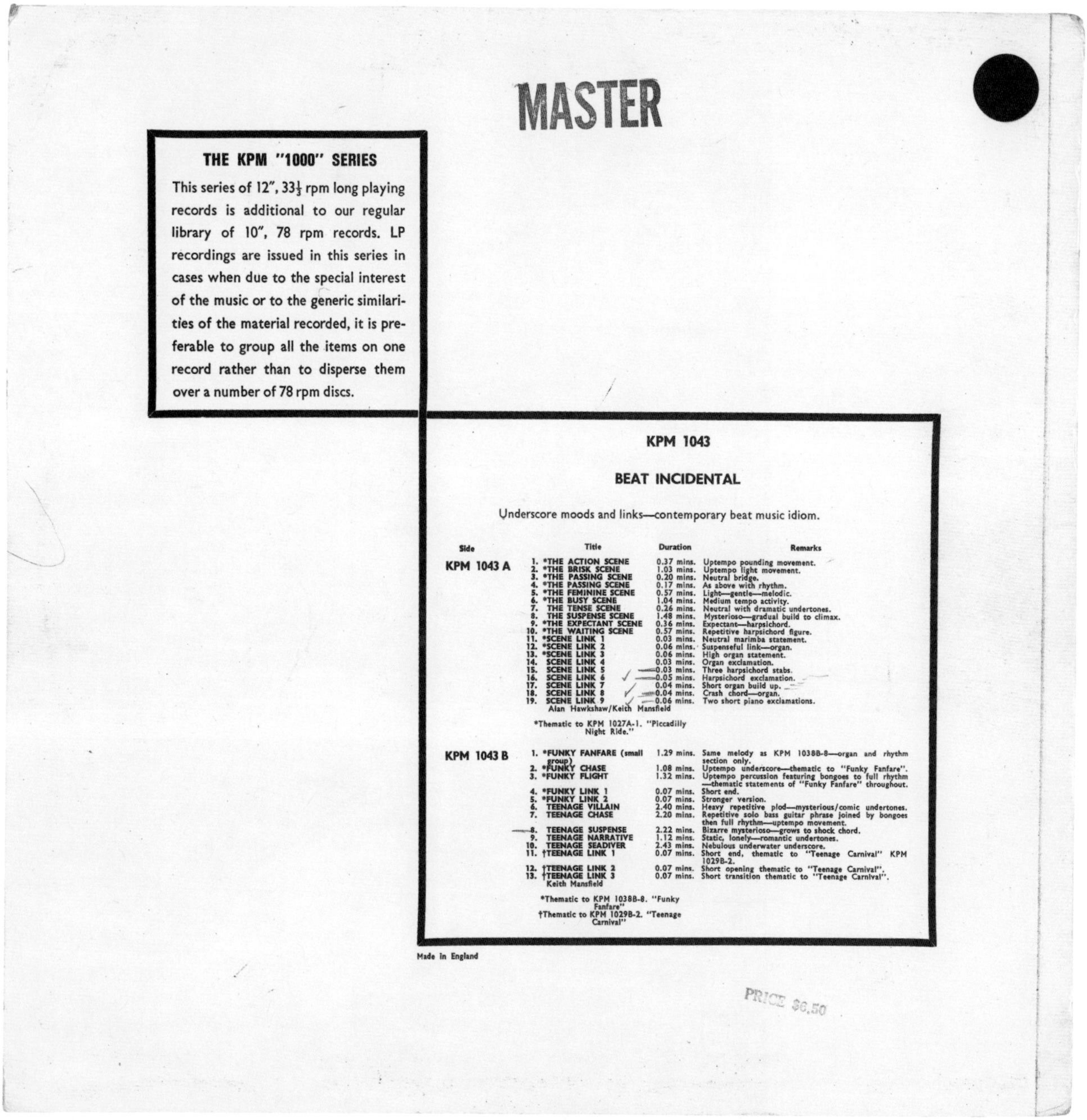

MASTER

THE KPM "1000" SERIES

This series of 12", 33⅓ rpm long playing records is additional to our regular library of 10", 78 rpm records. LP recordings are issued in this series in cases when due to the special interest of the music or to the generic similarities of the material recorded, it is preferable to group all the items on one record rather than to disperse them over a number of 78 rpm discs.

KPM 1043

BEAT INCIDENTAL

Underscore moods and links—contemporary beat music idiom.

Side	Title	Duration	Remarks
KPM 1043 A	1. *THE ACTION SCENE	0.37 mins.	Uptempo pounding movement.
	2. *THE BRISK SCENE	1.03 mins.	Uptempo light movement.
	3. *THE PASSING SCENE	0.20 mins.	Neutral bridge.
	4. *THE PASSING SCENE	0.17 mins.	As above with rhythm.
	5. *THE FEMININE SCENE	0.57 mins.	Light—gentle—melodic.
	6. *THE BUSY SCENE	1.04 mins.	Medium tempo activity.
	7. THE TENSE SCENE	0.26 mins.	Neutral with dramatic undertones.
	8. THE SUSPENSE SCENE	1.48 mins.	Mysterioso—gradual build to climax.
	9. *THE EXPECTANT SCENE	0.36 mins.	Expectant—harpsichord.
	10. *THE WAITING SCENE	0.57 mins.	Repetitive harpsichord figure.
	11. *SCENE LINK 1	0.03 mins.	Neutral marimba statement.
	12. *SCENE LINK 2	0.06 mins.	Suspenseful link—organ.
	13. *SCENE LINK 3	0.06 mins.	High organ statement.
	14. SCENE LINK 4	0.03 mins.	Organ exclamation.
	15. SCENE LINK 5	0.03 mins.	Three harpsichord stabs.
	16. SCENE LINK 6	0.05 mins.	Harpsichord exclamation.
	17. SCENE LINK 7	0.04 mins.	Short organ build up.
	18. SCENE LINK 8	0.04 mins.	Crash chord—organ.
	19. SCENE LINK 9	0.06 mins.	Two short piano exclamations.
	Alan Hawkshaw/Keith Mansfield		
	*Thematic to KPM 1027A-1. "Piccadilly Night Ride."		
KPM 1043 B	1. *FUNKY FANFARE (small group)	1.29 mins.	Same melody as KPM 1038B-8—organ and rhythm section only.
	2. *FUNKY CHASE	1.08 mins.	Uptempo underscore—thematic to "Funky Fanfare".
	3. *FUNKY FLIGHT	1.32 mins.	Uptempo percussion featuring bongoes to full rhythm—thematic statements of "Funky Fanfare" throughout.
	4. *FUNKY LINK 1	0.07 mins.	Short end.
	5. *FUNKY LINK 2	0.07 mins.	Stronger version.
	6. TEENAGE VILLAIN	2.40 mins.	Heavy repetitive plod—mysterious/comic undertones.
	7. TEENAGE CHASE	2.20 mins.	Repetitive solo bass guitar phrase joined by bongoes then full rhythm—uptempo movement.
	8. TEENAGE SUSPENSE	2.22 mins.	Bizarre mysterioso—grows to shock chord.
	9. TEENAGE NARRATIVE	1.12 mins.	Static, lonely—romantic undertones.
	10. TEENAGE SEADIVER	2.43 mins.	Nebulous underwater underscore.
	11. †TEENAGE LINK 1	0.07 mins.	Short end, thematic to "Teenage Carnival" KPM 1029B-2.
	12. †TEENAGE LINK 2	0.07 mins.	Short opening thematic to "Teenage Carnival".
	13. †TEENAGE LINK 3	0.07 mins.	Short transition thematic to "Teenage Carnival".
	Keith Mansfield		
	*Thematic to KPM 1038B-8. "Funky Fanfare"		
	†Thematic to KPM 1029B-2. "Teenage Carnival"		

Made in England

PRICE $6.50

OPPOSITE

Alan Hawkshaw / Keith Mansfield. *Beat Incidental*. KPM (UK): KPM 1043, 1969.

years—I really wish I had much more, because the editors would be gobbling it up now, but it did mean that on so many occasions when they needed important-sounding music, I was one of the few composers they could go to. A lot of the other writers, what would they want to write big stuff for when they could write this small stuff, which took no time and would earn just as much if not more money?

"Funky Fanfare" (from KPM 1043, *Beat Incidental*, 1969)

Keith Mansfield: I'm really proud of "Funky Fanfare," because it's nothing to do with who I was originally. And it was a product of that era, and it was so successful. So yeah, I'm really pleased I wrote that piece of music. It's one of these funny things. Often the things that you put the most effort into were not the most successful, and the ones where you had the least time [were], just like "Funky Fanfare."

There is no question that although you need expertise, you also need luck. And in this instance, the luck was a record company, Decca, that came to me to do an instrumental session with a very good pop drummer called Tony Newman, and they wanted to do two titles: a current tune, I forget what it was called, and the producer said we'd write the B-side—which meant I would write it—and we'd split it, but I would get paid for the arrangement. So, I wasn't really that keen to do it because I was already booked to go to Brussels or to Germany, one of the two, for KPM, and I wasn't taking sessions. In the end, I said OK. And I remember it was Decca, Monday afternoon—so Sunday afternoon, I had the morning off, I did the A-side. Monday morning, I get up, maybe 6:30, and I've got a piece of music to write for the B-side. So, hey, it's a B-side, I'm splitting it with the producer, what does it matter? So I get up, I put a record on to get me in the groove and the first thing that came into my head—it was the fanfare, or the tune. I just went along. That was it.

We spent two hours [at Decca] doing the A-side, had a break, then we did the B-side and I left. It turned out, of course, that they turned the record over and the B-side became the A-side. But before the session started I said to the producer, "Oh by the way, I didn't have time to write a new piece of music, I've had to write one of those that I've written for KPM." Of course, he thought that was fine. And then of course it became the A-side, but it wasn't called "Funky Fanfare," it was called "Soul Thing." So the first recording of "Funky Fanfare" is called "Soul Thing," and it's a Tony Newman record, a proper produced commercial recording done at Decca studios. Ten days later I record the same piece of music in Cologne for Robin [Phillips] and we called it "Funky Fanfare."

So that's how it started, I mean, I didn't second-guess myself—the first thing that came to my head, that's what I did. Because I had to come up with the idea, write it for the band, and get to London and be in time to do the session in the afternoon. When it's got to be that quick, there's no pressure. Just do whatever comes to your mind. I couldn't do that now. I'd take a month and I still wouldn't write it (*laughs*).

OPPOSITE

Keith Mansfield. *Night Bird*. Amphonic Music Ltd. (UK): AMPS 123, 1979.

"Grandstand" (from KPM 1173, *Solid Gold*, 1976)

Keith Mansfield: Another piece of music that doesn't mean that much in America, but means a great deal in England, because it was a famous theme tune: it's a combination of pop and brassy; I call it a "Las Vegas" sort of middle section. But it's proper orchestrated, with pop elements in the arrangement that make it fun; editors and people like those sorts of things. I'm pleased to have written that piece of music because of how much it's meant to other people: "Grandstand" was used for thirty-five years, every Saturday lunchtime, and sometimes Sundays, but the bonus there was, I can remember the time when my daughter was about twelve, and we were traveling in the car and she said, "Dad, did you really write 'Grandstand'?" And I'm thinking, *This is going to be some kind of windup*. And I said, "Yeah, why?" And she said, "All my friends at school love it." And then years later, when I was doing the KPM All-Stars, there's all these young guys there, and they grew up listening to all those theme tunes that I wrote.

Night Bird (Amphonic AMPS 123, 1979)

Keith Mansfield: Unfortunately, the cover mitigated against its usage. When it was done, there was a lot of criticism about the cover in America. They didn't like it—they said it was like some prostitute. You know, *What are they doing with that on the cover?* I don't think it helped the sales of the album. And that was also a little bit too adventurous maybe for library; it was too jazzy, funky... Good writing. Very good writing. But maybe it needed the sure hand of the producer sort of thinning out some of the stuff. But really, wonderfully executed by all the players.

Legacy

Peter Cox: [Keith] was a great person to work with, one of those people who actually specialized—unusually, almost fully—in library music, who found it a creative medium to work in.

Keith Mansfield: When you did library music, there was no contract. You weren't exclusive. But, if you worked like how I worked with Robin at KPM, I had plenty of work; I had no need to work elsewhere.

I had an office in Denmark Street, and I'd go across to KPM every day to have a cup of coffee or a cup of tea, and there would often be editors. And the editors would always be beefing about what they couldn't find in the library. So I'd listen to what they say, and rather than take offense, I'd think, *OK, next time I do this, I'll try and incorporate music that they are looking for.* And gradually, I realized, as the years went by, that I had all these friends all over the world that I'd never met. They were called editors. I mean, I have people use my music on a regular basis and they kind of see me evolve through different periods of my life. And they knew me and my friends, so that I could be somewhere, phone up, and immediately people would see me. And all they'd want to do is talk about the KPM recordings and all those other guys that were part

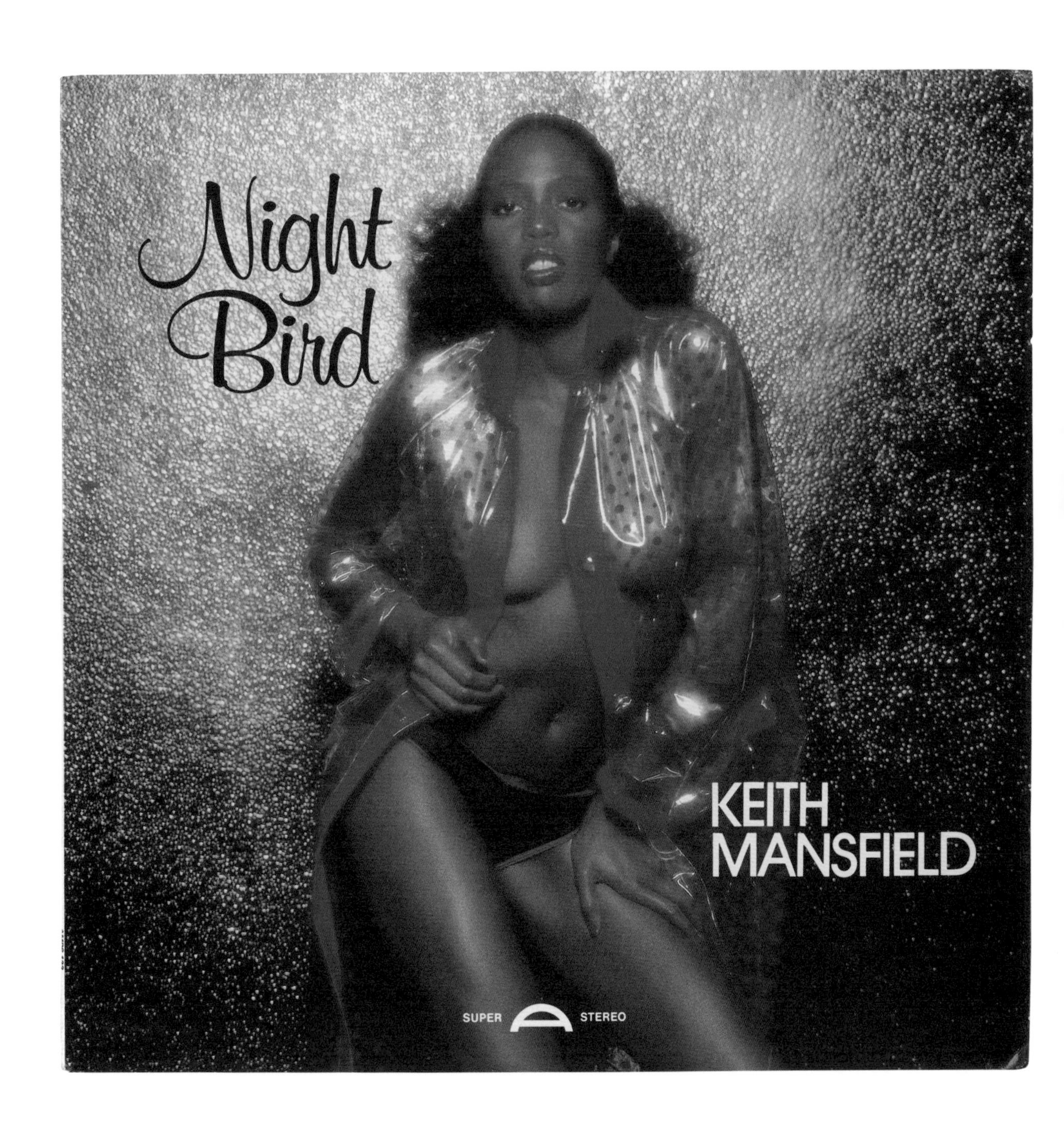
Night
Bird
KEITH
MANSFIELD
SUPER
STEREO

CONTACT
kpm
music
MODERNE INDUSTRIE
Rhythmische Synthesizer-Industriemusiken
Optimistisch, rhythmisch, plakativ
1304
Für Deutschland: SONOTON
Schleibingerstr. 10, 8000 München 80
Opitz Straße 22, 2000 Hamburg 60
UHJ AMBISONIC

OPPOSITE

Keith Mansfield / Richard Elen. *Contact*. KPM (UK): KPM 1304, 1983.

BELOW

Keith Mansfield / Alan Hawkshaw. *The Big Beat*. KPM (UK): KPM 1044, 1969.

of the sessions. It was a wonderful world. So, not only was there that social aspect of it, but there was an obligation. I had all these friends out there that I'd never met, and I had an obligation to give them music that they could use, even if it wasn't going to be the most overly successful.

I can remember meeting a lot of editors in America when APM [Associated Production Music] was formed. I remember going over there for the launch party and meeting all these editors, both in Los Angeles and in New York. And one of the things that was said by many of the editors was, "You're the editors' friend; you write music for the editors to be able to use." I loved hearing that—not for any ego, but because that's what I'd set out to do: I wanted to give them music that they could use, not just a thing that anybody could write.

The thing about the library was I could be whoever I wanted to be. I could be funky, I could be poppy, I could be big band, I could be orchestral, I could be angry, I could be happy, whatever I wanted to do. Because library music requires all those emotions. And, you know, particularly positive things—there's always a call for those—but the thing about library is you could always do those angst-ridden things as well, because somebody is going to need it somewhere; not everything is going to be happy. So as a composer I can't think of a better world to have been fortunate to live most of my life in.

JOHNNY PEARSON

Born in 1925 in Derbyshire, Johnny Pearson demonstrated an early aptitude for the piano: He won a scholarship to the London Academy of Music, formed a jazz band in his teen years, and played in the Royal Artillery Band and Orchestra during World War II. Over the ensuing two decades, he honed his skills and reputation in jazz combos, radio appearances, and concert orchestras, and in 1964, as part of the easy-listening ensemble Sounds Orchestral, he scored a hit with an orchestral version of Vince Guaraldi's "Cast Your Fate to the Wind." In 1966, Pearson recorded his first library records, and he would go on to a distinguished career in the field with numerous releases on KPM, Themes International, and Bruton yielding several classic library tracks (including "Heavy Action," known in the United States as the theme for *Monday Night Football*).

TOP

David Snell / Johnny Pearson. *Cottage Industry / Safari Rally*. Bruton Music (UK): BRL 8, 1981.

BOTTOM

Duncan Lamont / Johnny Pearson. *The Magic of Life*. Bruton Music (UK): BRD 21, 1982.

ALAN HAWKSHAW

BELOW

Hawkshaw performing as part of the KPM All-Stars in 2012.

Born in Leeds in 1937, Alan Hawkshaw began working as a band pianist in Liverpool in 1959. He soon had a regular gig with the pop group Emile Ford and the Checkmates, during which he rubbed shoulders with the Beatles and the Rolling Stones in their earliest days, before transitioning into studio sessions and recording for film and television. In 1963, Hawkshaw began working at KPM, where his prowess on piano, electric keyboards, and, especially, the Hammond organ (which he played with a trademark overdriven style) made him a key figure in the library's stable of musicians. One of Hawkshaw's best-known and most influential cuts, 1968's "The Champ," wasn't technically recorded for a library: The seminal funk track was delivered under the name "the Mohawks" for Pama Records (albeit on an album backed with KPM compositions), and has since become one of the most sampled recordings in history. Indeed, Hawkshaw's compositions are everywhere—Sugar Hill Gang even used one of his pieces (taken from a 1978 release as "Love De-Luxe and Hawkshaw's Discophonia") for "Rapper's Delight." He remains a true legend of the library music era, as well as an acknowledged godfather of hip-hop and sampling culture.

Peter Cox: Hawkshaw is the consummate Hammond king. Wonderful commerciality just tripped naturally off of Alan's fingers.

Alan Hawkshaw: With my music, with my funky stuff, I never copied anybody in America. I'd never listened to anybody—except the jazzers, but they weren't playing funk. Jimmy Smith didn't play funk; he's playing improvised jazz. So I'm not copying anything at that point... I toured with the Rolling Stones for two years, probably, during the early / mid-'60s. The group I was with had the same manager, so we toured with them. Mind you, they copied American blues music. So there was nothing original coming out of the Stones, in my opinion.

Peter Cox: He was fantastic in the advertising business, he absolutely cleaned up; that Hammond organ sound was so commercial. Alan was great—he just had the ability to write very, very commercial-sounding material. Anything from sort of very fast Hammond organ, which he wrote or cowrote with Alan Parker, through the things like "Girl in a Sports Car" (from *Friendly Faces*, KPM 1123, 1973), that sort of sound. Just so popular. And the way he plays that Hammond organ is just so effortless, just absolutely brilliant.

Alan Hawkshaw: When you're playing piano all the time, the electric piano, it's a gentle instrument. But when you get on the organ, you can really let rip; it's like a drum almost. That release of energy. And I felt that release a lot. You can hear it in the music. What I'm doing is just injecting my musicality, which was basically a very percussive way of playing the organ. Almost like a guy who can play conga drums, playing that on keyboard. Because I love the energy, I love the power of it. The difference, for me, was like being released out of a cage.

Peter Cox: Robin picked up immediately that [Hawkshaw's Hammond playing] had a wonderful commerciality, which it did.

Alan Hawkshaw: I got introduced to library music in about 1963, '64, by a guy called Guy Fletcher, my dear friend. Thank goodness he took me in there, because I met Robin Phillips. He was a young guy. He wanted to get more music of the times, especially the '60s. That's when I wrote "Senior Thump," "Beat Me 'Til I'm Blue" (from *The Big Beat*, KPM 1044, 1969)—all these things went together. I have no idea to this day whether he liked them or not, [but] he issued them. As it turns out, they were, in a way, a little bit ahead of themselves. Especially due to the fact they've all become highly popular in the twenty-first century. Which is one of those bizarre paradoxes that happens.

The "Hammond Sound"

Alan Hawkshaw: That was an accident. About 1967 or '68, I'm now beginning to get into session work. I'm just about still in [the Checkmates], but I'm now getting my feet wet by going into studio work, which was much more demanding—I could read music, but I wasn't a seasoned session person at that time. I was only doing maybe one or two a week, and they were quite easy sessions.

OPPOSITE

The Mohawks. *The Champ*. Pama Records (UK): PMLP 5, 1968.

But now, as my name's getting around, I'm beginning to get calls for more demanding sessions, more demanding fix-ups.

And I get booked on a session: Olympic Sound Studios, a famous studio in London. I turn up there, and I've borrowed an organ for this—because I haven't got one yet—and the guy was late delivering it, so I'm already very nervous. I look at the studio and it's packed with chairs. And there was going to be a big orchestra, which was probably one of my first orchestral sessions on Hammond; I did plenty later, but this would be my first. Now I'm really scared. The guy sets the organ up, the musicians are coming in, and I'm sitting with keyboard players like Ronnie Price, Laurie Holloway. These were keyboard players who were well-seasoned guys, British composers themselves, and they were there just as players. And French horns, big string section, woodwinds. Then the musical director walks in, Johnny Gregory. I don't know Johnny Gregory, he doesn't know me. It's a big Christmas album. And he hands the music out, which I'm trying to get my hands on to have a look at before we do the first thing. And the first number up is "God Rest Ye Merry Gentlemen." And it starts off, it's all strings and fugues, and very classical. And it's all this fugue-y stuff, very impressive. And then it says "organ solo," on bar sixteen or something. And I'm so scared at this point... I realize as I'm playing: I'm probably louder than the whole orchestra put together. I'm really loud. And it gets to the end of the run-through, and the musical director stops, turns to me, and says, "Excuse me, what's your name?" I said, "Alan Hawkshaw." He says, "That's great. That's just what this piece needs." And that was the beginning of where I overblew the Leslie speaker, kind of almost like a fuzz guitar. That was the beginning of that. That sound was born.

The Champ (by the Mohawks, Pama Records, PMLP 5, 1968)

Alan Hawkshaw: What happened was, I was booked on a session. I didn't know what it was 'til I got there. And it was the Mohawks, who were doing "The Champ" and a couple of other tunes, for Pama Records. Guy [Fletcher] was raving about the performance stuff then. So he said, "I'd really like to get an album out of this stuff as soon as possible." I said to him, "Well, I may be able to save you time," because I'd already recorded several titles in that vein for KPM anyway. Including "Beat Me 'Til I'm Blue," "Senior Thump," "Rocky Mountain Runabout," and so on. I said, "I could probably get you those tracks for no money; just put them on the album and do an agreement with Robin Phillips." And that's what happened. So the album was, in a sense, already made.

"Chicken Man" (from *Rock Comedy*, TIM 1017, 1976)

Alan Hawkshaw: We were doing a session in Munich. "Chicken Man" came out [of one of those sessions], and then it was picked up by *Grange Hill*, a popular TV theme that went on for about twenty years in England. Then I get a phone call one day from a producer at Thames Television, our commercial TV station in England. A woman said, "We want to use a piece of your music for a new TV series called *Give Us a Clue*." And it was going to

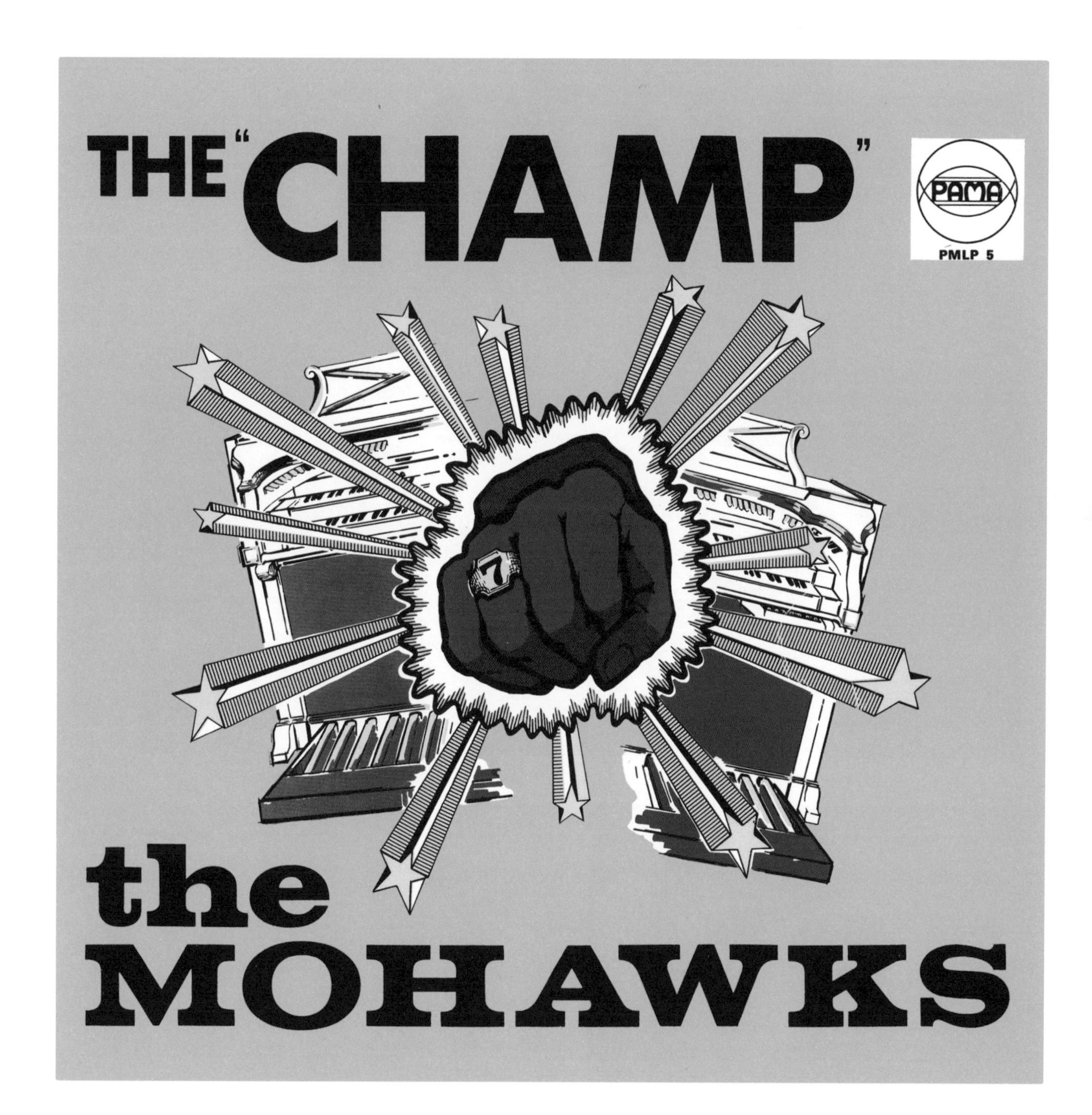
THE "CHAMP"
PAMA
PMLP 5
7
the
MOHAWKS

UNDERWORLD
BRUTON MUSIC
BRM 14
BRM 14

BRI 8
BRUTON MUSIC
KINETICS/VISION
BRI 8

BRD 4
BRUTON MUSIC
REFLECTIONS
BRD 4

OPPOSITE TOP

Alan Hawkshaw / Simon Benson / Eugenio Grandi / David Snell. *Underworld*. Bruton Music (UK): BRM 14, 1985.

OPPOSITE BOTTOM LEFT

Trevor Bastow / Alan Hawkshaw. *Kinetics / Vision*. Bruton Music (UK): BRI 8, 1980.

OPPOSITE BOTTOM RIGHT

Various. *Reflections*. Bruton Music (UK): BRD 4, 1978.

be presented by Michael Aspel, a well-known guy there. "And we want to use your piece 'Chicken Man.'" I said, "Really? Well, I've got to tell you that that piece is already being used as the TV show called *Grange Hill*." She said, "We're well familiar with that. We just want you to reorchestrate it and make it sound a bit more modern." And yet the same piece. I think it was the first time in history there's been two major TV shows with the same music.

Terrestrial Journey (BRI 1, 1978)

Alan Hawkshaw: If I was given [a theme of] "Wildlife," for instance, I'd get these mental images of wildlife. You know, whatever: spring and summer, birds flying, eagles swooping and so on... [*Terrestrial Journey*] was about space. It was about the cosmos. And it was all mainly electric piano and piano itself... at that time, synthesizers were beginning to come in.

Once I got something laid down, even if it was a very basic sound, I could then elaborate; I used to add to it with multitrack as I went along. So in other words, I didn't have a complete overall picture of what I was going to be doing, because I was literally being inspired by what I'd already done on a previous take. And that's how I did the whole of that album.

I would start off with, let's say, a Fender Rhodes, forming a pattern. We had no sequences; there was no real locking in to any click tracks. We had to literally play everything to a beat and whatever was featured at the time. I remember doing that album and really getting off on it, because the sound of the Fender, when you put some strain on it, immediately transported one into the heavens, into the skies. From then on, it was easy.

Peter Cox: I think it was Jimmy Phillips who was involved in asking Alan to write the *Countdown* theme ["Countdown," on *Terrestrial Journey*]. And Alan said, "Oh, don't even bother, Jimmy," and Jimmy said, "I think it's going to make some money." I think Alan said it took about ten minutes to just about dash this thing off. And it's now running today—you hear it every single day!

"Best Endeavours" (from *Televisual*, BRG 25, 1984)

Alan Hawkshaw: It's an orchestral piece, although it didn't start off as orchestral, with a piccolo trumpet playing. And incidentally, the piccolo trumpet [part] was the first sample that was ever done in England on the Synclavier synthesizer; we're talking about 1978, '79. That piece was picked up by Channel 4 News in England and they wanted to use it as their news theme. So: could they have an exclusive on it? Now this is just prior to when it's going to be issued. So Robin held it back, gave it a year or something like that, then issued it. The piece, Channel 4 News, is still on. It's still on after all these years: thirty-three, thirty-four years.

Actually, Clint Eastwood used it in a movie called *Pale Rider*, for the promotion of *Pale Rider*, which was being splashed all over TV in England at that time. So you'll get—and it happens—you'll

BELOW

Steve Gray / Zack Laurence / James Clarke / Alan Hawkshaw. *Televisual*. Bruton Music (UK): BRG 25, 1984.

OPPOSITE TOP

Alan Hawkshaw / John Cameron. *Odyssey*. Bruton Music (UK): BRI 27, 1985.

OPPOSITE BOTTOM LEFT

Various. *Comedy*. Bruton Music (UK): BRF 1, 1978.

OPPOSITE BOTTOM RIGHT

Alan Hawkshaw. *Alan Hawkshaw's Universal Bulletin*. New Southern Library (UK): NSL 1010, 1984.

get that jingle on commercial television just before or just after the news, and then get the same theme being played. So Channel 4 actually had a special announcement one night: The news announcer said, "We'd just like you to know that the Channel 4 music is not exclusively ours and, in fact..." And the news theme went out with a clip of Clint Eastwood riding off into the sunset with this theme going. It sounded very western, believe it or not.

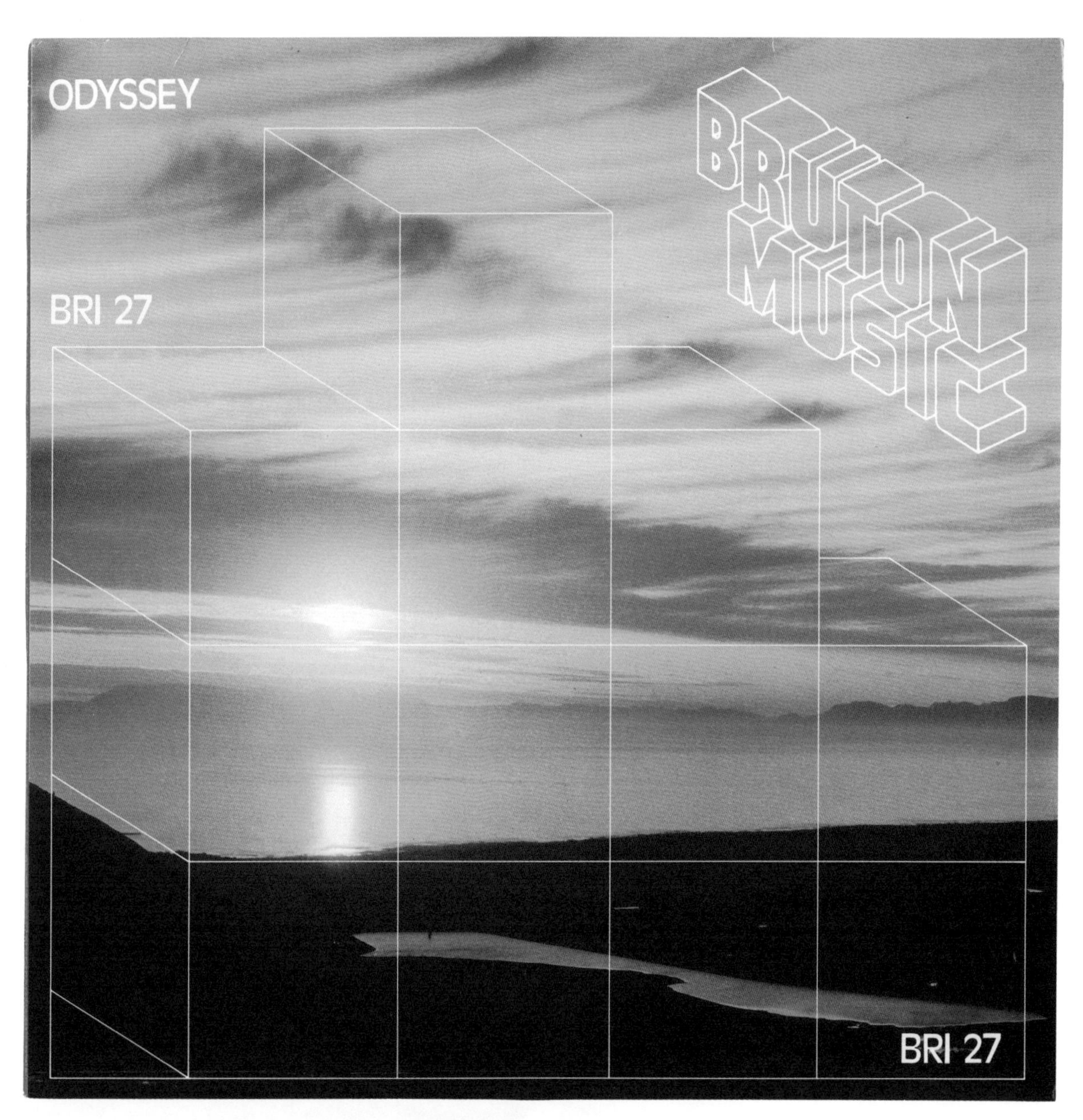
ODYSSEY
BRUTON MUSIC
BRI 27
BRI 27

BRF 1
BRUTON MUSIC
COMEDY
BRF 1

New Southern Library
ALAN HAWKSHAW'S
UNIVERSAL BULLETIN
Themes · Documentary · Drama · Panoramic · Impressive

JOHN CAMERON

A composer and producer who began as an arranger and music director for Donovan, John Cameron soon transitioned into film scoring (most notably for Ken Loach's seminal 1969 film *Kes*) and library music. Cameron's library credits include the enormously influential 1972 KPM record *Jazzrock*, as well as 1973's *Afro Rock* with Alan Parker and *Voices in Harmony* with Keith Mansfield, from the same year. Cameron was also musical director of the 1970s band Collective Consciousness Society, or CCS, whose version of Led Zeppelin's "Whole Lotta Love" served as the theme for *Top of the Pops* throughout that decade.

Peter Cox: John Cameron came up through CCS—that's where I knew him, through the reputation he built up with them. And he just wrote some wonderful stuff... A great writer, with a unique style, no doubt about it.

John Cameron: Quincy Jones was my favorite composer. "In the Heat of the Night," you know, I still listen to it. For me there are sort of iconic figures from the '60s and '70s. Oliver Nelson's work on television was something that I would listen to avidly; I mean, I fancied doing that. The whole Motown thing, actually, we'd go, "One minute, that bass line that they use in the second inversion..." or "What were they doing with the kick drum?" And every time a Stevie Wonder record came out, you'd go, "Hey, what's he doing there?" That was where my sources came from. I mean, during my degree in Cambridge, I used to sit with John Coltrane playing until four in the morning, that kind of album. And my roommate is in the next room going off with it (*laughs*). Or I had the

BELOW

John Cameron. *Badlands*. Bruton Music (UK): BRJ 28, 1984.

Moanin' album [by Art Blakey and the Jazz Messengers]; that's been imbued in me right from the early days. So when it came to something like that... it was a question of just dragging ideas out of my psyche, you know?

I came out of Cambridge not knowing what I was going to do, except I wanted to be in the music business. And library was quite a way down the road, you know. I actually signed [at KPM] with Robin's dad, Jimmy, as a songwriter first.

Peter Cox: I think the first time I really became aware of John was a track called "49th Street Shakedown" [from *Jazzrock*, KPM 1097, 1972], which he recorded in the old KPM Studios, down in the basement of KPM. And when I heard this, I was in a session that John was doing. It was so exciting; he had a driving energy. Taken straight from that CCS sort of vibe. And of course it was brilliant, and it went on and made shitloads of money, and quite rightly too. It was brilliant for sports, for action; it was so exciting, and so different from anything else that we produced.

Voices in Harmony (KPM 1125, 1973)

John Cameron: I was back and forth to L.A. during the early '70s; I suppose that [this record] was slightly homage to some of the music over there. In a way, "Half-Forgotten Daydreams" is an homage to Francis Lai. And, you know, the mix of Californian nice funk and country rhythm sections and strings, because I was working with Bobbie Gentry, and she had great arrangements by

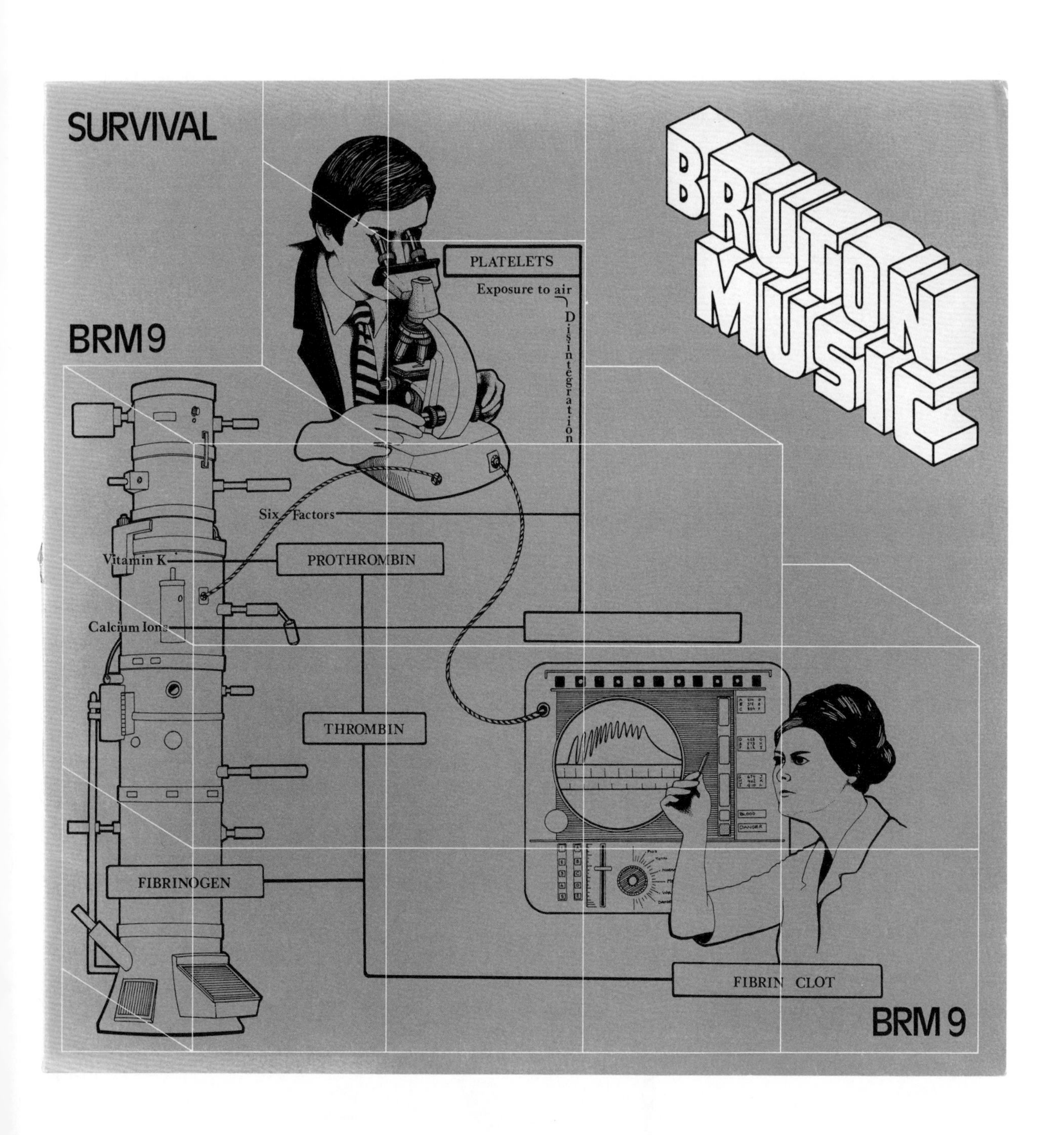
SURVIVAL
BRUTON MUSIC
BRM 9
PLATELETS
Exposure to air
Disintegration
Six Factors
Vitamin K
PROTHROMBIN
Calcium Ions
THROMBIN
FIBRINOGEN
FIBRIN CLOT
BRM 9

OPPOSITE

John Cameron / Jean Bouchéty / Robert Folk / Steve Gray. *Survival*. Bruton Music (UK): BRM 9, 1981.

TOP

John Cameron / Eric Allen. *Sketches of Africa*. Bruton Music (UK): BRR 19, 1984.

BOTTOM

Various. *Modern Africa*. Bruton Music (UK): BRR 20, 1984.

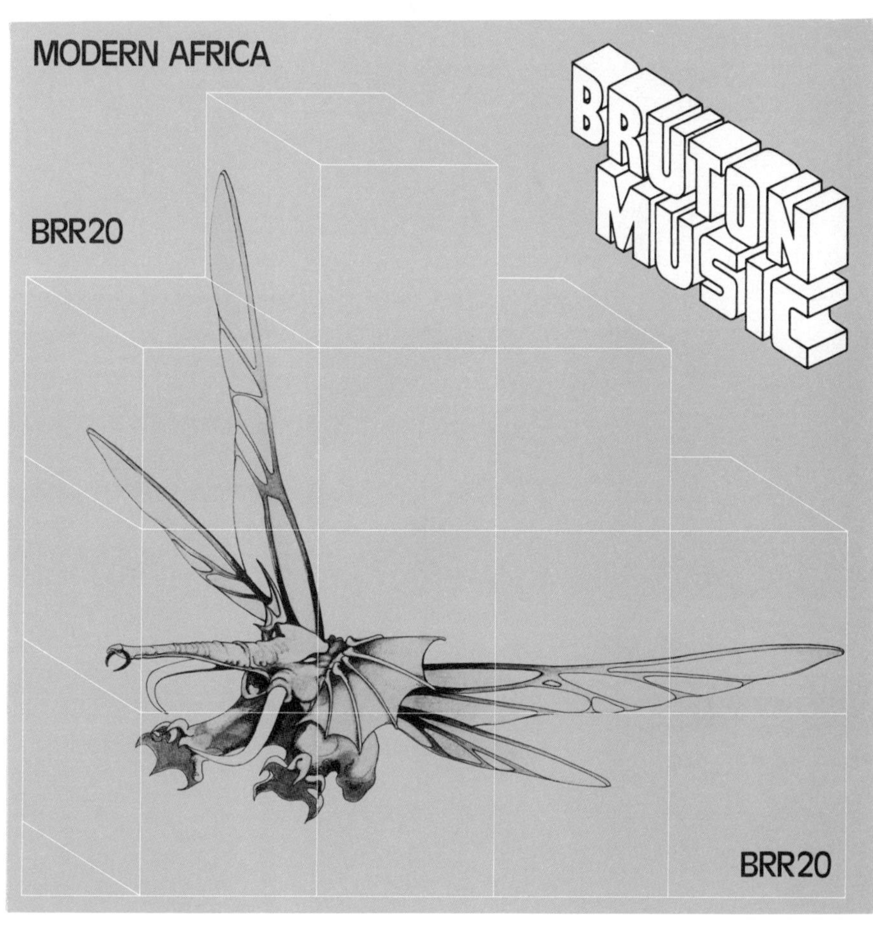

ATMOSPHERIC CHORALE
BRUTON MUSIC
BRM 10
BRM 10

EXPLORER
BRUTON MUSIC
BRI 25
BRI 25

BRI 9
BRUTON MUSIC
SUSPENSIONS/GALAXY
BRI 9

OPPOSITE TOP

Stephen St. Paul / John Cameron. *Atmospheric Chorale*. Bruton Music (UK): BRM 10, 1982.

OPPOSITE BOTTOM LEFT

John Cameron. *Explorer*. Bruton Music (UK): BRI 25, 1985.

OPPOSITE BOTTOM RIGHT

Trevor Bastow / John Cameron. *Suspensions / Galaxy*. Bruton Music (UK): BRI 9, 1980.

Jimmy Haskell—the arrangement on "Ode to Billy Joe" is a masterpiece. And a good friend of mine at the time was Perry Botkin, who was Nilsson's manager for some time; he wrote the arrangement on [Simon and Garfunkel's] "59th Street Bridge Song," you know, "Feeling Groovy." So I was very taken by this Californian gloss with strings, funky, nice, and I suppose that's what I tried to put into it.

"Swamp Fever" (from *Afro Rock*, KPM 1130, 1973)

I've always had an ability to write very fast. It's just why I've got a lot of work in movies and TV, where you have to produce stuff each week for each episode. And I tend to write as a jazz musician would write. So I'll think it, write it. I didn't—in those days especially—tend to sit down and hone and perfect, whatever. What came out first, then I'd get in the studio and then we would hone it. But I tended to go with gut reaction right from the start.

You know, you could go and write a symphony; you can go write a string quartet. But even those, I tend to end up writing it with a program or a poem—context is everything... When I put together a [library] project, I would sit down and write twenty titles that might apply to it, basically imagining situations that could be in a film or a TV series of that sort. And then I'd kind of think, *OK, what would I write for that situation?* Just a general idea. Because if you're too specific then it doesn't have the library use. You need something that can be applicable to this, applicable to that.

But, something like "Swamp Fever," I'd say, "I like that idea. Now, how's it going to feel?" Yeah, it's got to be steamy, it's got to be hot, it's got to be free, loose. It's got to have some of those elements of some of those scenes in *In the Heat of the Night*. You can actually feel the sweat on your arms. Just to convey that kind of atmosphere. Not specifically, *Guy goes into a bar, this happens, this happens*. But more, *What's that situation going to be?* Like the top of a screenplay where [it says] there's a bar in Havana, Cuba. It's late at night; it's heavy-duty drum-and-bass salsa music. There is a whole mess of different characters in there, some legal, most not. You know, so you build up the picture. And then you think, *OK, write some music to go with it*.

STEREO
DJL-7035
Brian Bennett
Voyage
a journey into discoid funk

COUNTERPOINT IN RHYTHM
BRUTON MUSIC
BRD 17
BRD 17

BRI 10
BRUTON MUSIC
FANTASIA
BRI 10

BRIAN BENNETT

OPPOSITE TOP

Brian Bennett. *Voyage (A Journey into Discoid Funk)*. DJM Records (UK): DJF 20532, 1978. Commercial release of Bruton LP *Fantasia* (*see below*).

OPPOSITE BOTTOM LEFT

Brian Bennett / Carlton Hall. *Counterpoint in Rhythm*. Bruton Music (UK): BRD 17, 1982.

OPPOSITE BOTTOM RIGHT

Brian Bennett. *Fantasia*. Bruton Music (UK): BRI 10, 1980.

As drummer of the popular and long-running British instrumental group the Shadows, Brian Bennett is perhaps the UK library composer with the most success outside the world of production music. Still, his work appears on many classic library recordings, including collaborations with Alan Hawkshaw for KPM and Themes International and solo compositions for Bruton Music.

Adrian Kerridge: Brian Bennett was the drummer with the Shads, and he was a very good composer—nice to work with, you know, he wasn't difficult. He was quite relaxed, but he knew his craft of writing; he knew exactly what to do, especially with the voicing of the instruments.

Peter Cox: Brian got his chance through Robin. Because Brian was in the rhythm section at a session in Brussels.

Adrian Kerridge: It was at Fonior Studios, in Belgium, where I first met him.

Peter Cox: Robin loved to get musicians and put them under a bit of pressure, but all for the right creative reasons. He said to each of the rhythm section, "Write me a couple of tracks, and you can [record them]. But the proviso is that you've got to sit in front of the band and conduct it." So Brian wrote these two themes, and anyway, after recording this—which was great, it was strings, and a lovely arrangement—I remember the orchestra all stood up and applauded. And I remember talking to Brian about it afterwards, and he said that was the one defining moment that turned him from a player into a writer. And Robin Philips was the one who gave him that break.

RON GEESIN

A Scottish composer and musician as well as a pioneer of electronic instrumentation, Ron Geesin gained recognition in the late 1960s and early '70s for his collaborations with Roger Waters and Pink Floyd, including the soundtrack album *Music from 'The Body'* and the multipart title track to Floyd's *Atom Heart Mother*. Geesin began his career in library music with the 1972 *Electrosound* album on KPM, which featured wildly innovative use of synthesizers, tape loops, and other techniques associated with musique concrète and the avant-garde. His lasting contributions to the fields of electronic music and sound design can be felt throughout today's musical landscape, from the most outré of modern composition to well-known film scores to commercial pop recordings.

Ron Geesin: There are no rules. For me, the only rule is good structure. Composition. You don't just do anything. It's got to mean a pattern. I think that most art is actually about building your own brain patterns, in the ideal. That's not to exclude the idea of acceptability in the public and everything else. But it's about building models of how you think. And since every human being is unique, if they're doing anything decent, it's going to come out unique to me. I've tried to copy stuff, and I can't do it. I can't copy things.

Peter Cox: I was always, in my heart of hearts, trying to turn Ron into a more commercial "writer," but Ron being Ron was unique and different. And Ron was unique in the correct sense of the word. There was nobody else like him.

Ron Geesin: One of my aphorisms about me is that I strive for "contented anonymity and complete uproar."

The Electro-Composer

Ron Geesin: I was so far away from the idea of having a musician sit there and play one line of dots. I was not double-tracking, I was not multitracking: I was making a whole world of sound. All of it was me, from—I devised this term much later on—"conception to reception"; the whole process, I made it. That's what you do: You think of the idea, you realize it.

I could not go anywhere near the British Musicians' Union... Because the Musicians' Union at one point had strict laws: You could play one instrument, and maybe if you applied specially, you could have a second instrument. And, you know, I had the equivalent of an orchestra... Through the '60s into the early '70s, there was plenty of antagonism. But it's the same as a school playground: You don't have to get involved in the fight. Some people like to pick fights, and some people like to just quietly get on with their lives.

I even was, for a short time, the chairman of the Association of Professional Composers. This problem came up. This was in the '80s, and it was obvious that there were quite a lot of composers who didn't use the old tools, the manuscript paper and the pencil. I actually wrote a booklet, *The Electro-Composer*; I wrote the whole booklet, anonymously, no name on it, logically arguing—not *arguing* because there really wasn't any argument, it was a fact of life—that if a machine is invented, you can't un-invent it. And what comes out of that is inevitable and unstoppable. So one has to learn how to use it for some kind of benefit to the human spirit, the human body and the human spirit. And that's how I made the argument about the fact that we'd gotten well beyond double-tracking. And I wrote that pamphlet thinking, *Right, that's it*. You know, to use that old cliché, *the shit will now hit the fan*. And I thought, *I think I'll stay under the duvet for a day or two*. And absolutely nothing happened. Because it was kind of obvious. It was so obvious that it had to happen.

I always talked about—I still do talk about—electronic methods of making sound structures as painting with sound, in fact. It's like having a palate and a brush: you paint, and you mess about and you experiment, and then something happens, if you're in a good mind. The structure emerges.

If you want to call it by its French term, *musique concrète, oooooh*, then you may, yes indeed. It was in that style. It is painting with sound. It is building sound. You're taking molecules of thought, and making a little structure, and then building those.

What is musique concrète? It's putting things together—first of all by editing, and then by mixing. But there are other times where you might have a microphone and hang it out the window, and there's no editing. And you might use the equivalent of a function in a synthesizer which would be a comb filtering, where you can take traffic noise and filter it down until you've just got a peak which could be a [*screech*] sound or a [*wind*] sound. As I often did.

OPPOSITE

Ron Geesin. *Electrosound*. KPM (UK): KPM 1102, 1972.

In fact, there are some things that were possible with magnetic tape and a bit of ingenuity that you'd be hard-pushed to get out of a synthesizer now.

Electrosound Vol. 1 (KPM 1102, 1972)

Peter Cox: [Geesin] was experimenting with new ideas, which of course for KPM was brilliant, because we had done enough of the mainstream material, and when we started to do the more electronic elements—Don Harper, people like that who were going in at that time—Ron was very much in the forefront of that. And he did create a lot of interest, because the use of synthesis was in its infancy, but it was novel. And with certain sorts of pictures, those new sounds were very much the avant-garde, cutting edge of music in the early '70s.

Ron Geesin: Jimmy Philips—nice old chap—was just about retiring at that time, and then Robin Phillips, and then, later on, Peter Cox took over. And they just came to me and said, "Well, you've done all this strange stuff on *'The Body'*, can you do us a music library album?" I said, "Of course I can"—because, being a solo survivor, I would tend to do that old classic thing of saying "yes" to anything, and go and find out how to do it afterwards (*laughs*).

And for me it was easy, because I didn't have any preconceived pictures to work to. I just made patterns. Some of them were rhythmic patterns, but some were just texture patterns, you know, things flowing over other things. All done with what I had in my little studio: certainly magnetic tape, and editing—slash razor blade stuff—mixing, running tape out through loops, doing different things. I'd already developed, by that time, a method of playing with tape between two machines, so that it wasn't like a loop where you've only got one thing going around; the sound was looped, but you could add into it all the time. You fed the sound back in, but the tape was running from one machine across to another machine. You had to get the tension right, so you needed the right kind of machine. Now when I started off, I had the "great" British ferrograph tape recorder, which was not great at all: It was built like a German tank, and they said you could drop it out of a first-floor window and it would still work, but as a piece of musical technical equipment, it wasn't any good at all. So the ReVox came in from Switzerland, and the ReVox was a baby Studer. Studer was the parent company. And when the ReVox came in you could have a control to micro-adjust speed, so that you could get the tension of the feed machine just right so that the second machine—you'd watch the little guides and things just get the tension bang on. And magic was made. I can't tell you how I did it (*laughs*).

Some of the pieces I did for KPM, on the albums, I don't think they were ever picked up, you know, on commercial work in the media. And that meant they didn't fit anywhere. But there were other ones that did; one had no idea which would be picked up and which would not. And that was one of the thrills for me in doing that library, particularly *Electrosound* volume one. There's one piece that I did called "Syncopot"—because it was to do with moving a potentiometer slightly to get a certain rhythm going, and then multi-multi-multitracking. And it was one of my favorite pieces; it's a real hot rhythm piece. It relates to my passion for black jazz. And then years later, I'm watching the television, and it's a nature documentary, and there's a certain species of beetle in the desert. And the beetle was digging in for the night, because it had to go into the sand. And there's two beetles, and they're going like this [*digging motions*] and here it is, what's been used? "Syncopot"! And it was absolutely perfect for this. And then I became friends with the director; I contacted him and I said, "Fantastic!" I never would have believed it. So that was the joy of it, you know, you make patterns and someone perceives that pattern as something else.

KPM 1102

Stereo
playable Mono

ELECTROSOUND

I present some tunes, untunes, anti-tunes, delightful and undelightful sounds for all sorts of purposes and state that:

The pieces herein displayed may be combined with themselves (as much out of sync as possible) to achieve thicker diffuse atmosphere, and playing things at different speeds would not be wrong!

RON GEESIN.

KPM 1102A

Title	Duration	Remarks
1. **GLASS DANCE**	1:53	Fast flowing complex rhythmic tinkling sound.
2. **U.F.O.**	2:03	Fuzz background with descending electronic scales.
3. **SONG OF THE WIRE**	1:46	Echoing organ sound over a neutral modulating bass.
4. **INDUSTRIAL JUNGLE**	2:05	Industrial sound, suggesting heavy machining, with deep tonal interjections
5. **BOTTLING PLANT**	2:03	Repetitive background sound suggesting busy activity.
6. **SLOW SONG**	2:03	Slow droning organ-like chords with metallic background.
7. **SYNCOPOT**	2:31	Rhythmic rubbing sound with electronic overlay in syncopated time.
8. **ENZYMES IN YOUR EAR**	2:09	Harsh dischordant notes in a random form over a repetitive riff.
9. **TROGLODYTE**	1:39	Slow muffled chords played over a neutral background with distorted interjections.
10. **SLOW SPRINKLE**	2:09	Random staccato notes suggesting droplets falling on water.

Composed by: RON GEESIN

KPM 1102B

Title	Duration	Remarks
1. **ORGAN IN THE CLOUDS**	2:32	Rhythmic, tuneful organ sound with repetitive bass line.
2. **DUCK FIGURES**	2:25	High pitched squawks over a neutral modulating background.
3. **ELECTRIC BARBED WIRE**	2:08	Metallic rhythmic drumming over a high-pitched modulating background.
4. **COMMUTER**	1:19	Rhythmic piano sound on a deep metallic syncopated background.
5. **CAR CRUSHER**	2:13	Grating dischordant metallic rasps with random high-pitched electronic background.
6. **SKY HIGH**	2:03	A series of gradually increasing harsh oscillations.
7. **DUET FOR CHOIR AND TUNNEL**	2:07	Echoing empty sound in a repetitive sequence.
8. **SPIROGRAPH A.**	1:52	Slow wistful clarion in random time with fuzz chord interjections.
9. **SPIROGRAPH B.**	2:33	As above at different pitch.

Composed by: RON GEESIN

This album is one of the "KPM 1000 Series" twelve inch long playing transcription discs produced especially for the film, television and radio industries, to the highest professional standards. The music contained herein is copyright of KPM Music Ltd., and licence must be obtained prior to usage. Stereo and Mono tapes are available from KPM and their world wide agents.

PRICE $6.50

MADE IN ENGLAND

KPM MUSIC LTD., 21 Denmark St., London, W.C.2.

Printed by West Brothers · Printers · Limited · London, S.W.19

Another one that's been used quite a lot, but I don't know where, is "Song of the Wire." It's a strange, eerie melody. Now, that was done with tape editing from the VCS3 [synthesizer]: I got the tones, and then literally editing every note. That was made just after we moved out of London, and I remember that there was a strange sound that comes in occasionally, and years after that, I realized that I had subconsciously recorded the sound of a jackdaw. When we first moved to this house in the country and there were empty rooms, there was nothing in the place, this jackdaw—in the mornings in May, because the sun was in a certain position—went up against the window and tried to attack its image in the window. And it made that sound. And I subconsciously reproduced that sound in the VCS3, and it's that on there. So things come from strange places.

Electrosound Vol. 2 (KPM 1154, 1975)

There's a couple of pieces [that have been used often], and I think one of them is "Frenzy." That's a cracking piece, because again, it's violent screeching, but rhythmic; it's a basic beat. I think that was used on a porno film recently. But I don't know, it's the kind of area where I'd say, "I've done it and it's out there." Or as I often say, I make interestingly shaped leaves that go on trees, and they get blown off in the autumn; they fall, and they can either end up as decoration on the front of a house, or in the gutter. You make stuff, and you don't know—it can go anywhere. And provided one has a sense of balance, a life philosophy of balance, then the failures are as good as the successes.

Legacy

Peter Cox: It was great having people like [Geesin] on board, and he was pioneering things that he'd done early, with his experiences obviously with Pink Floyd. He is an unforgettable person—he's a wonderful jazz aficionado, tremendous knowledge on a whole range of subjects, and a very, very fun person to work with.

Ron Geesin: I put a lot of humor into my work; I can't help it. Because that's a part of what's going on. I think that that's one of the great messages for life, especially now, in this turmoiled world. Keep the humor. Keep the lightness. Enjoy life, because it's bloody soon over.

LES BAXTER

BELOW

The Exotic Rhythms of Les Baxter Orchestra and Chorus. *African Blue*. GNP Crescendo (US): GNPS 2047, 1969.

An American composer and bandleader of remarkable prolificacy, Les Baxter wrote more than one hundred film soundtracks and was a pioneer of the late '50s, early '60s embrace of exotica. In 1970, KPM released Baxter's celebrated library record *Bugaloo in Brazil*, a Latin jazz exercise replete with samba flourishes and South America–referencing track names, but backed by Baxter's famous name, the record was rereleased in the United States by GNP Crescendo under the title *African Blue*. The record—given wholly different, African-inflected song titles on rerelease ("Girl from Uganda," "Johannesburg Blues")—may be a good example of the cultural nonspecificity of the era's so-called "world music" releases, but it also demonstrates the growing trend of library and commercial versions of records being released side by side.

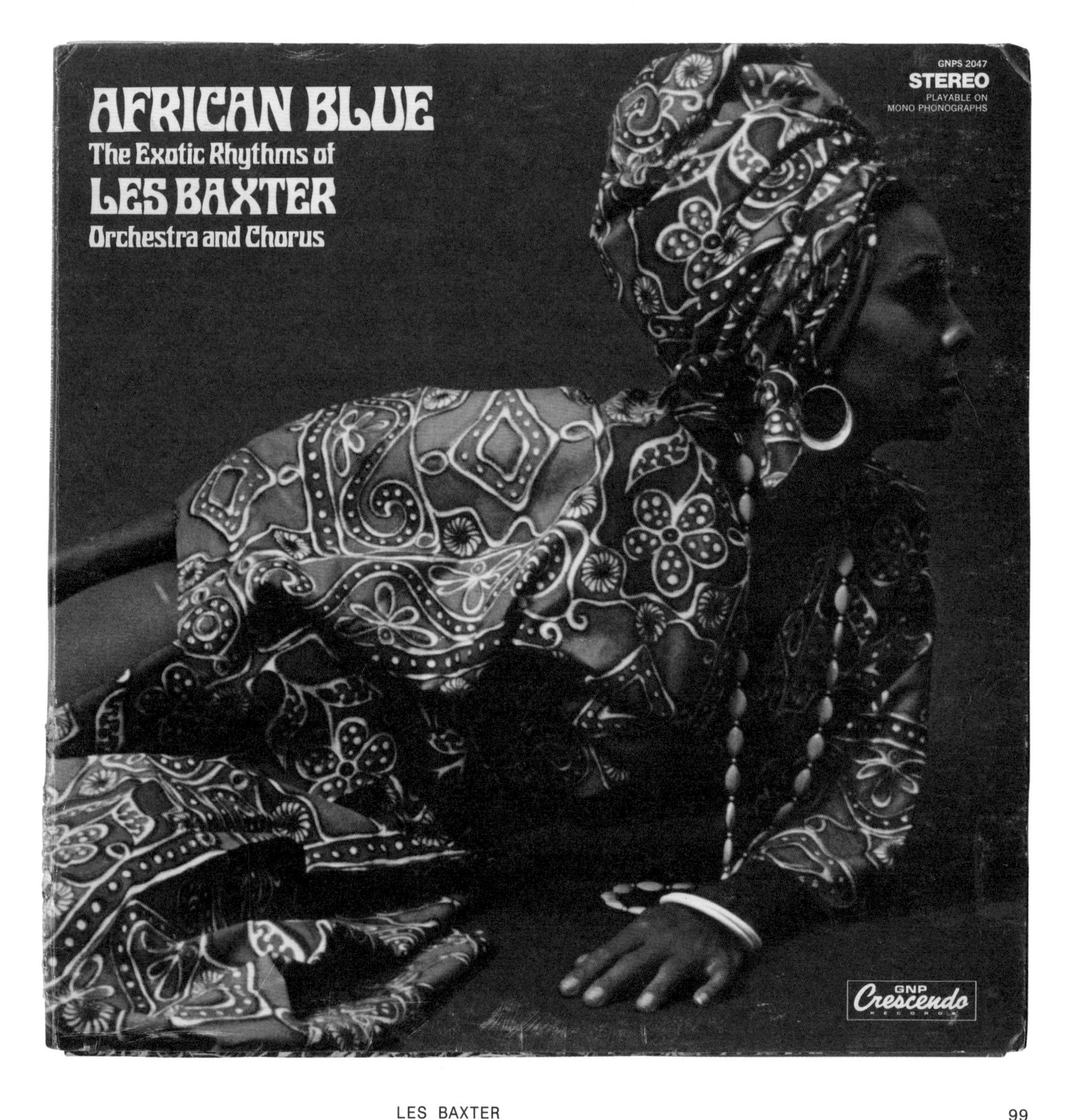

DELIA DERBYSHIRE

OPPOSITE

Derbyshire cutting tape in the BBC Radiophonic Workshop studios. Image courtesy BBC Photo Library.

Born to a working-class family in 1937, Delia Derbyshire managed to transcend her humble beginnings and launch a career as a renowned sonic innovator, seminal composer of early electronic and musique concrète, and pioneer of scoring and sound design. After early studies at Cambridge in mathematics, Derbyshire switched to a music degree and attempted to embark on a career in the field, only to be stymied by barriers in the male-dominated industry, which did not then employ women in recording studios. After stints teaching piano and other subjects to primary school students for the UN in Geneva and in her hometown of Coventry, England, Derbyshire worked briefly as an assistant at the Boosey & Hawkes publisher (and music library)—but it was only after she joined the BBC, in 1960, that her musical gifts found expression in the workplace. Derbyshire went to work for the then-new BBC Radiophonic Workshop, founded in 1958 by company employees (including fellow electronic music legend Daphne Oram) to provide themes, jingles, and sound design across the BBC's many broadcast platforms. In 1963, Derbyshire crafted her most widely known composition: the evocative and singular theme to *Doctor Who*, which BBC soon released on LP to lasting popularity.

With her work firmly in place in mainstream British culture, Derbyshire turned in the late 1960s to the creation and promotion of electronic music across all media, and teamed with fellow Radiophonic Workshop composer Brian Hodgson and the experimental musician David Voraus to form the band White Noise, which released its seminal debut album, *An Electric Storm*, in 1969 for Island Records. The group also pseudonymously recorded for music libraries (with Derbyshire credited as "Li de la Russe," a partial anagram of her first name), releasing music for the Standard Music Library as well as KPM, which put out the trio's *Electrosonic* (KPM 1104) on its famed KPM 1000 series in 1972. Though her library work constitutes a sideline in a storied and historic career, Derbyshire's contributions to the field of production music are prime examples of the industry's desire to incorporate sounds from the furthest vanguard of musical experimentation into its catalogs, even if only as the pseudonymous creations of a massively influential (but still underappreciated) giant of the field. Derbyshire died in 2001, leaving behind a legacy whose import is only now beginning to be felt.

THEMES

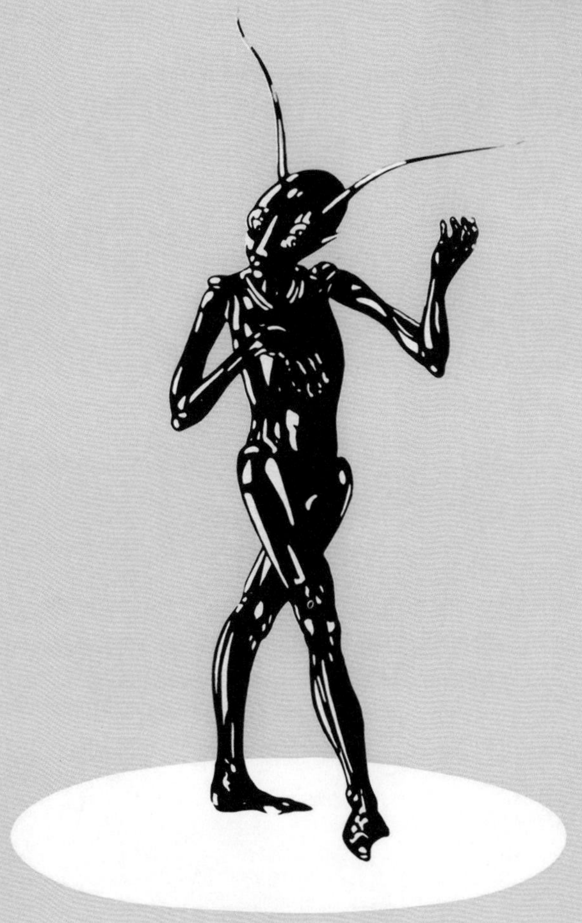

New Blood

THEMES INTERNATIONAL

OPPOSITE

Alan Parker / Alan Hawkshaw / Jon Watts / Mike Cox. *New Blood*. Themes International Music (UK): TIM 1002, 1973.

BELOW

Alan Hawkshaw / Alan Parker. *The Rock Machine*. Themes International Music (UK): TIM 1011, 1973.

Founded in 1973 by guitarist / composer and KPM stalwart Alan Parker, Themes International was created with the intention of bringing more of the unique, diverse sounds of the era into the library world. The library was distinguished by its arresting, often extraordinarily designed yellow sleeves, as well as its musical innovations (such as the dual release in 1976 of *The Voice of Soul*, a vocal record, and *The Sound of Soul*, its corresponding instrumental, which allowed production clients to cut between the two for greater effect). Themes International continued to occupy a distinct space in the world of UK library recordings until 1985, when its catalog was absorbed by EMI.

TOP

Various. *The Romantic Mood*. Themes International Music (UK): TIM 1006, 1973.

BOTTOM

Various. *Light Activity*. Themes International Music (UK): TIM 1007, 1973.

TOP

Various. *Jingles*. Themes International Music (UK): TIM 1010, 1973.

BOTTOM

Alan Hawkshaw / Brian Bennett. *Synthesizer and Percussion*. Themes International Music (UK): TIM 1012, 1974.

THEMES
The Sound Of Soul

ALAN PARKER

OPPOSITE

Alan Parker. *The Sound of Soul*. Themes International Music (UK): TIM 1022, 1976.

A session guitarist who cut his teeth playing on pop hits as well as film scores, Alan Parker's initial renown as a library composer came as a part of KPM, where he was hired on the basis of his renown as a session player. Once he'd joined the company, Parker became extremely prolific, writing and recording numerous highly popular recordings, including 1973's seminal *Afro Rock* with John Cameron. After founding Themes International, Parker continued to release classic recordings, among them 1976's *The Voice of Soul*, one of the best-known library recordings to feature vocals. Parker remains active in the field today, having contributed to the recent recordings in memory of former KPM manager Robin Phillips.

Peter Cox: Alan Parker, yes, another wonderful player. Did some very successful albums, and is a wonderful guitarist; there's no two ways about it. [He] captured that commerciality of the time by just playing the right stuff at the right moment, and enjoyed, quite deservedly, a very, very successful career.

Keith Mansfield: [Parker] was the guitar player through all the early years. He was one of these people who could play classical guitar with strings and have a really busy part written for him, or could do electric guitar, distorted, and do all sorts of things. He was a really good reader, and very, very adaptable. So without question, Alan was the guitar player in those early years... And he was always the first call in our sessions in the early days.

Alan Parker: I started professionally in the business as a studio session musician. I was a professional studio boy when I was about seventeen and a half, about eighteen, not quite. And I developed—to cut it down into a bit of a nutshell—I developed a very good reputation, guitar-wise. Really, Big Jim Sullivan and myself were rated about the top two session guitarists and such for many years. And through doing sessions with absolutely everybody throughout the years—having worked with so many varied types, and not just recording artists, or groups or whatever, but also some of the best film composers in the world—I got very interested in composing.

And it started from there, really, my writing career. And also in those days, remember, in England, the various TV networks, OWT, Yorkshire, Granada, Thames, they all had their own heads of music in those days. And I was very lucky that I got quite a few commissions. And it developed from there, to be quite honest. It's as simple as that.

You couldn't record library music in the UK, because of the MU, you know, the union laws. So about a couple of times a year at least, Robin would take a rhythm section and it might be a lead trumpet or something, whatever. And we used to go to Cologne a lot. And that's how I met Robin. It was one day—I can't remember when to be honest—but we finished early, basically, and Graham Walker said to Robin, "Why don't you get Alan to do some stuff?" You know, because rock guitar was coming in and such, in those early days. So I went back to the hotel, and I went into the bedroom, leaned in and wrote about three or four pieces and came back the next morning and recorded them. And that's how I really started into the library bit, and then it developed from there. He gave me other things to do, and it got better and better, you know, and so it went... it just took off, really.

Peter Cox: [Parker] and Rob were very close, good friends, as Robin was with all the writers. And that friendship transcended merely being colleagues; it was much, much deeper than that. That's what gave KPM its spirit. And I think that's one of the lessons you learn working for a company like that, that if you do have the ability to create a real spirit of friendliness and affection between you, it brings out the best in people's creative talent.

The Voice of Soul* and *The Sound of Soul
(TIM 1021 and TIM 1022, 1976)

Alan Parker: Themes International, yeah. There was a lot of success in a lot of that stuff. It was fantastic. We used to go to Munich to record a lot of it, and some of it we recorded at Morgan Studios in Willesden, in London. And that was Madeline Bell, as you know, singing on it—she cowrote a lot of stuff. I mean they were crazy days; I remember when we were doing those sessions, we were laying down five or six tracks in a three-hour session. The whole thing. And then Madeline would just stick her vocals on afterwards. They were quite incredible days actually when you think about them...

When we [added Bell's vocals], if I'm really honest, I think some people thought, *Oh, this won't get used, this won't be popular*. But we just did it. It's as simple as that. We thought, *No, we're going to do this project*. And lo and behold, it became incredibly, incredibly popular. And got a lot of usage, absolutely. It was taking a chance to try to be a bit different. And of course what happens? Everybody jumps on the bandwagon and tries to do a similar thing.

"You've Got What It Takes," that track we laid down as one of the tracks in those multiple recordings and then—and then the composer would guide Madeline about how they wanted it sung, the interpretation, and she was amazing. I mean, she would do about four or five tracks in a three-hour session. In all truth, it's the musicianship of those sorts of people that was staggering. Stunning, you know. I mean, you don't get that these days, to be quite frank.

MADELINE BELL

BELOW

Alan Parker / Madeline Bell. *The Voice of Soul*. Themes International Music (UK): TIM 1021, 1976.

Known to library collectors as a collaborator with Alan Parker, Madeline Bell has also enjoyed a long and distinguished career in popular music. Born in Newark in 1942, Bell grew up performing gospel, and at eighteen she joined the well-known Alex Bradford Singers. After the group toured the UK in 1962, Bell settled in England and began work as a backing vocalist for pop artists, eventually recording with Dusty Springfield, Elton John, and the Rolling Stones (on the enduring "You Can't Always Get What You Want"). Bell's involvement in Themes International's *The Voice of Soul* came amidst the singer's branching into advertising jingles and other music-for-hire recordings; the innovative album solidified Bell's standing in the world of library music, even as her voice has remained omnipresent across the pop landscape.

ALAN TEW

BELOW

Alan Tew. *Drama Suite Part I*. Themes International Music (UK): TIM 1024, 1976.

OPPOSITE

Alan Tew. *Drama Suite Part II*. Themes International Music (UK): TIM 1025, 1976.

Though best known in library circles for a few specific compositions, Alan Tew led a varied and prolific career across many musical genres. He began his career as a pianist in the late 1950s Len Turner Band, after which he became an arranger for various pop acts of the day. This development led—as it did with many of Tew's peers in pop arrangement—to a profitable sideline in production music. Tew's library recordings (largely of the "cop funk" variety) have been synchronized in high profile British television programs and films including *The Hanged Man*, *The Sweeney*, and *The Two Ronnies*. Tew's 1976 *Drama Suite*, a two-part release on Themes International, is considered one of the greatest library records of all time and yielded his most famous composition: "The Big One," known in the United States as the theme to *The People's Court*.

THEMES

Drama Suite Part II

MUSIC DE WOLFE

BELOW

Meyer de Wolfe with orchestra, circa 1910.

Founded in 1909 by Dutch musical director Meyer de Wolfe upon his emigration to London, Music De Wolfe did big business early on as a sheet music publisher, providing written soundtracks to be played alongside many of the most popular silent films of the era. When the "moving pictures" added sound, De Wolfe stayed at the industry forefront, publishing recordings of earlier sheet music hits onto 35mm nitrate film and, later, quarter-inch tape, a more stable (and decidedly less flammable) medium. As the century wore on, the company continued to expand its reach to new industries, and in 1955, a De Wolfe composition soundtracked the UK's first television commercial, a one-minute spot for Gibbs toothpaste. Numerous notable film and TV synchronizations followed, including works for *Doctor Who* and *Monty Python*. As the exploitation boom of the 1970s turned B-movies into a high art form, De Wolfe music was on full display, from the scores for seminal kung fu films by the Shaw Brothers to the music for 1978's *Dawn of the Dead*, the zombie classic by legendary filmmaker George A. Romero.

In 1974, the library birthed the popular sublabel Rouge Music, run by Rosalind de Wolfe, and it has since added imprints specifically for jazz, classical, and sound effects releases. In the present day, more than a hundred years after its founding, De Wolfe has retained its status as a leading production library, while samples from its catalog have been employed by many of today's most popular commercial artists.

TOP

Spinning Wheel. *Lorry Load*. Music De Wolfe (UK): DWS/LP 3353, 1977.

BOTTOM

André Ceccarelli. *Rythmes*. Music De Wolfe (UK): DWS/LP 3328, 1976.

BELOW

The International Studio Orchestra. *Double or Quits*. Music De Wolfe (UK): DW/LP 3209, 1971.

OPPOSITE TOP

Keith Papworth. *Hard Hitter*. Music De Wolfe (UK): DWS/LP 3318, 1975.

OPPOSITE BOTTOM LEFT

Jack Trombey. *Spinechiller*. Music De Wolfe (UK): DWS/LP 3300, 1975.

OPPOSITE BOTTOM RIGHT

Various. *Creeps*. Music De Wolfe (UK): DWS/LP 3269, 1973.

"Eye Level"

Originally released as part of the 1971 De Wolfe LP *Double or Quits*, the peppy instrumental "Eye Level" was composed by Jan Stoeckart (under the pseudonym Jack Trombey) and performed by the De Wolfe session musicians, credited as "the International Studio Orchestra." The recording originally gained traction when it was featured as the title music for the UK detective show *Van der Valk*, but its popularity exploded when, upon the start of the show's second season in 1973, Columbia pressed a 7" single for the commercial market—credited this time to the Simon Park Orchestra. The record (which had charted on the UK singles chart eight months prior at #41) this time raced up the charts and spent four weeks at number one, becoming the first television theme—and certainly the only library recording—to ever achieve such a feat.

music de wolfe
HARD HITTER

SPINECHILLER
music de wolfe

CREEPS
music de wolfe

BELOW

Printed Rouge catalog for 1982-83.

OPPOSITE TOP

Unit Eight. *Glass Head*. Rouge Music Ltd. (UK): RMS/LP 130, 1981.

OPPOSITE BOTTOM LEFT

Chameleon. *Superdoop*. Rouge Music Ltd. (UK): RMS/LP 131, 1981.

OPPOSITE BOTTOM RIGHT

Rubba. *Some Shufflin'*. Rouge Music Ltd. (UK): RMS/LP 149, 1983.

GLASS HEAD
Rouge

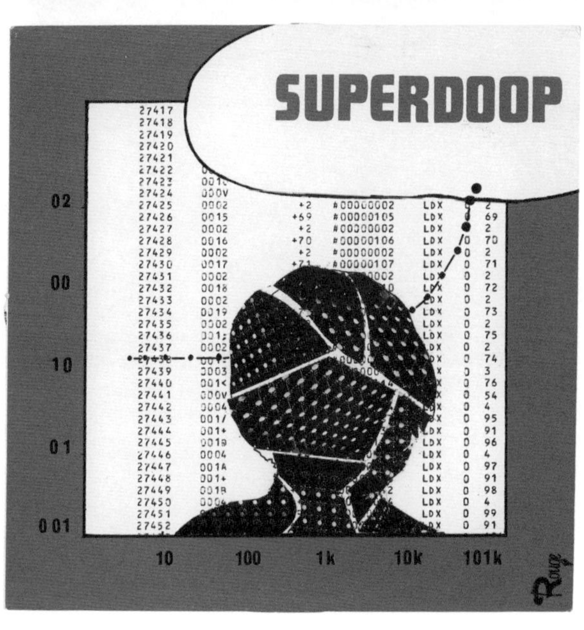
SUPERDOOP
02
00
10
01
001
10
100
1k
10k
101k
Rouge

Rouge
SOME SHUFFLIN'

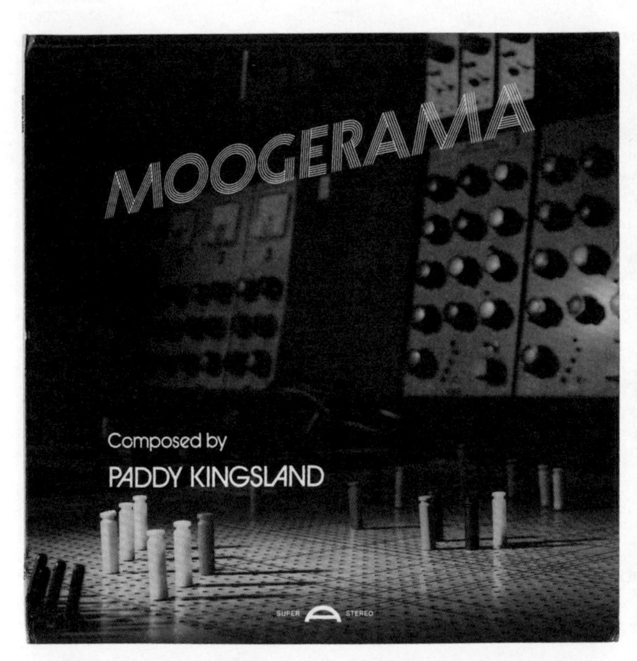

MOOGERAMA
Composed by
PADDY KINGSLAND
SUPER STEREO

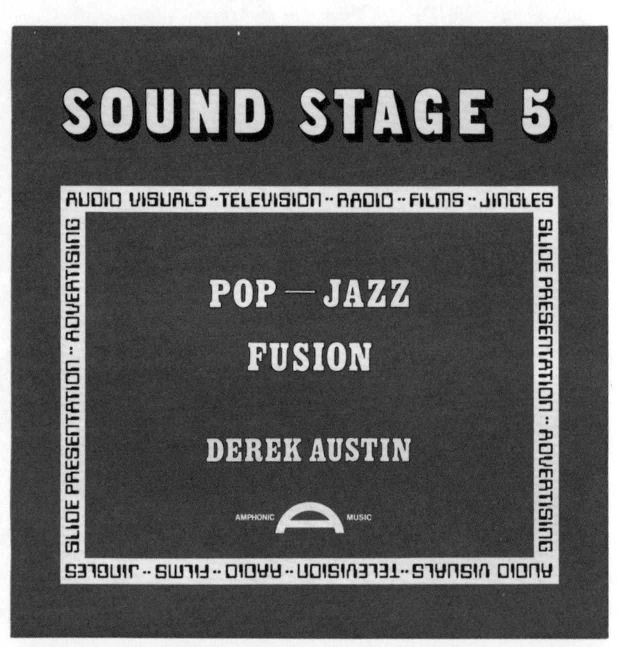

SOUND STAGE 5
AUDIO VISUALS··TELEVISION··RADIO··FILMS··JINGLES
SLIDE PRESENTATION··ADVERTISING
POP — JAZZ
FUSION
DEREK AUSTIN
AMPHONIC MUSIC

MELODY ALL THE WAY
AMPHONIC MUSIC LTD.
80 MORTIMER STREET
LONDON W1
01-580 5020

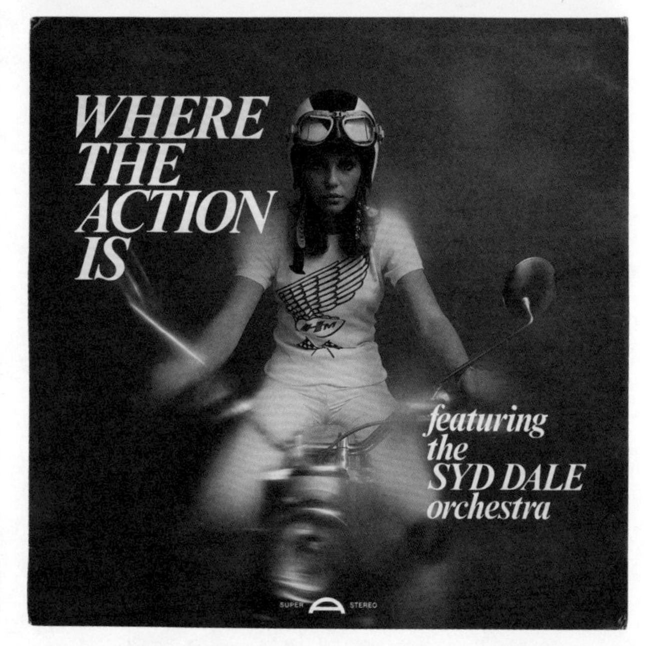

WHERE THE ACTION IS
featuring the SYD DALE orchestra
SUPER STEREO

AMPHONIC MUSIC

OPPOSITE TOP LEFT

Paddy Kingsland. *Moogerama*. Amphonic Music Ltd. (UK): AMPS 121, 1978.

OPPOSITE TOP RIGHT

Derek Austin. *Sound Stage 5: Pop-Jazz Fusion*. Amphonic Music Ltd. (UK): AVF 5, 1981.

OPPOSITE BOTTOM LEFT

Concert Pop Orchestra. *Melody All the Way*. Amphonic Music Ltd. (UK): AMPS 113, 1975.

OPPOSITE BOTTOM RIGHT

The Syd Dale Orchestra. *Where the Action Is*. Amphonic Music Ltd. (UK): AMPS 120, 1977.

BELOW

Syd Dale / Steve Gray. *Moodsetter, Pacesetter*. Amphonic Music Ltd. (UK): AMPS 1005, 1973.

Founded by erstwhile KPM artist Syd Dale in 1970, Amphonic found early success during the heyday of British library. Dale, a composer known for his intricate, melodic arrangements, was already a veteran of the world of production music, having helped arrange themes across the landscape of British TV and film, including the James Bond series; with Amphonic, he sought to establish a home for his compositions under his independent ownership. As the label grew, however, many of Dale's peers (including KPM and Themes International veterans, like Alan Parker) began contributing to the library, soon building a catalog that emphasized the funk and disco sounds of the era while also embracing new musical directions, such as the dawning electronic era with its new age and easy listening–inflected sounds. Syd Dale died in 1994, but Amphonic—still a family business—is now run by his son Ian.

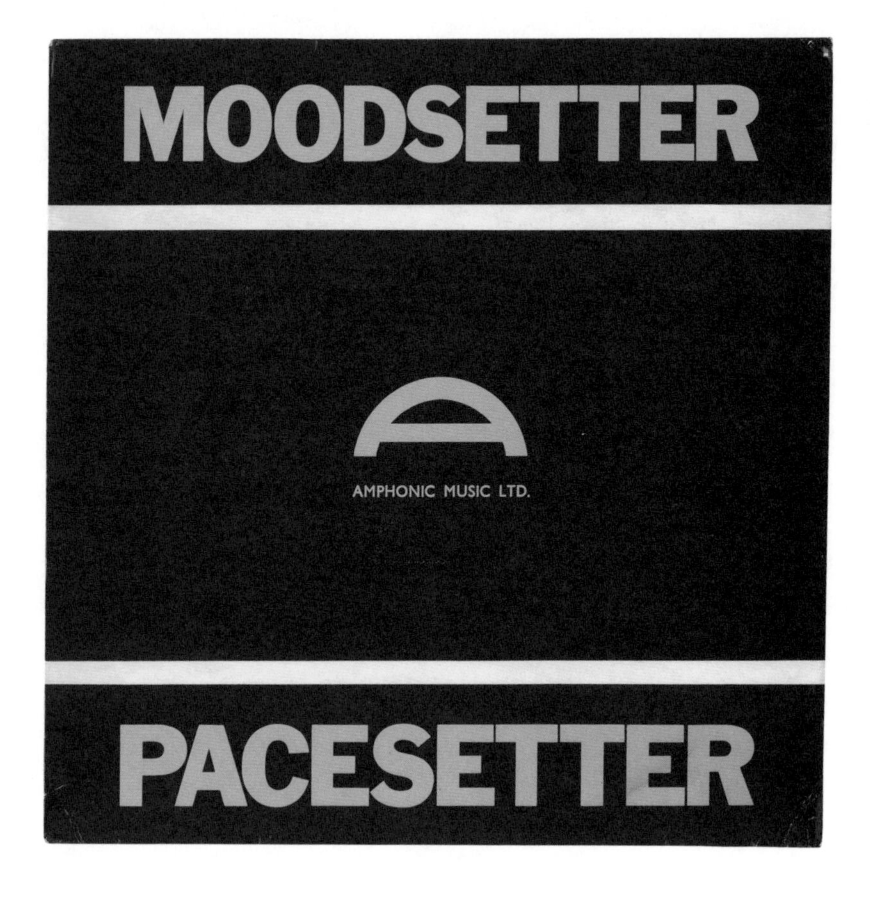

SOLAR FLARES
SVEN LIBAEK
and his Orchestra
Peer
International
Library
Limited

SVEN LIBAEK

OPPOSITE

Sven Libaek and His Orchestra. *Solar Flares*. Peer International Library Limited (UK): P.I.L. 9026, 1974.

BELOW

Cover of the box containing the tape master of *Solar Flares*.

Born in Norway in 1938, Sven Libaek has enjoyed a dizzyingly storied career in the arts: After being trained as a pianist and actor (eventually appearing in the 1958 Norwegian film *Windjammer*), Libaek immigrated to Australia in 1960 and three years later had become head of A&R for CBS Records Australia. There, he produced records for surf pioneers the Atlantics and crossed paths with a pre-fame Bee Gees, but when he got an offer to score a film, Libaek was asked to choose between A&R or composing and picked the latter. By the mid-'70s, Libaek had created scores for several TV productions, including most famously the nature documentary *Inner Space*, whose soundtrack is now an acknowledged "underwater exotica" classic. Libaek had also branched into library music in 1970, writing and recording the *My Thing* album for Peer / Southern, and in 1974 he followed it up with the masterful *Solar Flares*. Today, Libaek is counted among the giants of lounge jazz, soundtrack exotica, and production music as a whole.

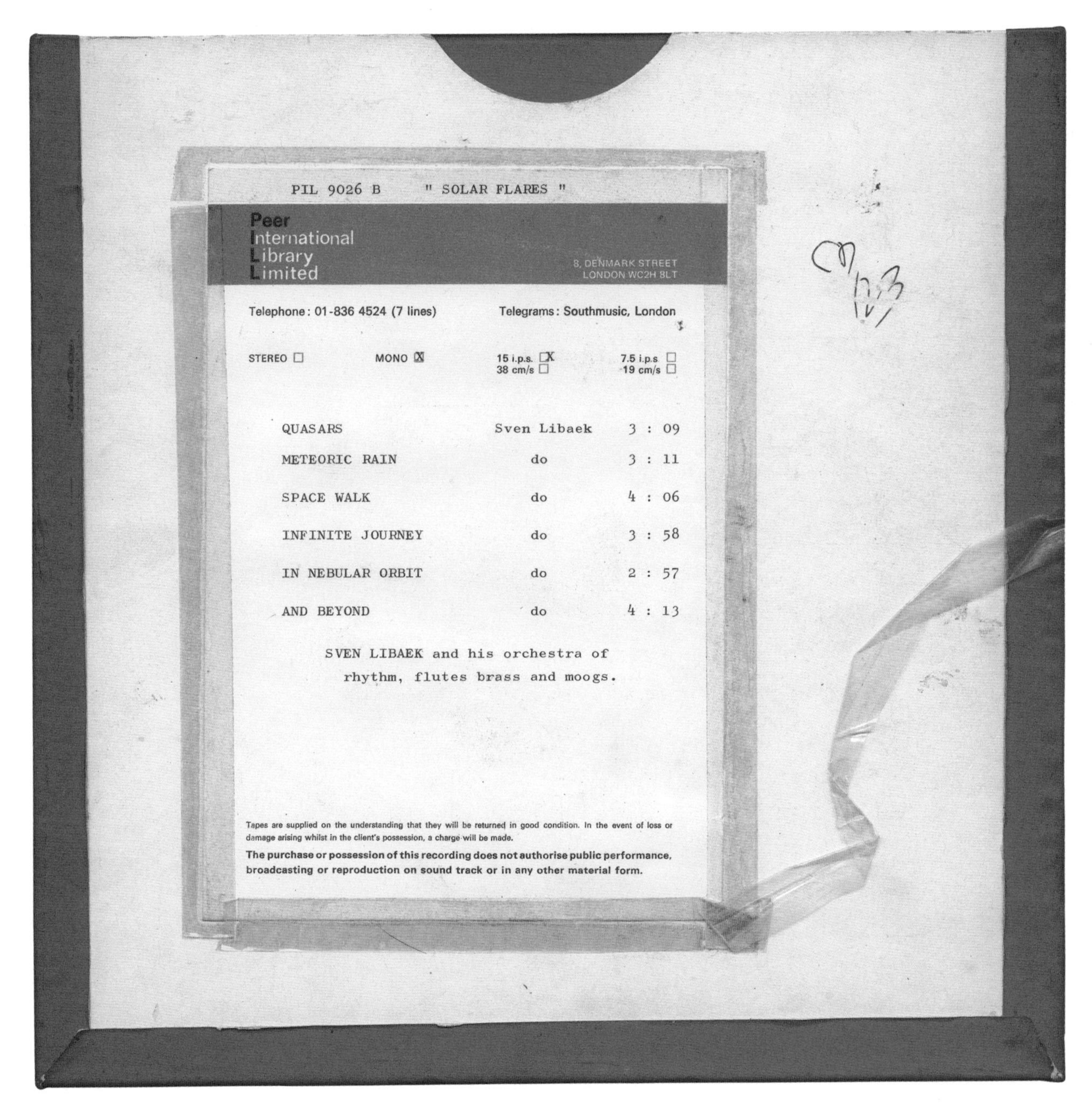

PIL 9026 B " SOLAR FLARES "

Peer International Library Limited

8, DENMARK STREET
LONDON WC2H 8LT

Telephone: 01-836 4524 (7 lines) Telegrams: Southmusic, London

STEREO ☐ MONO ☒ 15 i.p.s. 38 cm/s ☒ 7.5 i.p.s. 19 cm/s ☐

QUASARS	Sven Libaek	3 : 09
METEORIC RAIN	do	3 : 11
SPACE WALK	do	4 : 06
INFINITE JOURNEY	do	3 : 58
IN NEBULAR ORBIT	do	2 : 57
AND BEYOND	do	4 : 13

SVEN LIBAEK and his orchestra of rhythm, flutes brass and moogs.

Tapes are supplied on the understanding that they will be returned in good condition. In the event of loss or damage arising whilst in the client's possession, a charge will be made.

The purchase or possession of this recording does not authorise public performance, broadcasting or reproduction on sound track or in any other material form.

PEER / SOUTHERN

BELOW

Catalog of the Peer-Southern publishing library circa 1966, containing the sheet music for hundreds of compositions owned by the company.

OPPOSITE TOP

The Barrie Moore Combo. *Gemini*. Peer International Library Limited (UK): P.I.L. 9016, 1972.

OPPOSITE BOTTOM LEFT

The Westway Studio Orchestra. *Industry (Light), Industry (Heavy)*. Southern Library of Recorded Music (UK): MQ LP 3, 1971.

OPPOSITE BOTTOM RIGHT

Stringtronics. *Mind Bender*. Peer International Library Limited (UK): P.I.L. 9013, 1972.

Founded by Ralph S. Peer in 1928 as the Southern Music Publishing Company, Peer (or as it is now known, Peermusic) has become the largest independent music publisher in the world, with control over hundreds of thousands of copyrights worldwide. In the library world, the organization is known for developing several production music labels and sublabels—most notably, Peer International Library Limited, the Southern Library of Recorded Music, and the New Southern Library—featuring releases by industry stalwarts including Nino Nardini, Sven Libaek, and Alan Hawkshaw.

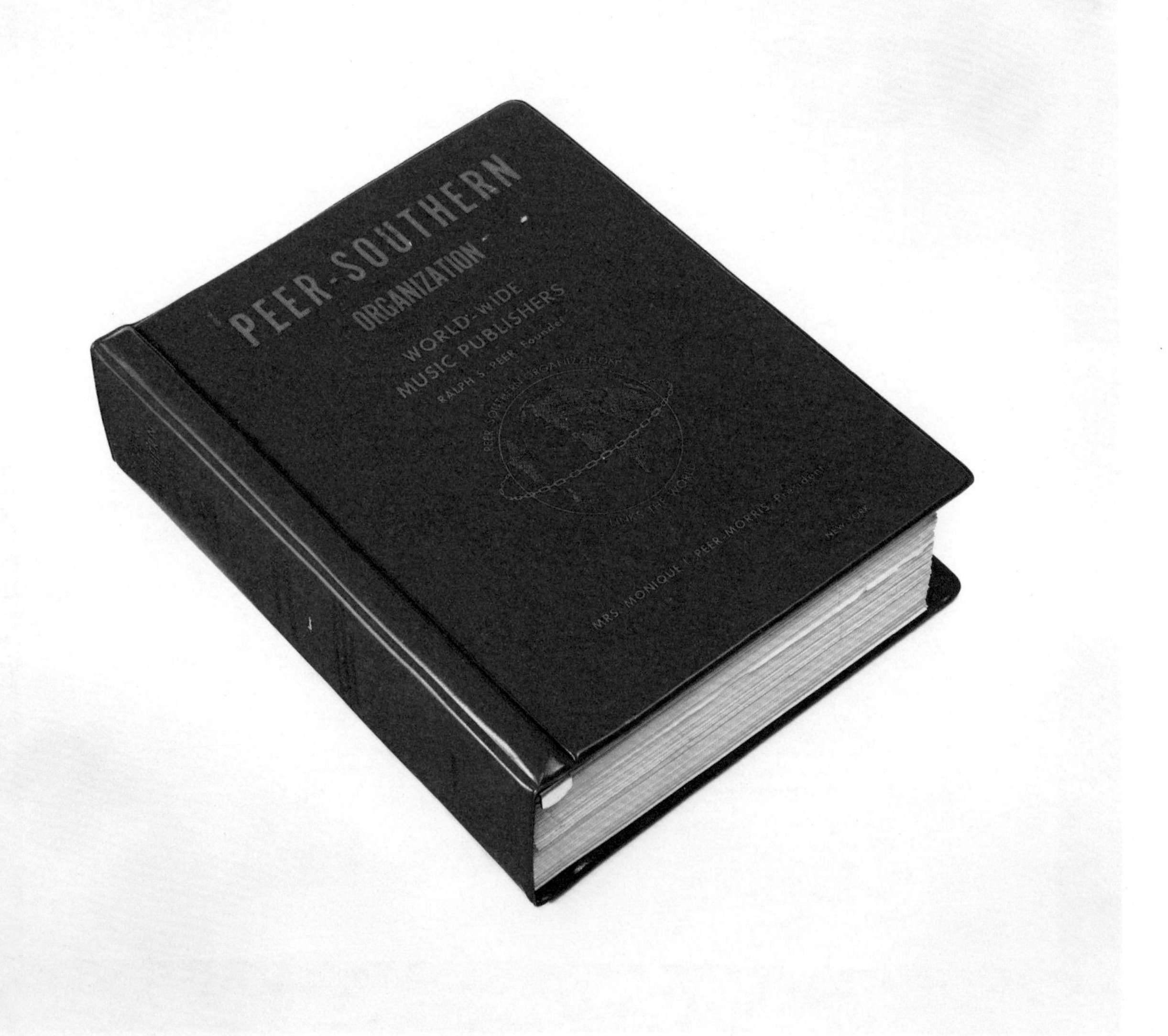

GEMINI
THE BARRIE MOORE COMBO

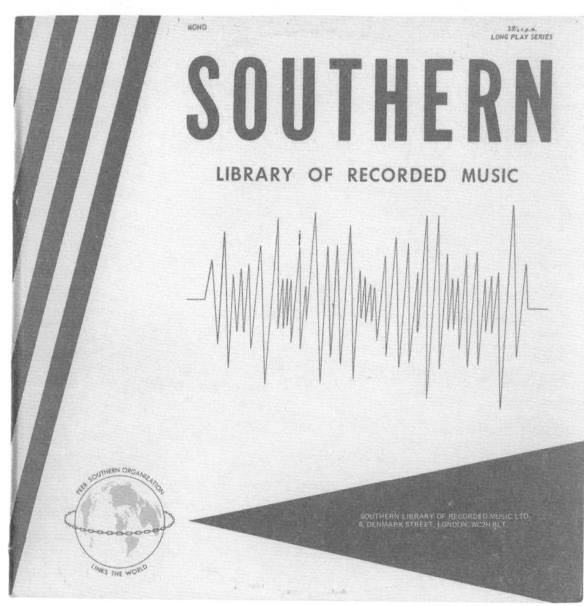
MONO
33⅓ r.p.m.
LONG PLAY SERIES
SOUTHERN
LIBRARY OF RECORDED MUSIC
PEER SOUTHERN ORGANIZATION
LINKS THE WORLD
SOUTHERN LIBRARY OF RECORDED MUSIC LTD.
8, DENMARK STREET, LONDON, WC2H 8LT.

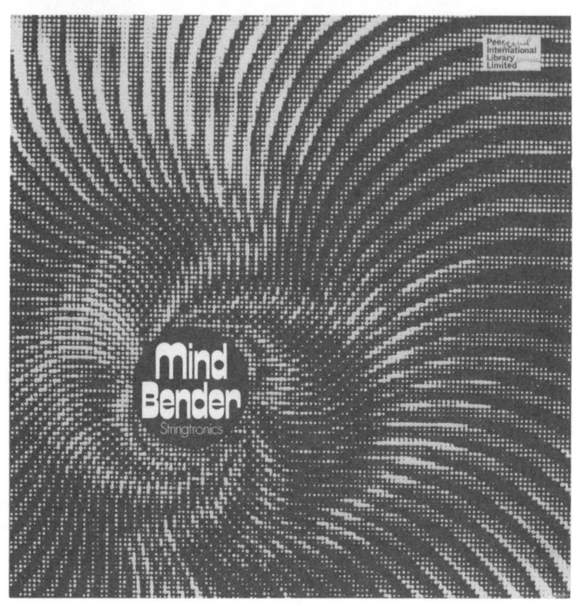
Peer
International
Library
Limited
Mind
Bender
Stringtronics

JOSEF WEINBERGER / IMPRESS

BELOW

Ray Russell. *Master Format*. JW Music Library (UK): JW 500, 1983.

OPPOSITE TOP

Peter Thomas. *The Electric Stringmobile*. JW Theme Music (UK): JW 410, 1976.

OPPOSITE BOTTOM LEFT

Sydney Dale. *Inversions / Melody in Percussion*. Impress (UK): IA 398, 1970.

OPPOSITE BOTTOM RIGHT

Reginald G. Wale & Art Morgan / Tony Carr. *Go-Go-Go! / Rhythm-Rhythm-Rhythm!* Impress (UK): IA 399, 1972.

Founded in 1885 Vienna in order to license the operettas of Johann Strauss, Josef Weinberger's eponymous publishing house initially focused on live performance and musical theater. The company grew with the times, however, and by the mid-twentieth century had begun branching into the field of production music via its JW Media Music subsidiary.

In the mid-'50s, JW in turn acquired the label Impress, which had until then been financially backed by a British postcard firm. Like other UK libraries of the day, Impress had to contend with a British Musicians' Union ban on library performances; as a result, its recording sessions during the ban took place in Stuttgart, Germany, enabling the label to employ highly skilled European players. Impress folded in the mid-'70s, though its recordings are still used in synchronization and sampling today; JW Media Music, for its part, is still in operation.

JW 410

the electric stringmobile

composer: peter thomas

JW 410

THEME MUSIC

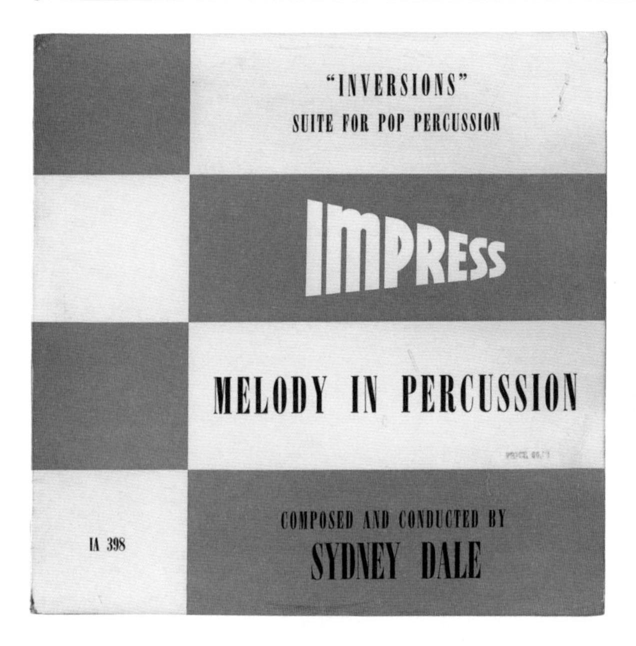

TOD DOCKSTADER

OPPOSITE

Tod Dockstader. *Recorded Music for Film, Radio & Television: Electronic Vol. 1.* Boosey & Hawkes (UK): SBH 3073, 1979.

Born in Saint Paul, Minnesota, in 1932, Tod Dockstader is one of comparatively few highly regarded American library composers. He's also a musician whose career trajectory highlights the strange, somewhat paradoxical relationship between avant-garde composition and corporate production music: In addition to his seminal contributions to the Boosey & Hawkes library, Dockstader is an iconic figure in the history of experimental electronic music.

After a degree in psychology and art at the University of Minnesota, Dockstader found work in Hollywood as a film editor—putting him well in mind of the relationship between film production and sound—before moving to New York in 1958 and becoming a recording engineer. In the off-hours of his apprenticeship at Gotham Recording Studios, Dockstader began the tape manipulation experiments that would lead to his first album, 1960's *Eight Electronic Pieces* (later used, in a further crossover with filmic high art, as the soundtrack to Fellini's *Satyricon*). In spite of his lack of an academic musical background and his isolation from other early electronic composers like John Cage, Pierre Henry, and Karlheinz Stockhausen, Dockstader's work began to enjoy some recognition in the avant-garde. In 1979, he composed and recorded the two-volume *Electronic* series of releases for Boosey & Hawkes (the same library that had briefly employed fellow tape manipulator Delia Derbyshire two decades prior). These records—acknowledged masterpieces of early electronic music and library landmarks—were reissued in 2012, three years before Dockstader's death at eighty-two in 2015.

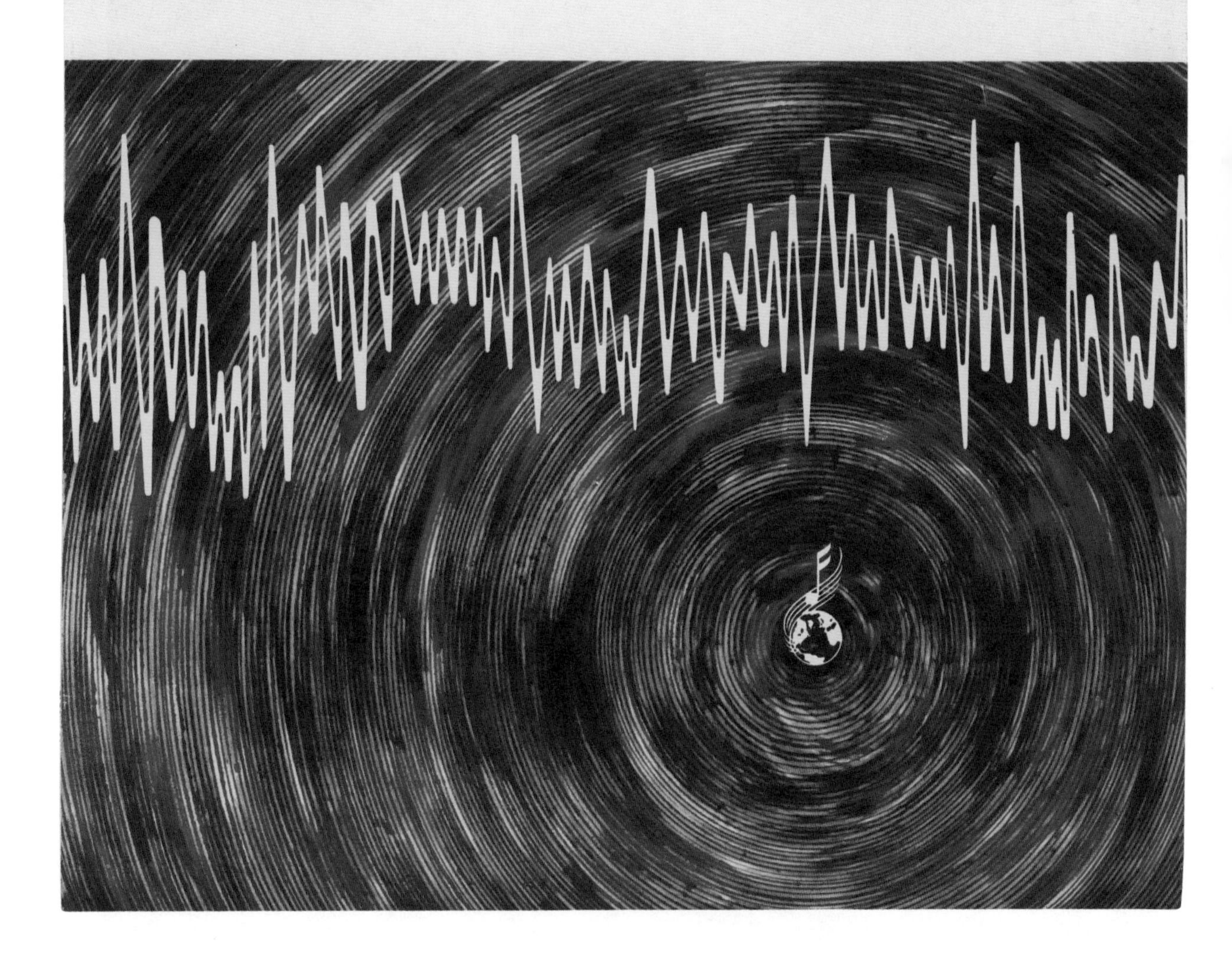
SBH 3073
March '79
Boosey & Hawkes
ELECTRONIC
Recorded Music for
Film Radio & Television

programme music

PM 011

Music to varnish Owls by

Composer:
GEOFF BASTOW

programme music

PM 008

On the Side of the Angels

Composer:
DAVID SNELL

programme music

PM 012

Light and Shade

Composer: Bill Geldard

OPPOSITE TOP

Geoff Bastow. *Music to Varnish Owls By*. Programme Music (UK): PM 011, 1975.

OPPOSITE BOTTOM LEFT

David Snell. *On the Side of the Angels*. Programme Music (UK): PM 008, 1975.

OPPOSITE BOTTOM RIGHT

Bill Geldard. *Light and Shade*. Programme Music (UK): PM 012, 1975.

TOP

Iota Music. *Background Music Library - Atmospheric Electronic*. Iota Records (UK): IOTA 1001, 1986.

MIDDLE LEFT

Various. *Activity / Travel / Dramatic*. Standard Music Library (UK): ESL 126, 1974.

MIDDLE RIGHT

Roger Spell Ensemble / Enzo Scoppa. *Untitled*. BBC Coded Music Scheme (UK): CMS 104, no date.

BOTTOM

Alain Debray. *Variations on a Theme*. Shepherds Bush Library Music (UK / Netherlands): SHEP 004, 1984.

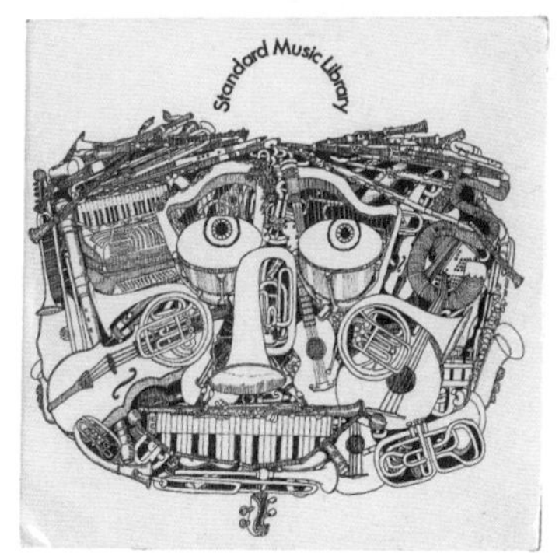

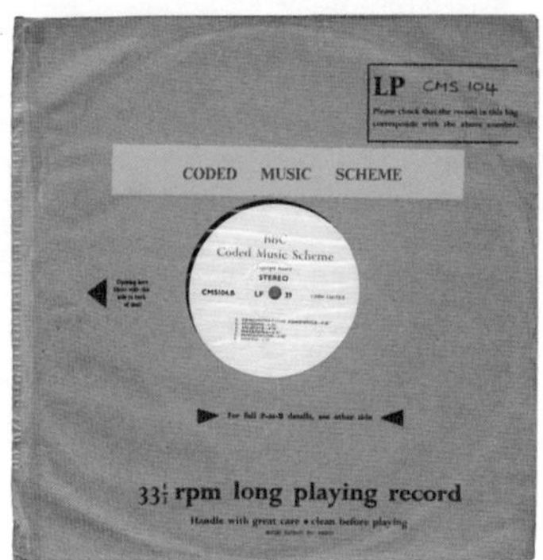

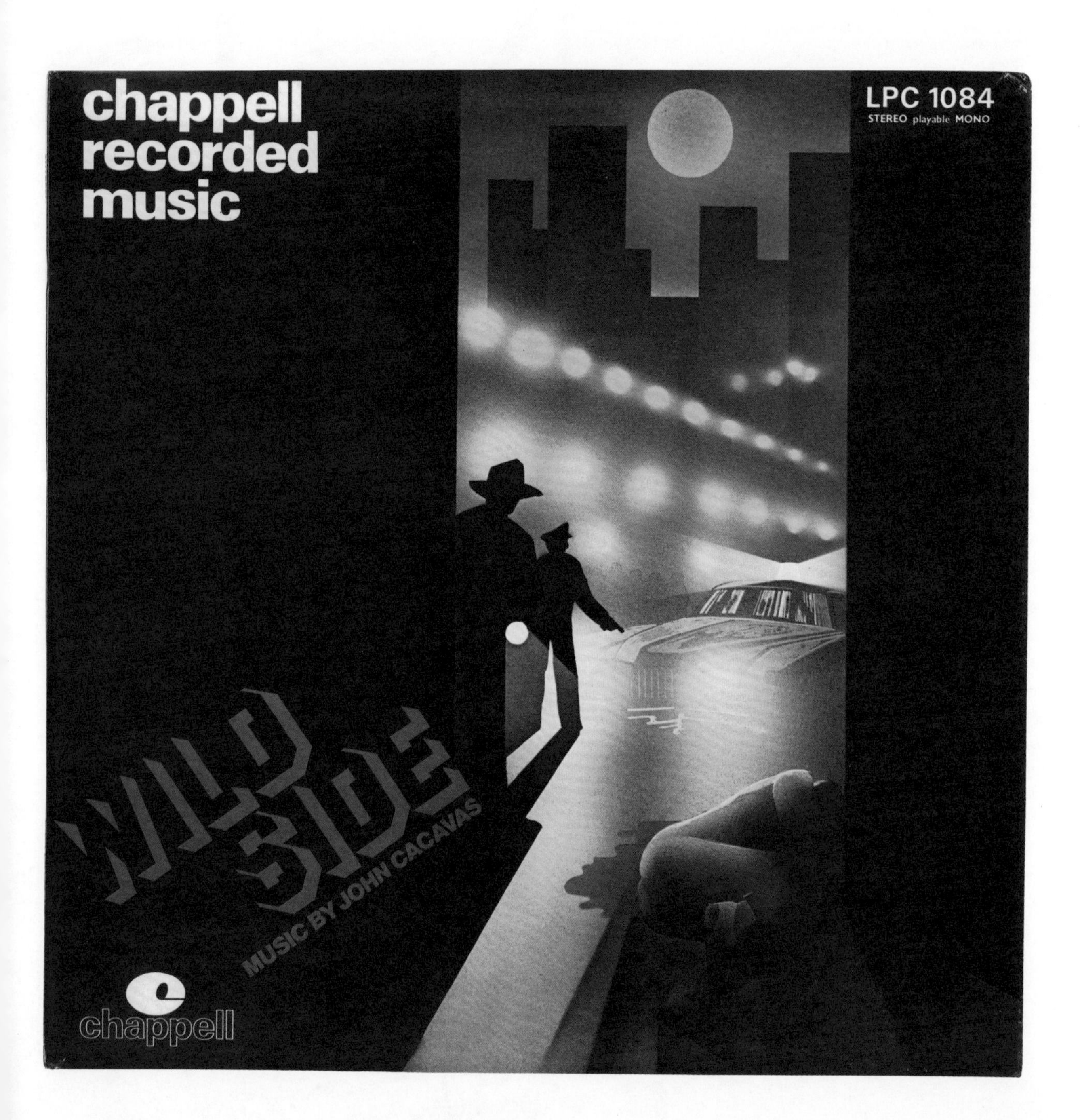
chappell
recorded
music
LPC 1084
STEREO playable MONO
WILD SIDE
MUSIC BY JOHN CACAVAS
chappell

OPPOSITE

John Cacavas and His Orchestra. *Wild Side*. Chappell (UK): LPC 1084, 1976.

TOP

John Cacavas and His Music. *Music for Drama (Orchestral)*. Chappell Recorded Music Library (UK): CAL 4014, 1974.

BOTTOM

The Boneschi Electronic Combo. *Sounds Electronic*. Chappell Recorded Music Library (UK): CAL 4004, 1973.

TOP

Larry Robbins' Dynamic Drums Plus. *Larry Robbins' Dynamic Drums Plus*. Conroy Recorded Music Library (UK): BMLP 102, 1973.

BOTTOM

Various. *Rhythmic Underscores - Solo Instruments*. Conroy Recorded Music Library (UK): BMLP 086, 1972.

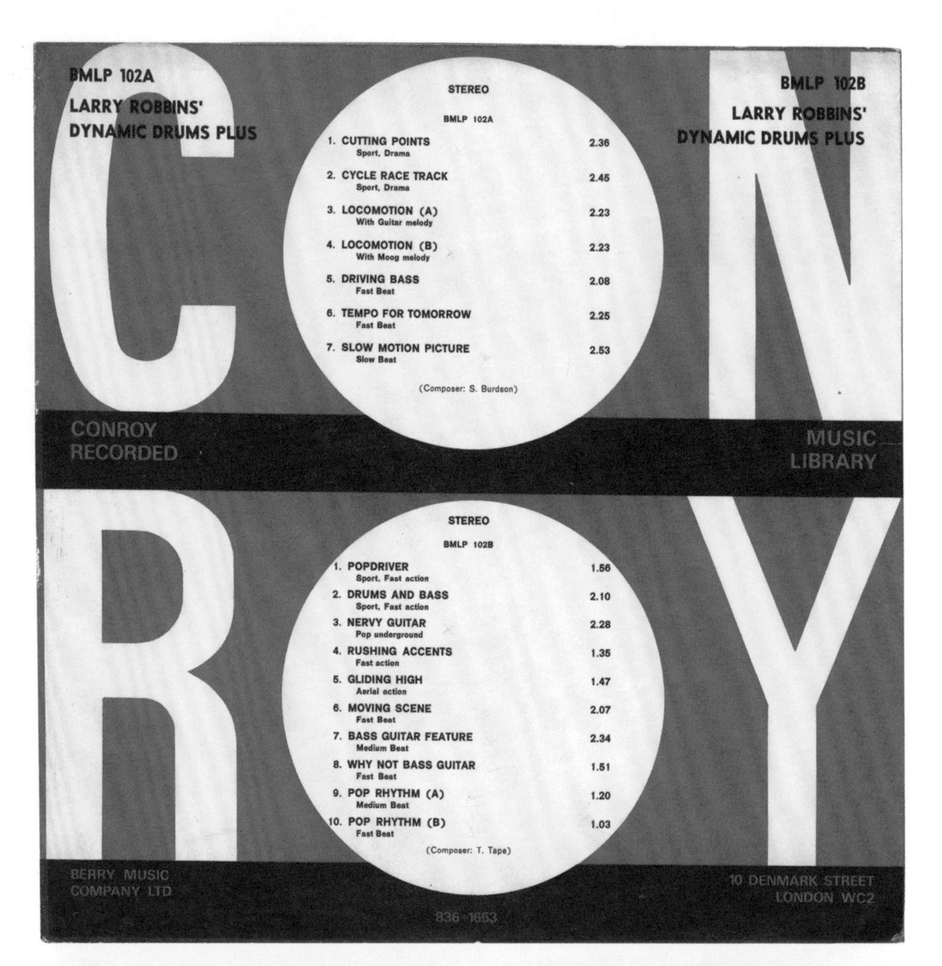

CONROY RECORDED MUSIC LIBRARY

BELOW

Spiral-bound print catalog for the Conroy Recorded Music Library.

A British library that began releasing records in 1965, Conroy was a sublabel of the larger UK publisher Berry Music, and its catalog typified the library industry's strange mixture of tradition and experimentation from the start. Conroy's early releases included compositions by big band stalwarts like Eddie Warner (founder of the French IM library) as well as early electronic recordings by Arsène Souffriau (a Belgian experimental pioneer and peer of experimental godfathers Pierre Schaeffer and Pierre Henry). Due to its parent company Berry's status as a distribution partner for the German label Sonoton, Conroy (as well as fellow sublabels like Studio One) functioned as a means by which German library recordings found their way into the UK market: among many other major German recordings, it published seminal albums by Sonoton founder Gerhard Narholz under pseudonyms such as Walt Rockman and Tony Tape. Conroy ceased production in the 1980s, but its history and its catalog offer an excellent window into the trends and eccentricities of a highly unique industry at the height of its international appeal.

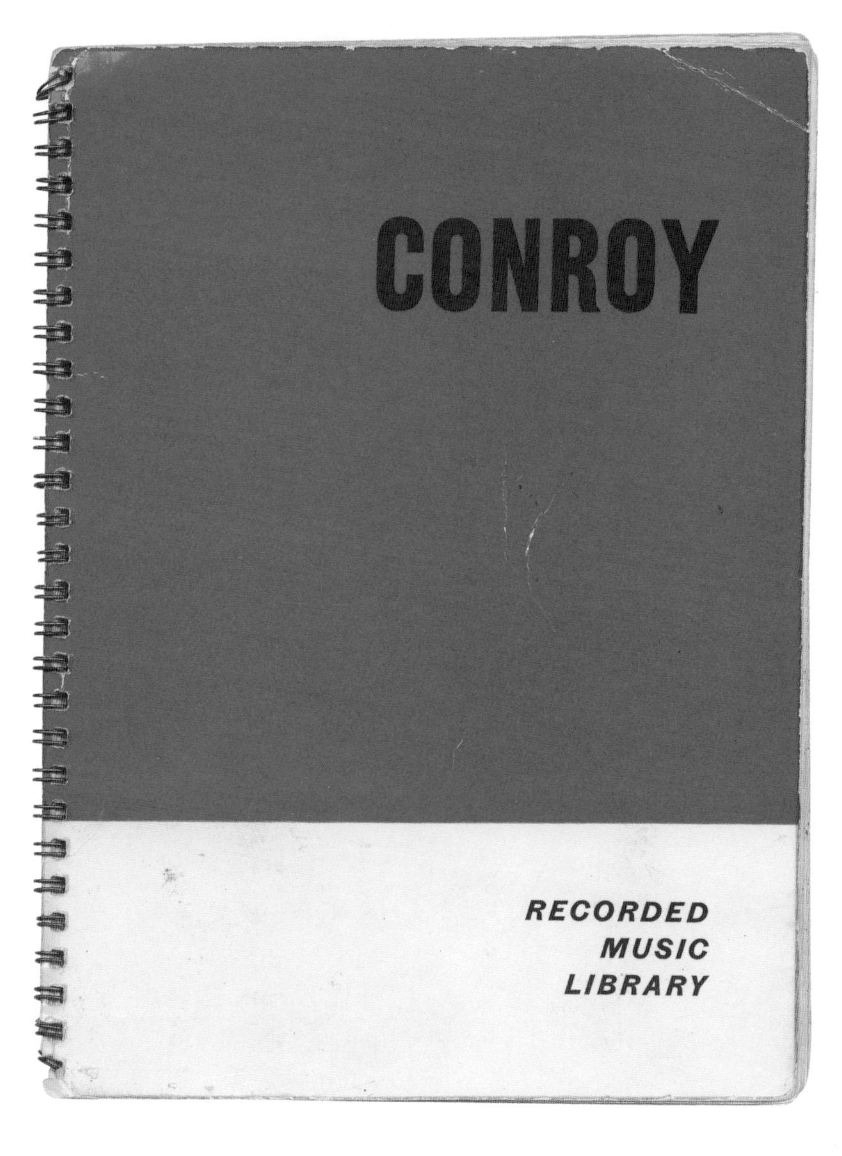

TOP AND BOTTOM

Front and back cover of Walt Rockman's *The Walt Rockman Moog Moods*. Conroy Recorded Music Library (UK): BMLP 118, 1975. "Rockman" was one of scores of aliases used by Sonoton's Gerhard Narholz.

BMLP
118A
CONROY
RECORDED
MUSIC
LIBRARY
THE WALT ROCKMAN MOOG MOODS
BMLP
118B

BMLP 118

This record is from the Conroy Library of Recorded Music produced on twelve-inch long playing discs especially for the radio, television and film industry to the highest possible professional standards. The music is copyright of Berry Music Co. Ltd and licence must be obtained prior to usage. Stereo and Mono tapes are available from Berry Music Co. and their agents.

THE WALT ROCKMAN MOOG MOODS

Track No.	Title	Time	Composer	Sound
1.	DUCK POND (1)	2.47		Beat - Synthesizer + Rhythm
2.	,, (2)	2.35	W. Rockman	Grotesque - Melodic ex Rhythm
3.	,, (3)	0.24		As above - short version
4.	HEN PARTY (1)	3.00		Beat shake - Synthesizer + Rhythm
5.	,, (2)	1.00	W. Rockman	Synthesizer melody with bass
6.	,, (3)	0.08		"Effect"
7.	ELECTRONIC APPLE (1)	3.37		Happy Beat - Synthesizer + Rhythm
8.	,, (2)	1.27	W. Rockman	- Synthesizer ex Rhythm
9.	,, (3)	1.23		- Fast moog figure + Rhythm
10.	THE THREE BEARS (1)	2.55		Slow Beat - Synthesizer + Rhythm
11.	,, (2)	1.22	W. Rockman	- Synthesizer + Rhythm
12.	,, (3)	1.14		- Moog melody ex Rhythm

Track No.	Title	Time	Composer	Sound
1.	CLOCKWORK ELEPHANT (1)	2.40	W. Rockman	Medium beat-Synthesizer + Rhythm
2.	,, (2)	1.58		Synthesizer ex Rhythm
3.	RUBBER DUCKS (1)	2.20	W. Rockman	Medium pop rhythm Synthesizer Rhythm
4.	,, (2)	0.53		Synthesizer ex Rhythm
5.	PLASTIC PENGUINS (1)	1.52		Beat-Synthesizer + Rhythm
6.	,, (2)		W. Rockman	Synthesizer melody (solo)
7.	,, (3)			Synthesizer
8.	,, (4)			Moog solo (Happy)
9.	SOFT TOYS (1)	1.52	W. Rockman	Slow Rock Synthesizer + Rhythm
10.	,, (2)	1.19		Gentle Synthesizer melody (solo)
11.	MOON MONKEY (1)	2.05		Pop Rhythm Synthesizer + Rhythm
12.	,, (2)	0.48	W. Rockman	Synthesizer melody (Bass)
13.	,, (3)	0.49		Synthesizer melody (Treble)

©Berry Music Co. Ltd., 10 Denmark Street, London, W.C.2 (01-836 1653)

CONROY RECORDED MUSIC LIBRARY

GERMAN
LIBRARIES

SONOTON

BELOW

Sonoton studios in Munich.

Established in Munich in 1965 by Gerhard and Rotheide Narholz, Sonoton introduced library music to Germany. Initially intended to cater to the country's new TV market, the library also provided an avenue for Gerhard Narholz's astonishing musical prolificacy, and soon became a haven for a wide range of European composers and musicians. In 1969, Sonoton struck a deal with the British label Berry Music for international publishing rights, exposing its catalog to a worldwide audience; when Berry was bought out by EMI in 1973, Sonoton transitioned into a full-fledged international label, with successes in the library and commercial fields and many innovations to its credit. Now a worldwide operation with hundreds of producers and composers under its employ, Sonoton nonetheless remains an independently run business still helmed by its founders—a remarkable achievement in an era when nearly every other major library has been absorbed by a multinational conglomerate.

SHIP AHOY
SLOW
the brain
augustyn bloch
A MUSICAL WILDLIFE
Vol.1 PASTORAL
POLLUTION
Themes and
Panoramic
SPACE FICTION
INDUSTRIAL
THEMES & UNDERSCORES VOL.1
J. FIDDY
VOL.1
UNDER WATER
SOFTLY
Dramatic
Sounds
and
Movements
Vol.1
Pastoral
Scenes and Underscores
modeste moussorgsky
Swinging
Centuries
Soft And Tender
Norman Candler
Vol.3 Slapstick
SONOTON
SONOTON
SONOTON
SONOTON

OPPOSITE

Cover of a Sonoton print catalog.

TOP

Mladen Franko. *Amazing Space Vol. 1*. Sonoton (Germany): SON 101, 1980.

BOTTOM

The Sammy Burdson Group. *Space Fiction*. Sonoton (Germany): SON 106, 1980.

TOP

Walt Rockman. *Underwater Vol. 1*. Sonoton (Germany): SON 113, 1980.

BOTTOM

Various. *Underwater Vol. 2*. Sonoton (Germany): SON 114, 1980.

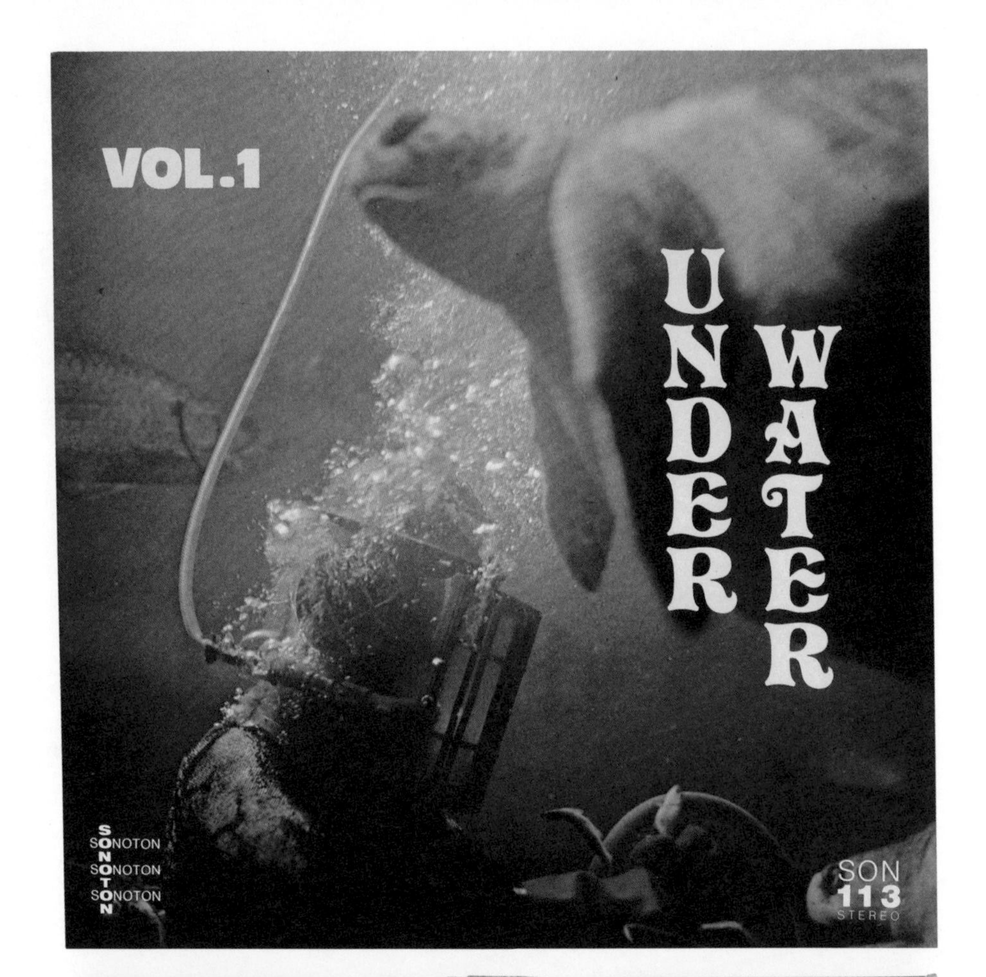

TOP

Ted Atking / Alain Feanch / Cecil Wary. *Scoop*. Sonoton (Germany): SON 153, 1981.

BOTTOM

Various. *A Musical Wildlife - Vol. 1: Pastoral*. Sonoton (Germany): SON 107, 1980.

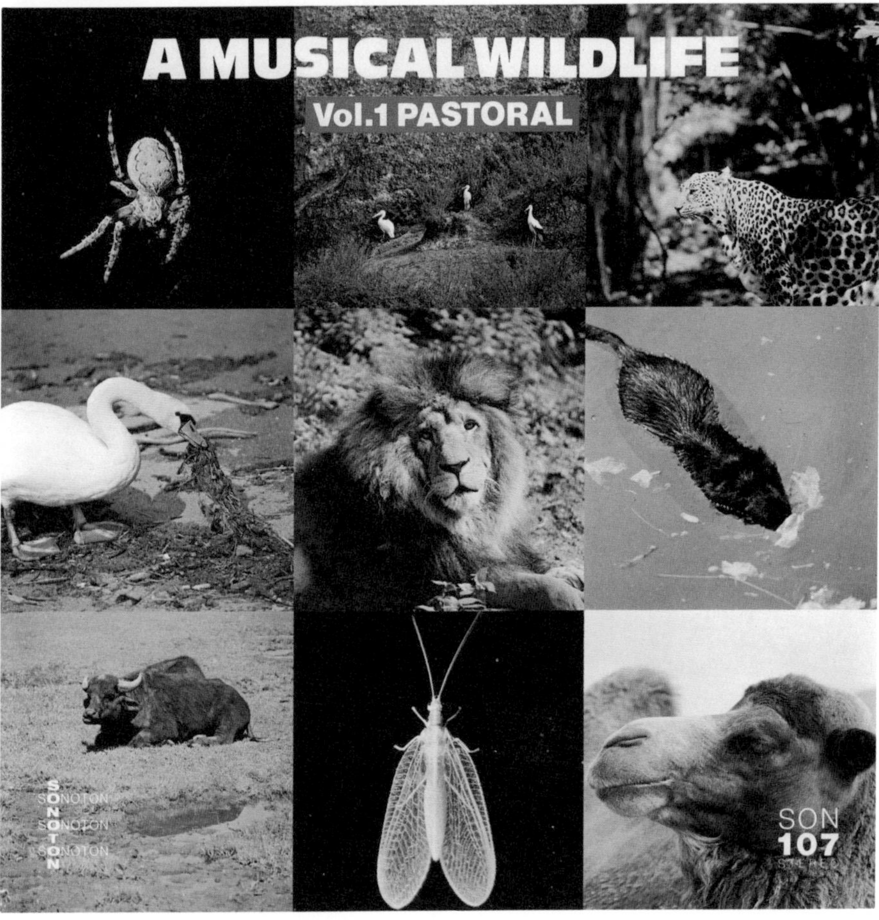

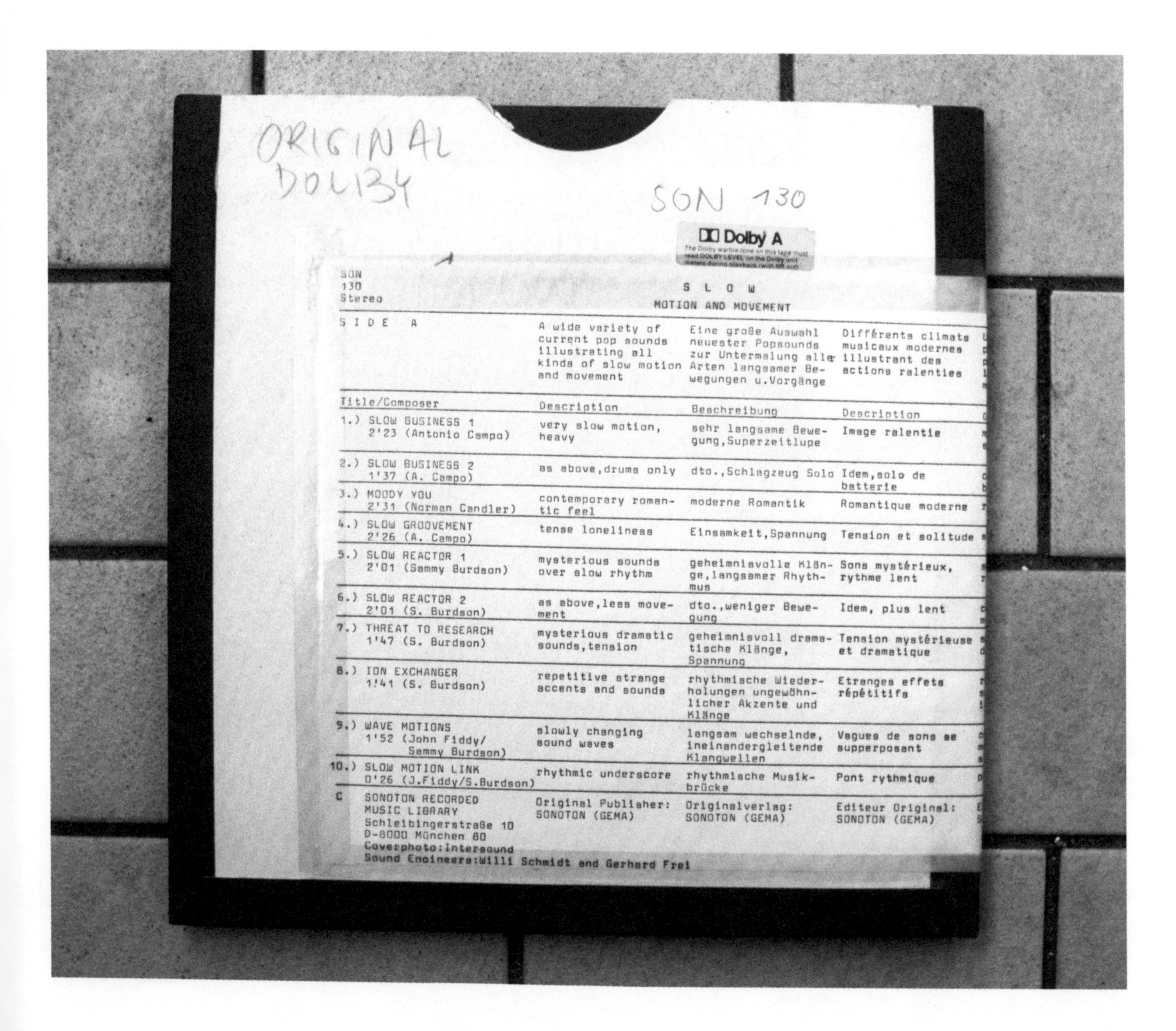

SON
130
Stereo

S L O W
MOTION AND MOVEMENT

S I D E A	A wide variety of current pop sounds illustrating all kinds of slow motion and movement	Eine große Auswahl neuester Popsounds zur Untermalung aller Arten langsamer Bewegungen u.Vorgänge	Différents climats musicaux modernes illustrant des actions ralenties
Title/Composer	Description	Beschreibung	Description
1.) SLOW BUSINESS 1 2'23 (Antonio Campo)	very slow motion, heavy	sehr langsame Bewegung,Superzeitlupe	Image ralentie
2.) SLOW BUSINESS 2 1'37 (A. Campo)	as above,drums only	dto.,Schlagzeug Solo	Idem,solo de batterie
3.) MOODY YOU 2'31 (Norman Candler)	contemporary romantic feel	moderne Romantik	Romantique moderne
4.) SLOW GROOVEMENT 2'26 (A. Campo)	tense loneliness	Einsamkeit,Spannung	Tension et solitude
5.) SLOW REACTOR 1 2'01 (Sammy Burdson)	mysterious sounds over slow rhythm	geheimnisvolle Klänge,langsamer Rhythmus	Sons mystérieux, rythme lent
6.) SLOW REACTOR 2 2'01 (S. Burdson)	as above,less movement	dto.,weniger Bewegung	Idem, plus lent
7.) THREAT TO RESEARCH 1'47 (S. Burdson)	mysterious dramatic sounds,tension	geheimnisvoll dramatische Klänge, Spannung	Tension mystérieuse et dramatique
8.) ION EXCHANGER 1'41 (S. Burdson)	repetitive strange accents and sounds	rhythmische Wiederholungen ungewöhnlicher Akzente und Klänge	Etranges effets répétitifs
9.) WAVE MOTIONS 1'52 (John Fiddy/ Sammy Burdson)	slowly changing sound waves	langsam wechselnde, ineinandergleitende Klangwellen	Vagues de sons se supperposant
10.) SLOW MOTION LINK 0'26 (J.Fiddy/S.Burdson)	rhythmic underscore	rhythmische Musikbrücke	Pont rythmique
C SONOTON RECORDED MUSIC LIBRARY Schleibingerstraße 10 D-8000 München 80	Original Publisher: SONOTON (GEMA)	Originalverlag: SONOTON (GEMA)	Editeur Original: SONOTON (GEMA)

Coverphoto:Intersound
Sound Engineers:Willi Schmidt and Gerhard Frei

OPPOSITE TOP LEFT

Various. *Slow (Motion and Movement)*. Sonoton (Germany): SON 130, 1980.

OPPOSITE TOP RIGHT

Various. *Fast (Motion and Dramatic Movements)*. Sonoton (Germany): SON 131, 1980.

OPPOSITE BOTTOM

Box containing the tape master for *Slow*.

TOP

Jeff Newman. *Impact Vol. 2*. Sonoton (Germany): SON 286, 1988.

BOTTOM

Laszlo Bencker. *Robot Couture - Underscores 1*. Sonoton (Germany): SON 296, no date.

TOP

Gerhard Narholz. *Mini Takes Vol. 1*. Sonoton (Germany): SON 208, 1984.

BOTTOM

Gerhard Narholz. *Mini Takes Vol. 2*. Sonoton (Germany): SON 255, 1986.

OPPOSITE TOP LEFT

Claude Larson. *Digital Patterns*. Sonoton (Germany): SON 181, 1982.

OPPOSITE TOP RIGHT

Claude Larson. *Middle East Impressions Vol. 1*. Sonoton (Germany): SON 197, 1983.

OPPOSITE BOTTOM LEFT

Claude Larson. *Far East Impressions Vol. 1*. Sonoton (Germany): SON 196, 1983.

OPPOSITE BOTTOM RIGHT

Claude Larson. *Soundscapes Vol. 2*. Sonoton (Germany): SON 247, 1986.

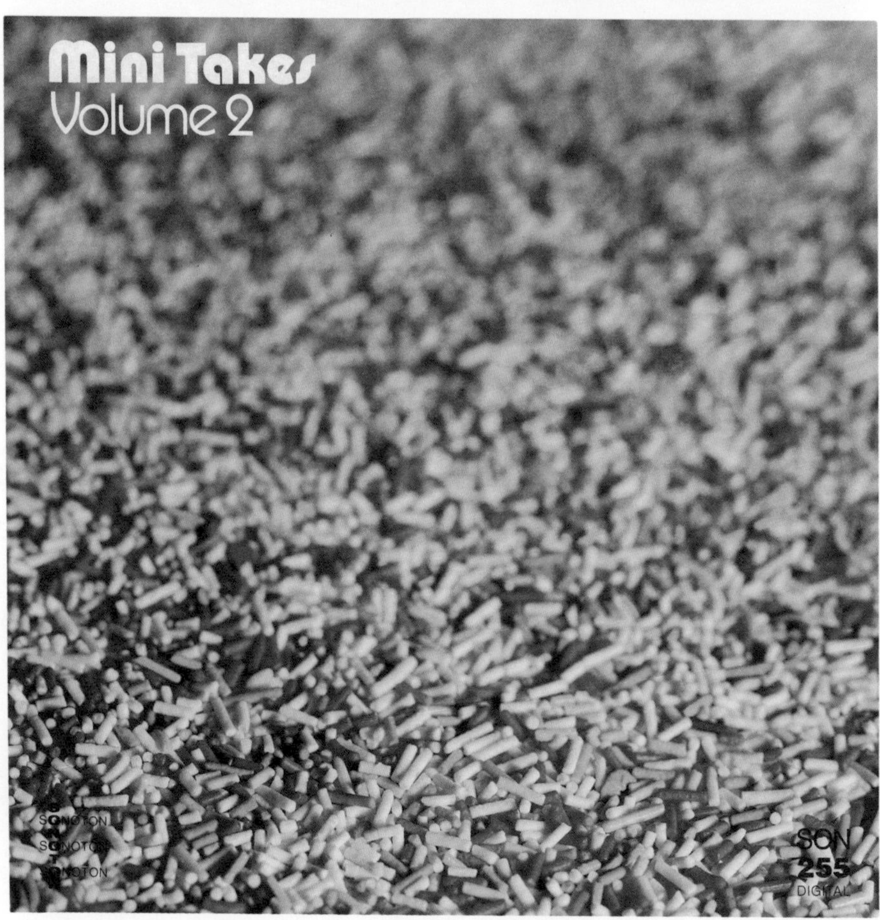

3000
IGITAL PATTERNS
INDEX ** PAGE D - READY **
COMMAND: C L A U D E L A R S O N
8168 03 80 00 0D 80 34 0D 01 20 1A 0A 00 FF 08 00 FF
WAVEFORM DUMP FORMAT:A B
VOICE: SINWAVE MODE: 4 END SEG: 128 64 32 STEP:1 2 4 8
SONOTON
SON 181 STEREO

claude larson
Middle East Impressions
Volume 1
SONOTON
SON 197 STEREO

claude larson
Far East Impressions
Volume 1
SONOTON
SON 196 STEREO

SOUNDSCAPES VOL.2
Claude Larson
SONOTON
SON 247 DIGITAL

TOP

John Epping. *Testimony to the Past Vol. 2*. Sonoton (Germany): SON 284, 1987.

BOTTOM

Jean-Claude Madonne. *Beautiful World*. Sonoton (Germany): SON 209, 1984.

TOP

J. Fiddy. *Industrial - Themes & Underscores Vol. 2*. Sonoton (Germany): SON 118, 1980.

BOTTOM

John Epping / Wolf Nanssen / Mac Prindy. *New Waves Underscores - Flow*. Sonoton (Germany): SON 203, 1983.

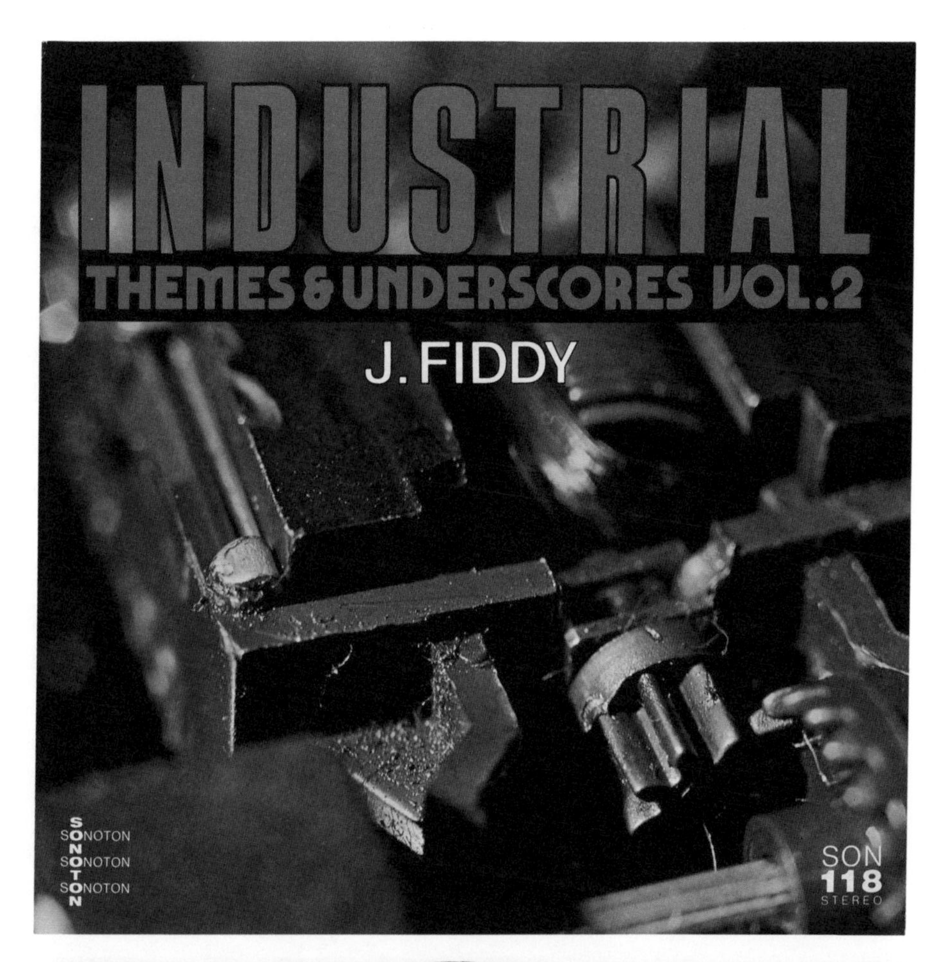

TOP

Walt Rockman. *Pollution*. Sonoton (Germany): SON 116, 1980.

Says Narholz of the cover art: "That's my son Robert. We had to go through the fire brigade to get this mask for him."

BOTTOM

Walt Rockman. *Biology*. Sonoton (Germany): SON 115, 1980.

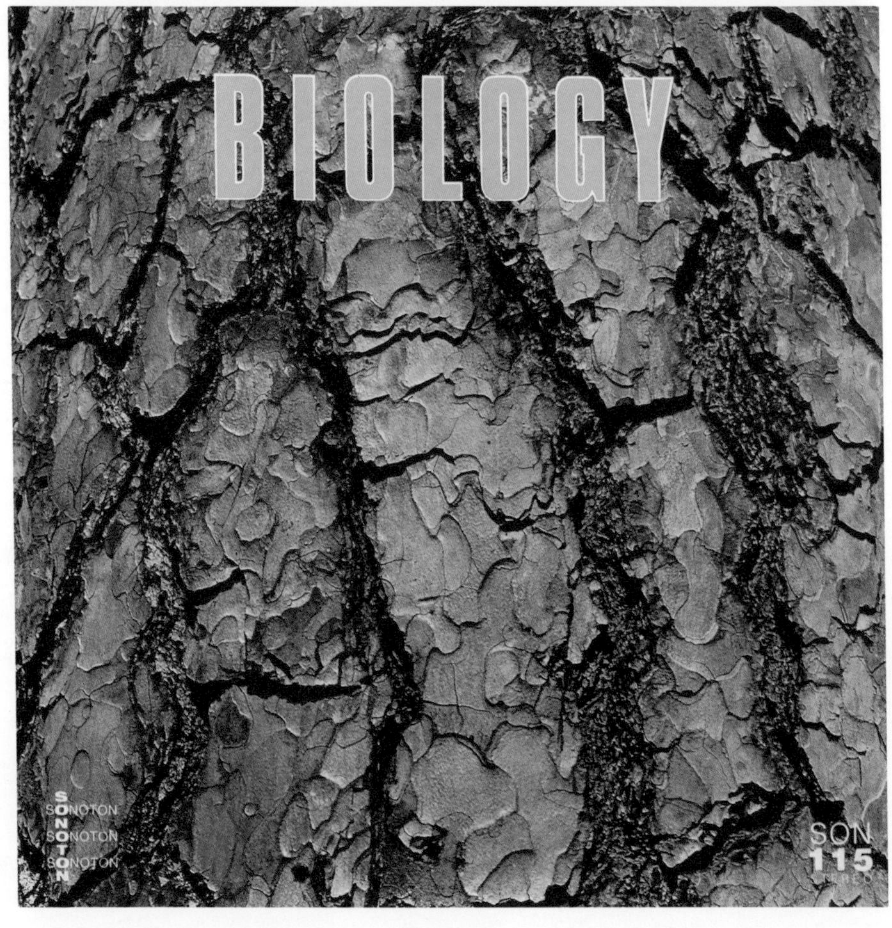

GERHARD NARHOLZ

A former music teacher and classically trained composer, Gerhard Narholz worked as a pop songwriter in the European music scene of the late 1950s before transitioning into film and television scoring. Finding that the early days of German television provided endless opportunity for music synchronization, Narholz formed Sonoton, his own music library, with his wife, Heidi Narholz, in 1965. Since then, he has been responsible for thousands of library recordings, whether as composer—either under his own name or one of his countless pseudonyms, which include Norman Candler, Walt Rockman, and Tony Tape—or through his hands-on involvement in the hundreds of releases in the Sonoton catalog, which often included photographing the label's now-iconic LP covers. In a field replete with prolific composers and storied labels, Narholz and Sonoton stand out for both their astonishing productivity and the high quality of their releases.

Origins

Gerhard Narholz: I already had some pop songs, some hits in Germany, as a songwriter, so I never had enough time to write really serious music, which I studied. I immediately went into the pop kind of scene in Germany, and from there I went into the film business; based on my pop songs, I got commissioned to write scores for films in Germany which have been very popular, featuring pop songs. Those have been kind of local themes—the Alps, love stories, funny stories, but always a lot of music in it.

Obviously, business-wise for the producers of those movies, it was a double effect: First of all, they wanted to sell the music, and people went there to see the pop artist, and the other side, those pop songs became popular by the movies. Television was not there, or was very young, in the early days, so the movies [were] the media to transport and to make songs popular in the late '50s, early '60s.

It's clearly a waste of efforts to write and produce music for a film that is shown once or twice and never again, so I thought, *Let's reuse these kinds of productions*. And I got the commission from German television to reuse tracks, which we organized in categories and copied on big tapes. We then distributed tape copies to German television—which was very young in those days, and didn't have any music at all and urgently needed music of all kinds. It developed quickly: They needed music, we had it. And soon it was not enough to compose my own music; we commissioned other composers to write for us. And in order to do so we had to form a company.

Sonoton was formed in 1965. It developed quickly. Television people needed music, other producers of industrial films—there was no video at that time—needed music for their product. So Sonoton expanded in Germany; I wouldn't say quickly, but continuously, gradually. And having quite a lot of material, we [were] looking out to other countries. But we didn't have any experience, no contacts at all. I don't remember how we got the first contact to the English label Conroy, Berry Music [Conroy's parent company], but this label was interested in our productions. Berry Music released our German productions worldwide on the label Conroy, and then we created, in cooperation with Barry Music, other labels, such as Studio One—where we had our happy songs, happy instrumentals released—or Pro Viva Productions. Until Mr. Berry retired and decided to sell his company to EMI. And this was the moment we decided to do our own label and our own distribution. This was about '72.

Recording

Gerhard Narholz: Most of the recordings were done in Trixi Studio. This was a legendary place for musical recordings in the early '60s, until the mid-'80s when they had to close because of all the synthesizer businesses that came in. Big studios [were not] needed anymore, because people are now sitting on their computers doing their music, mixing it themselves, so the studio had to close unfortunately. But in the old days it was a really great studio [with] a wonderful sound engineer—Willi Schmidt was his name—who did all the big TV shows in Germany, and of course our recordings. Musicians came in, whole big bands, and rehearsed the thing and "let's go," we recorded it. It was wonderful; they really played well. Nowadays, musicians know that they don't have to care so much—they can make mistakes because it can be repaired on tracks, so this wonderful feeling, that an orchestra has to play and that's it, is not there anymore.

There were productions that had to be made with very primitive means. Because there were no synthesizers available. [For *Underwater* volumes 1 and 2 (SON 113 and SON 114, 1980)], we manipulated all kinds of technical sounds that came out of the desk. I actually don't remember how it all was made, but it was all done with primitive equipment.

We had all kinds of musical combinations, from small groups up to full symphony orchestras. In the old days, musicians used to get paid after the session. So Heidi walked in, in the evening, with a bunch of Deutschmarks, and musicians stood in line to sign the receipt and get paid. This took an hour or more after sessions, which is unbelievable now, but in the old days it was like that. They came in, played, got paid, and went out again.

Composing

Gerhard Narholz: If you're doing certain music styles, you don't have to have a picture in mind; you concentrate on the style of music. If you do a jazz piece, that's jazz. But if you're doing descriptive music, you have to have the imagination of a possible scene. That's the nature of library music: you have to have all possible scenes in mind, different scenes in mind. Whatever could happen, you have to have the music for that.

And the requirements of the markets are changing all the time. Things that were needed five years ago may be out today. So we always have to try to be current and continue asking people, "What are you using? What do you need? What don't you like?" These are important questions. And we try to tell our composers what the clients want, and how they should do their productions.

In the old days, it was necessary [for clients to preview the music in person], because on the LPs, all those cracks and noises had not really been the thing they wanted; they wanted tape copies. They came into the offices and we had a music director who played the music for them, and they selected what they wanted.

I found out that people think that if a composer is writing classical music, he cannot write a jazz tune, or if he's writing romantic music how could he write a rock tune. So I simply used for certain kinds of music, a certain pseudonym, like Norman Candler, who did all the romantic big orchestra stuff, and so on and so on... Walt Rockman, that was a kind of rock music in the '70s... The initial idea was to combine every pseudonym with a certain kind of music. Just a basic idea.

I [also] make up my mind and try to find a title that somehow suits the possible usage for the track. So that the user can see from the title what kind of music he may expect from the track. I'm really running out of titles sometimes. Because in Germany, we have over 300,000 tracks in the library. And the number of suitable words to describe music is limited. So it's not easy sometimes.

OPPOSITE

The original photograph for the *Unusual Sounds* covers. Says Narholz: "These were kind of experimental photos which I did with the Hasselblad [camera]. It was really fun to create all kinds of images with primitive means. Today with the computer technology, it's easy to do things like that, but in the old days I tried all kinds of tricks to manipulate pictures. It was fun.

"There's a custom in Austria and Germany, to heat lead on the first night of the year, and drop it into water, and the figures that come out will tell you if you will be lucky, if you will earn money, and so on and so on. I don't know if they still do it, but in the old days they did it. And these are such products, which came from melting lead into water."

TOP

Augustyn Bloch. *Unusual Sounds Vol. 1 - Reflections*. Sonoton (Germany): SON 102, 1980.

BOTTOM

Augustyn Bloch. *Unusual Sounds Vol. 2 - The Brain*. Sonoton (Germany): SON 133, 1980.

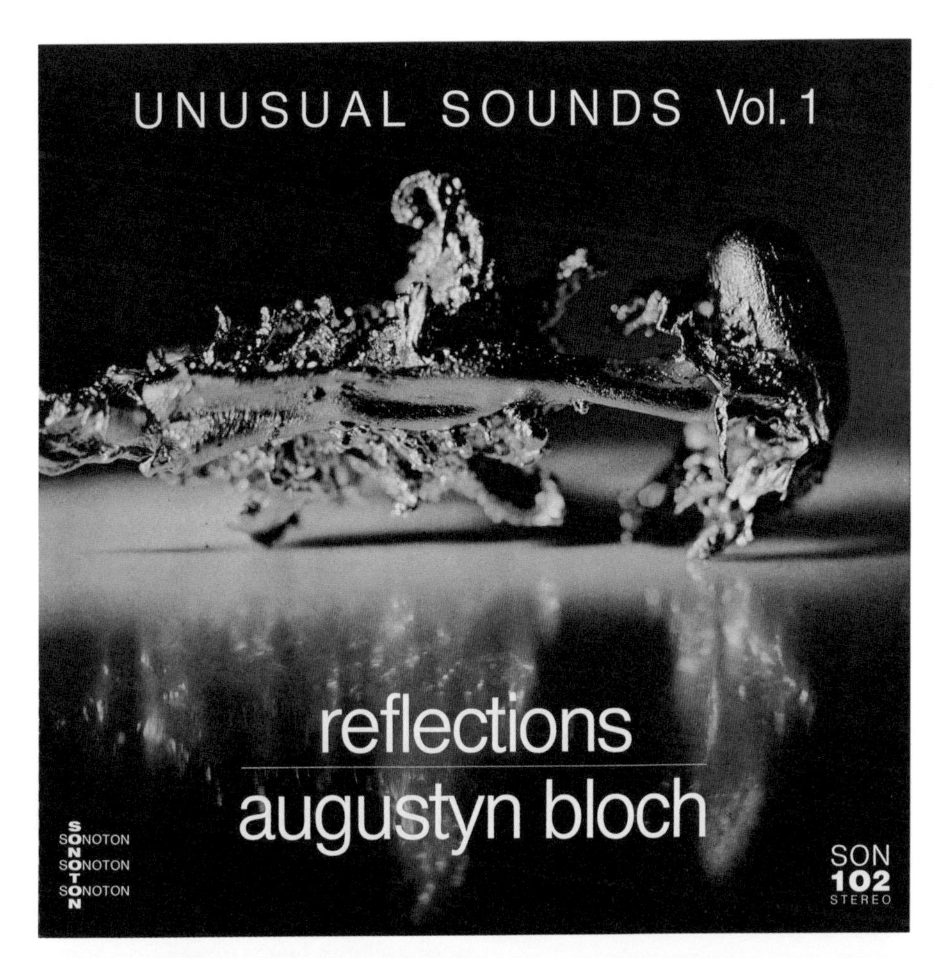

OPPOSITE TOP LEFT

Narholz's son playing with magnetic tape, 1968.

OPPOSITE TOP RIGHT

Rotheide (Heidi) Narholz in 1994.

OPPOSITE BOTTOM

Narholz with two of his sons.

Usage

Gerhard Narholz: We have no way of influencing the usage of our music. That's the nature of library music: that any producer can take any track at any time, provided he is licensing correctly. So we have no idea if our music is used in a porn or in a church production. But we have to write music for each possible application in the library.

I've composed over 4,000 works, and they've been spread all over the world. I couldn't say I've been especially impressed by a usage, but I don't know all the usages; I have no idea where the music has been used. It's impossible to know. All I can see is—I get some royalties from Japan, so I can see, OK, it's been used in Japan, but I don't know where.

Of course, coincidentally, sometimes I hear music on television, and think, *Oh, that sounds familiar, somehow*. But, you know, I write a piece of music and forget it. I may hear it once when I make a compilation for CD for release, but then never again.

Packaging and Reissues

Gerhard Narholz: [To create LP covers] I simply purchased a Hasselblad camera with all the necessary lenses and tricks, and made my own pictures for the LP series. Which was really fun and nice. You could be very creative, and there was the huge display on the album cover where you could show the picture. Since the picture got smaller with the CDs, it was not as attractive anymore; I more or less stopped the photographical thing. Now we have three or four graphic designers doing the graphics for CD covers.

The whole thing is a business method. Library is a business thing. Of course we need all the creativity and artistic input and thinking, but if it really comes to the source, it's business... If there is a demand, we will reissue for sure; if not, we won't.

COLOURSOUND

BELOW

Spiral-bound "Edition Show Business" catalog of the Coloursound library.

OPPOSITE TOP

Branislav Zivkovic. *Moods for Flutes*. Coloursound Library (Germany): CS23, 1982.

OPPOSITE BOTTOM LEFT

Gil Flat. *Action Tracks*. Coloursound Library (Germany): CS39, 1983.

OPPOSITE BOTTOM RIGHT

Various. *Soft Moods for Romantic Sequences*. Coloursound Library (Germany): CS53, 1982.

Founded in 1979 by composer, music lawyer, and vibraphonist Gunter Greffenius, Coloursound was a Munich-based library catering largely to the market for experimental sounds; its first release was 1980's *Biomechanoïd*, an abstract synthesizer excursion by Joel Vandroogenbroeck, of the pioneering *kosmische* band Brainticket. The record—complete with imposing, anonymous title and unearthly H.R. Giger cover art—set the tone for the label's progressive leanings, and Vandroogenbroeck, thrilled with the openness that library work offered, would go on to record several innovative records for Coloursound. The label's catalog (which also featured recordings by, among others, Klaus Weiss, Sonoton's Gerhard Narholz, and label boss Greffenius) now stands as a tribute to the unfettered creative license that libraries were able to provide to forward-thinking musicians who, frustrated by the whims and constraints of the commercial scene, found complete freedom in the world of production music.

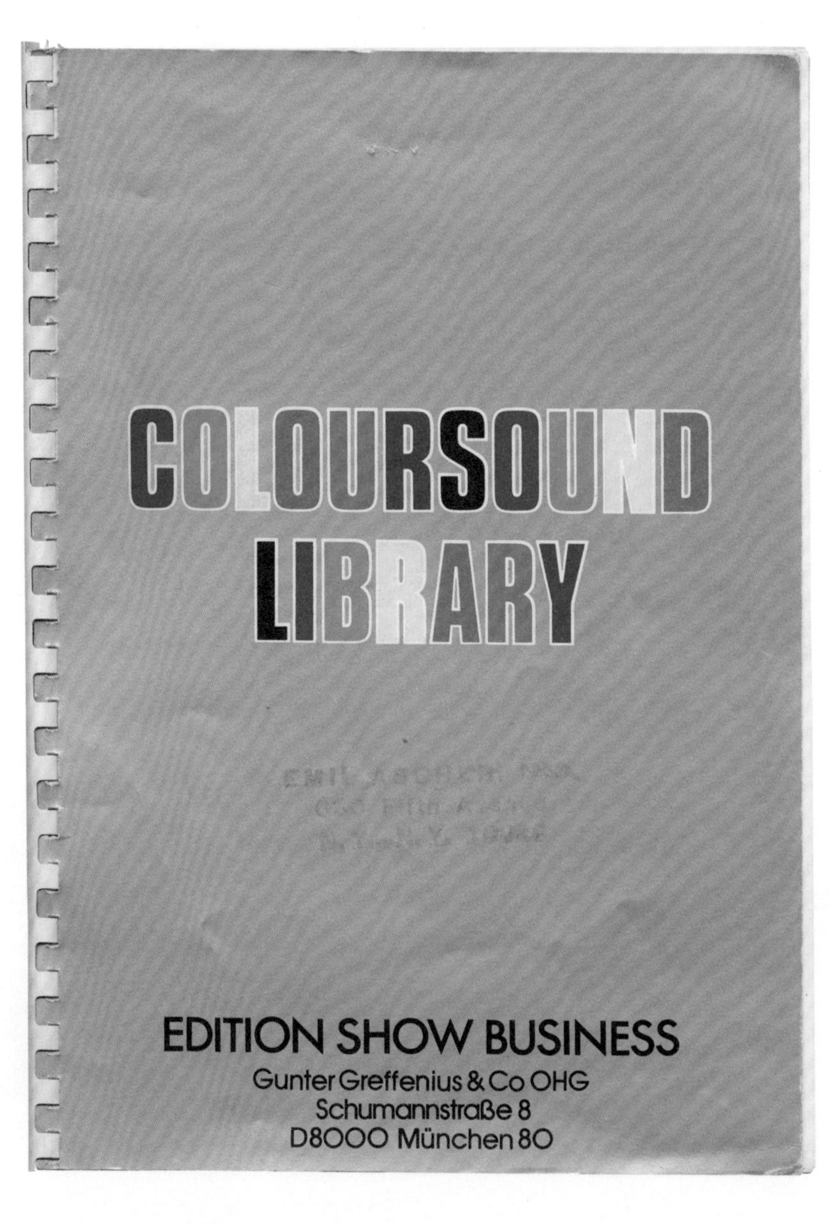

COLOURSOUND
LIBRARY
EDITION SHOW BUSINESS
Gunter Greffenius & Co OHG
Schumannstraße 8
D8000 München 80

MOODS FOR FLUTES
WG.

ACTION TRACKS Gil Flat

SOFT MOODS FOR ROMANTIC
SEQUENCES

BIOMECHANOÏD

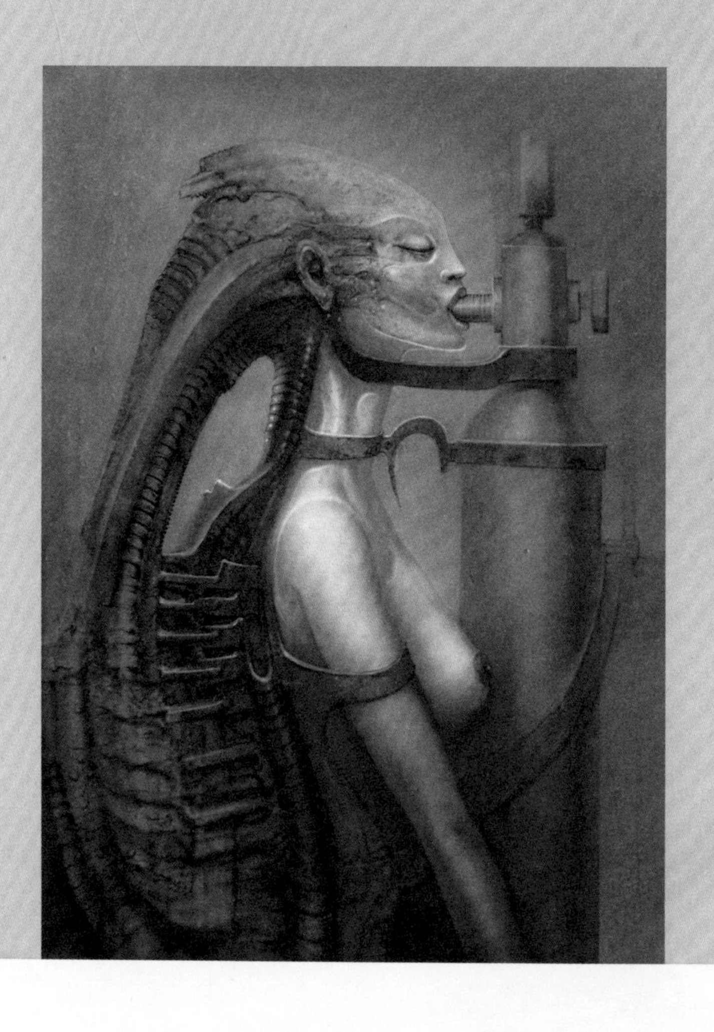

JOEL VANDROOGENBROECK

OPPOSITE

Joel Vandroogenbroeck. *Biomechanoïd*. Coloursound Library (Germany): CS1, 1980.

BELOW

Joel Vandroogenbroeck. *Birth of Earth*. Coloursound Library (Germany): CS7, 1980.

Born in Brussels in 1938, Joel Vandroogenbroeck began his music career with extensive training in classical jazz, which he parlayed into a gig as a touring pianist with performances throughout Europe. In the late 1960s, Vandroogenbroeck became enamored with the krautrock era of German psychedelia and formed the Swiss group Brainticket, whose early work demonstrated the members' progressive, experimental approach to psych rock but attracted controversy for its references to the drug culture. In 1972, continuing a lifelong obsession with world music and exotic instruments, Vandroogenbroeck traveled to Bali to study the gamelan, and upon his return to Switzerland he developed a complementary fascination with synthesizers. Upon signing with Coloursound, he put these disparate skills to use, churning out innovative and wide-ranging records for the library under a variety of pseudonyms, among them Eric Vann, J.V.D.B., and V.D.B. Joel.

TOP

Joel Vandroogenbroeck. *Lost Continents*. Coloursound Library (Germany): CS8, 1980.

BOTTOM

Joel Vandroogenbroeck. *Mesopotamia Egypt*. Coloursound Library (Germany): CS22, 1982.

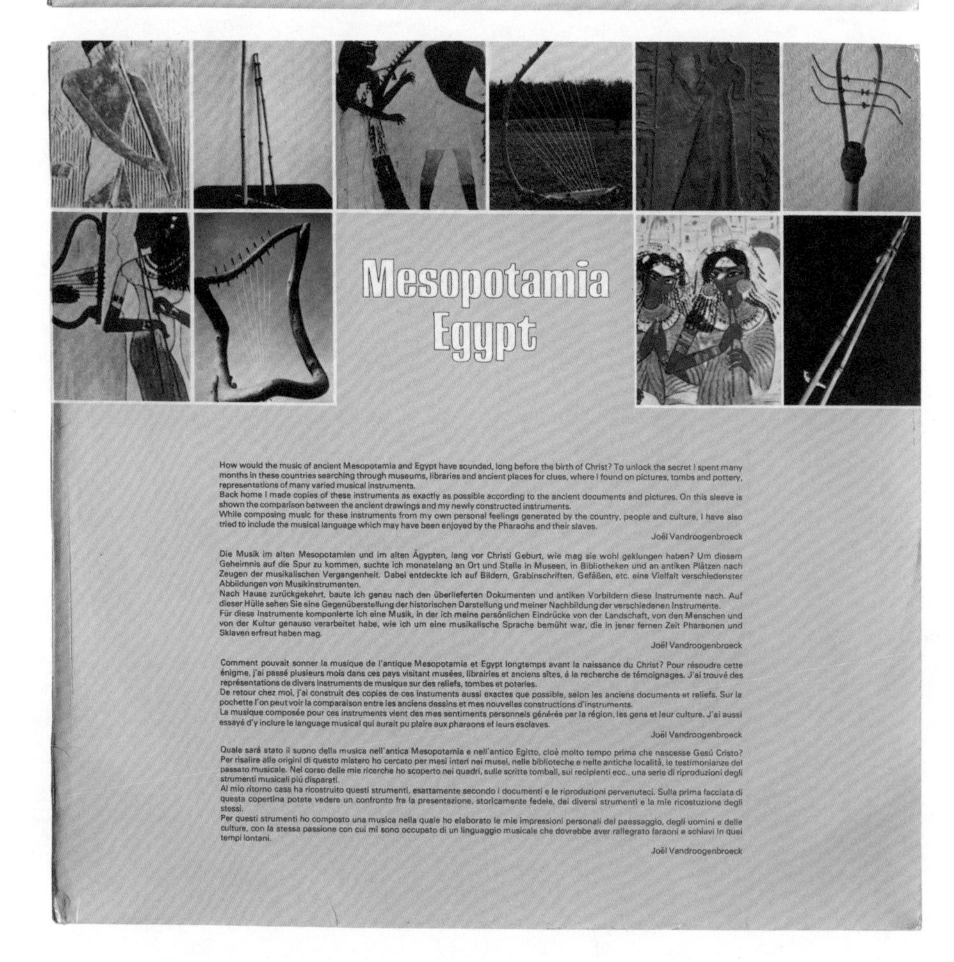

TOP

Joel Vandroogenbroeck.
Meditations Vol. 2.
Coloursound Library (Germany):
CS4, 1980.

BOTTOM

Joel Vandroogenbroeck.
Video Games & Data Movements.
Coloursound Library (Germany):
CS74, 1987.

SONOTON
SONOTON
SONOTON
SONOTON
Klaus Weiss
TRAILERS SPOTS SIGNATURES
SON
204
STEREO

KLAUS WEISS

OPPOSITE

Klaus Weiss. *Trailers Spots Signatures*. Sonoton (Germany): SON 204, 1983.

BELOW

Klaus Weiss. *Open Space Motion (Underscores)*. Coloursound Library (Germany): CS18, 1981.

Born in 1942, Klaus Weiss began his career as a jazz drummer at sixteen (with a group called the Jazzopators) before working with the internationally successful '60s groups the Klaus Doldinger Quartet and the Erwin Lehn Big Band. In 1965 he formed his own trio, the first of many groups to bear his name, and as his renown as a bandleader grew over the next decade, he began working in production music, contributing recordings to German libraries like Selected Sound, Coloursound, and Sonoton.

Gerhard Narholz: Klaus Weiss was a great drummer. He was a very—how should I say it to be polite?—a very strong-minded person. He was not popular with producers because he had his own mind. If he didn't like a producer, he took his drums and walked out during the session! He was not easy to work with. But he was a wonderful player, wonderful musician, and unfortunately he passed away a few years ago.

selected sound
RECORDED MUSIC LIBRARY
MUSIKARCHIV
CATALOGUE NO. 2
Long-Playing 33 1/3 Discs Stereo
Stereo-Langspielplatten No. 9049 – 9075
+ Special-Program ST 101 – 118

SELECTED SOUND
RECORDED MUSIC LIBRARY
CATALOGUE
Radio – Television – Films – Advertising – Backgrounds

Stereo 9067
selected sound
TIME SIGNALS
KLAUS WEISS RHYTHM & SOUNDS
Journal
Time Signals
Scoria
Rhythm & Sounds
Sequent
Just Walk Easy
Walk Easy
Join In
The Rocker
Hot Cake
Shuffling
The Hunters
Drums Around
Survivor
Different Strokes
Reports
Humming
Eternity
Swinging Skins
Machinery
The Searchers
Space Waltz
Kind Of Bossa
Rudiments
Heavy Weights
67

TIME SIGNALS
KLAUS WEISS RHYTHM & SOUNDS
selected sound 9067
Side A
1. SL 1370 JOURNAL Klaus Weiss 0'36
2. SL 1371 TIME SIGNALS Klaus Weiss 1'27
3. SL 1372 SCORIA Klaus Weiss 2'29
4. SL 1373 RHYTHM & SOUNDS Klaus Weiss 1'23
5. SL 1374 SEQUENT Klaus Weiss 1'39
6. SL 1375 JUST WALK EASY Klaus Weiss 1'00
7. SL 1376 WALK EASY Klaus Weiss 1'01
8. SL 1377 JOIN IN Klaus Weiss 1'33
9. SL 1378 THE ROCKER Klaus Weiss 1'28
10. SL 1379 HOT CAKE Klaus Weiss 1'19
11. SL 1380 SHUFFLING Klaus Weiss 1'18
12. SL 1381 THE HUNTERS Klaus Weiss 1'18
13. SL 1382 DRUMS AROUND Klaus Weiss 1'52
Side B
1. SL 1383 SURVIVOR Klaus Weiss 2'43
2. SL 1384 DIFFERENT STROKES Klaus Weiss 1'12
3. SL 1385 REPORTS Klaus Weiss 1'10
4. SL 1386 HUMMING Klaus Weiss 1'19
5. SL 1387 ETERNITY Klaus Weiss 1'20
6. SL 1388 SWINGING SKINS Klaus Weiss 1'22
7. SL 1389 MACHINERY Klaus Weiss 1'37
8. SL 1390 THE SEARCHERS Klaus Weiss 1'09
9. SL 1391 SPACE WALTZ Klaus Weiss 1'40
10. SL 1392 KIND OF BOSSA Klaus Weiss 1'29
11. SL 1393 RUDIMENTS Klaus Weiss 1'16
12. SL 1394 HEAVY WEIGHTS Klaus Weiss 1'44
Original published 1978 by SELECTED SOUND, D-2000 Hamburg 70
Rhythmusgruppe + Synthesizer, Schlagzeug-Solo, verschiedene Tempi und Klangfarben. Für Dokumentationen, Reportagen, Berichte, Nachrichten, Sport, Industrie, Technik, Elektronik, Forschung und Wissenschaft, Kriminalität, Abenteuer, Weltraum, Zukunftsbilder, Umweltprobleme, Rauschgift – Aktion, Geschwindigkeit, Stress, Verfolgung, Spannung, Hochleistung, Gewalt, Angst, Kraft, Entwicklung, Entstehung, Aufbau, Wiederkehr, Unendlichkeit, Tiefe, fremde Welten, Weite, Zeitlupe.
selected sound 9067

SELECTED SOUND

OPPOSITE TOP ROW

Two catalogs for the Selected Sound library, printed with the same glossy gold covers as their LPs.

OPPOSITE BOTTOM ROW

Front and back cover of Klaus Weiss' celebrated *Time Signals*. Selected Sound (Germany): 9067, 1978.

BELOW

Victor Cavini. *Japan*. Selected Sound (Germany): ST 144, 1983.

PAGES 166–167

Print catalogs for the Stereo Tape AG label, which specialized in recording and licensing classical and symphonic music out of a studio in Hamburg's famous Musikhalle concert space.

Founded by Sonoton alumnus Klaus Netzle (who recorded for libraries under the alias Claude Larson), Selected Sound started out as a production music company in the mold of libraries like KPM, with jazz, orchestral, and electronic recordings released in eye-catching but standardized sleeves—in this case, the gold covers of the label's 9000 series. Over time, the Hamburg-based library's catalog broadened considerably to encompass numerous genres and themes, including a series of releases based on traditional and indigenous styles from countries around the world (catering to the growing market for so-called "world" or "ethnic" music). Now a part of the EMI Production Music conglomerate, the Selected Sound library continues to release albums, and its recordings are still used in productions in Europe and around the world.

STEREO TAPE AG

STEREO TAPE AG

MUSIK MOSAIK

1

Musikverlag Octave · Alfred K. Schacht · Adolfstr. 45 · 2000 Hamburg 76 · Tel. 040 / 22 51 43 - 45 · Telex 21 37 23

MUSIK MOSAIK

2

Musikverlag Octave · Alfred K. Schacht · Adolfstr. 45 · 2000 Hamburg 76 · Tel. 040 / 22 51 43 - 45 · Telex 21 37 23

MUSIK MOSAIK

3

Musikverlag Octave · Alfred K. Schacht · Adolfstr. 45 · 2000 Hamburg 76 · Tel. 040 / 22 51 43 - 45 · Telex 21 37 23

MUSIK MOSAIK

4

Musikverlag Octave · Alfred K. Schacht · Adolfstr. 45 · 2000 Hamburg 76 · Tel. 040 / 22 51 43 - 45 · Telex 21 37 23

MUSIK MOSAIK

5

Musikverlag Octave · Alfred K. Schacht · Adolfstr. 45 · 2000 Hamburg 76 · Tel. 040 / 22 51 43 - 45 · Telex 21 37 23

MUSIK MOSAIK

6

Musikverlag Octave · Alfred K. Schacht · Adolfstr. 45 · 2000 Hamburg 76 · Tel. 040 / 22 51 43 - 45 · Telex 21 37 23

OPPOSITE

Various. *Musik Mosaik* (vols. 1-6). Musikverlag Octave (Germany): MM1-MM6, no date.

TOP

Klaus Weiss. *Sound Music Album 26*. Golden Ring (Germany): S 5261 20, 1979.

BOTTOM

Ralph Haldenby. *Wide World*. UBM Records (Germany): UBM 1002, 1982.

PAGE 170

Various. *Spots* (vols. 1-9). Intersound (Germany): 1-9, no date.

SPOTS
1

SPOTS
2

SPOTS
3

SPOTS
4

SPOTS
5

SPOTS
6

SPOTS
7

SPOTS
8

SPOTS
9

FRENCH
LIBRARIES

MONTPARNASSE 2000

BELOW

Various. *Montparnasse 2000 vous présente un échantillon de son catalogue*. Éditions Montparnasse 2000 (France): DMP 1, no date.

Founded in 1968 by club and cabaret owner André Farry, Montparnasse 2000—named for the famous arts district of Paris in which it was based—was originally treated as little more than a financial venture. The library began its musical innovations, however, when Farry recruited composer and musician Louis Delacour to act as label manager and head of A&R. Delacour had found success in the 1950s as bandleader for a Latin orchestra (Pépé Luiz y su Orquesta Hispana), and he was determined to take MP 2000 in a new sonic direction, recruiting prolific and innovative composers in the hopes of quickly building a successful library of modern sounds. Delacour's determination (and Farry's funds) did the trick, and MP 2000 attracted iconic talent to its roster, including Janko Nilović, Yan Tregger, Camille Sauvage, and Jean-Jacques Perrey. In 1970, Delacour began the commercial label Neuilly, another successful venture that shared many artists with his former library over the course of the 1970s. Neuilly and its equally popular sublabel Crea Sound Ltd continued releasing seminal records after MP 2000 closed its doors in the early '80s. Other notable MP 2000 sublabels included IML (International Music Label) and St. Germain des Prés.

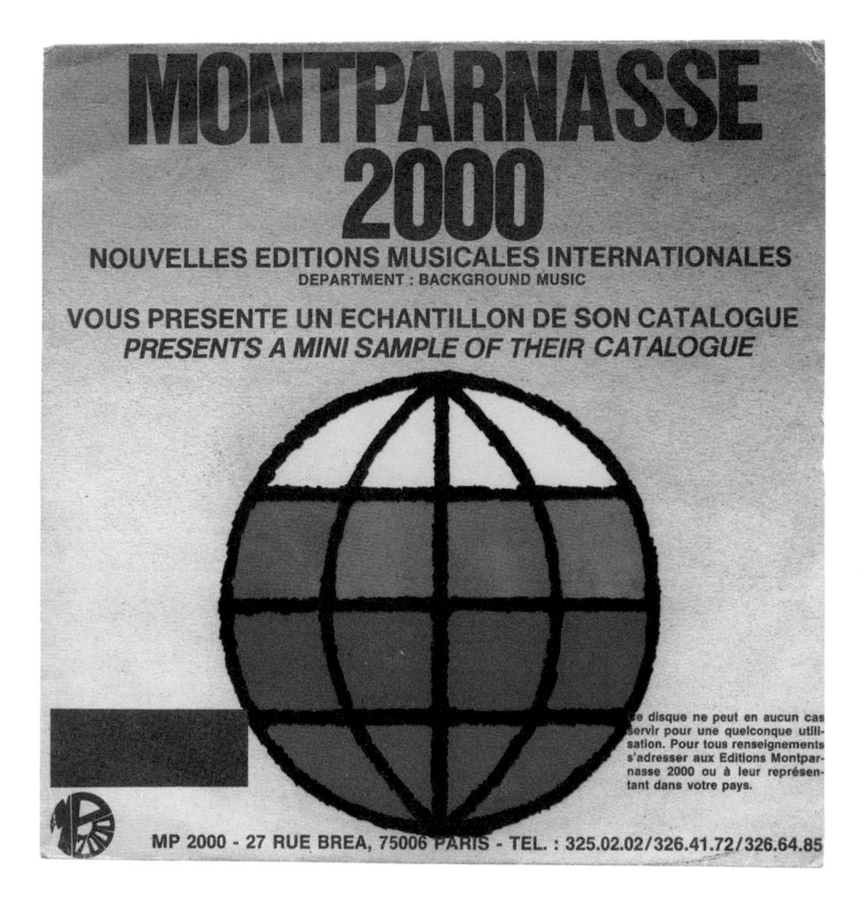

TOP

Eric Framond. *Univers 2000*. Éditions Montparnasse 2000 (France): MP 21, 1973.

BOTTOM

Various. *Stylissimo*. Éditions Montparnasse 2000 (France): MP 40, 1974.

OPPOSITE TOP

Eric Framond. *Palpitations*. Éditions Montparnasse 2000 (France): MP 76, 1976.

OPPOSITE BOTTOM LEFT

Camille Sauvage, Roger Roger, Nino Nardini. *Circus Parade*. Éditions Montparnasse 2000 (France): MP 90, 1977.

OPPOSITE BOTTOM RIGHT

Ariel Kalma. *Interfrequence*. Éditions Montparnasse 2000 (France): MP 120, 1979.

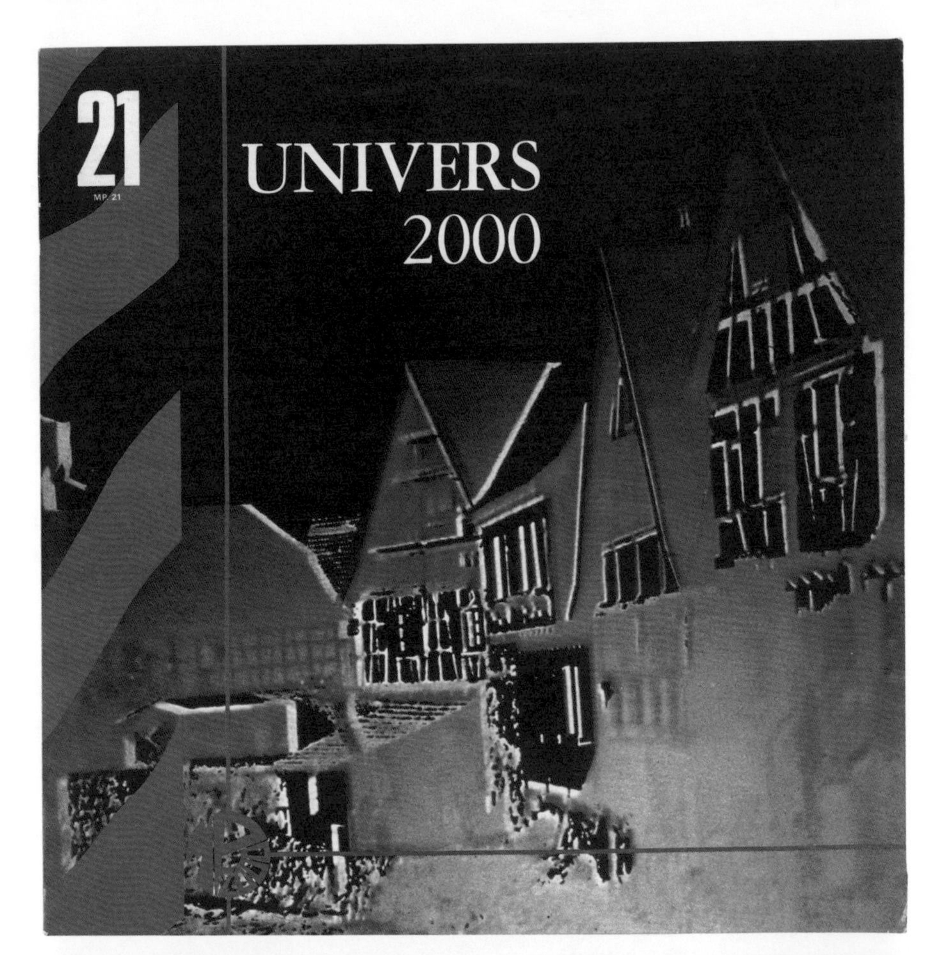

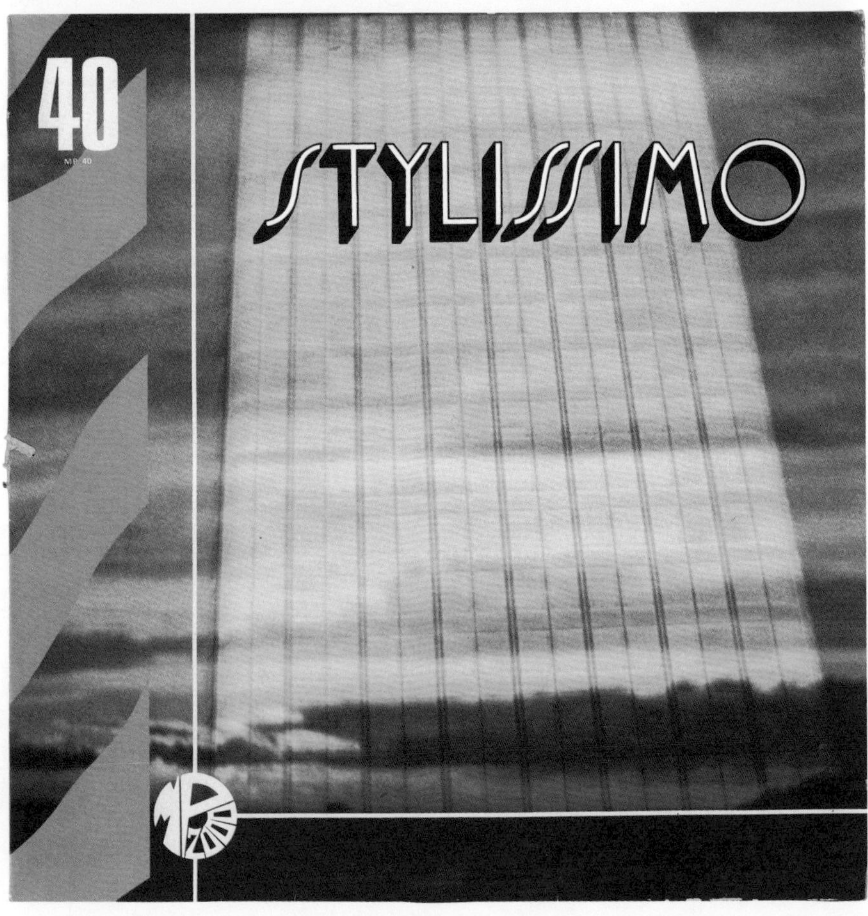

76
MP 76
palpitations

90
CIRCUS PARADE

120
INTERFREQUENCE

121
Suspense

09
SUPRANATURAL

104
vin, bière
carnaval
T R F PRODUCTION MUSIC LIBRARIES
747 Chestnut Ridge Road
Chestnut Ridge, NY 10977
(914) 356-0800 Fax: (914) 356-0895
Toll Free: (800) 899-MUSIC
trfemail@aol.com

122
MP 122
Rêve
abyssal

OPPOSITE TOP LEFT

Gerard Gallo / Guy Pedersen. *Suspense*. Éditions Montparnasse 2000 (France): MP 121, 1979.

OPPOSITE TOP RIGHT

Marie-Claude Robert. *Supranatural*. Éditions Montparnasse 2000 (France): MP 09, 1971.

OPPOSITE BOTTOM LEFT

Daniel J. White. *Vin, bière et carnaval*. Éditions Montparnasse 2000 (France): MP 104, 1978.

OPPOSITE BOTTOM RIGHT

Gaston Borreani. *Rêve abyssal*. Éditions Montparnasse 2000 (France): MP 122, 1979.

TOP

Andy Loore. *Water Show*. Éditions Montparnasse 2000 (France): MP 55, 1976.

BOTTOM

Jacky Giordano. *Pop-In... Devil's Train*. Éditions Montparnasse 2000 (France): MP 107, 1976.

125
HYPOTHESE
SYNTHETISEUR
MP2000

130
TRANSLATION
MP2000

126
FOLKLORE
MP2000

OPPOSITE TOP

Various. *Hypothese*. Éditions Montparnasse 2000 (France): MP 125, 1980.

OPPOSITE BOTTOM LEFT

Various. *Translation*. Éditions Montparnasse 2000 (France): MP 130, no date.

OPPOSITE BOTTOM RIGHT

Daniel J. White / Claudine White. *Folklore*. Éditions Montparnasse 2000 (France): MP 126, 1980.

TOP

Various. *Hypnose*. International Music Label (France): IML 04, 1974.

BOTTOM

Claude Engel, Teddy Lasry, Bernard Lubat. *More Creative Pop*. International Music Label (France): IML 06, 1971.

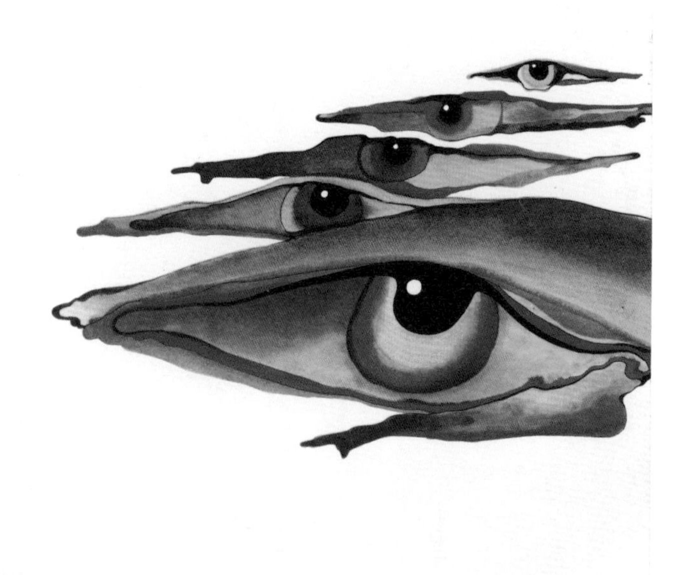

TOP

Daniel Humair. *Drumo Vocalo.* International Music Label (France): IML 02, 1971.

BOTTOM

Jean Claudric. *Génériquement votre.* International Music Label (France): IML 07, 1976.

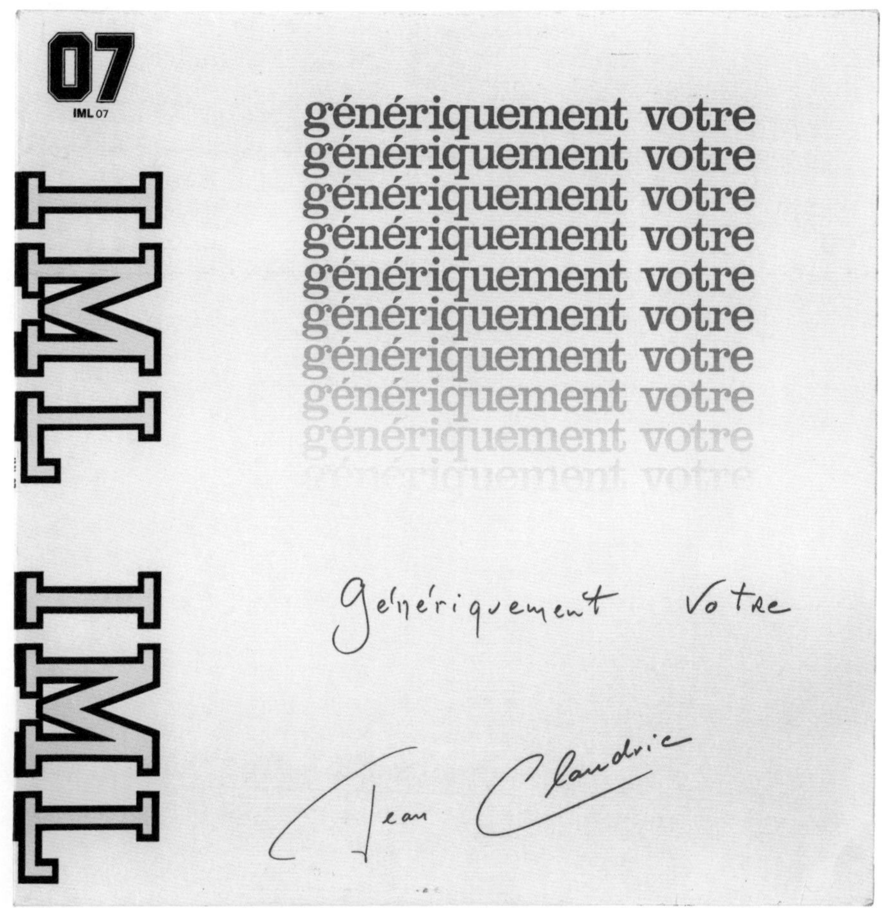

TOP LEFT

Jean Claudric. *Escapade*. International Music Label (France): IML 05, 1974.

TOP RIGHT

Maxi Baratas / Agathe Neel. *Romantico*. St. Germain des Prés (France): St GDP 109, no date.

MIDDLE

Jacques Siroul. *Midway*. St. Germain des Prés (France): St GDP 123, 1973.

BOTTOM LEFT

Gerardo Iacoucci. *Symbolisme Psychédélique*. St. Germain des Prés: St GDP 107, 1970. LP center label.

BOTTOM RIGHT

Gerardo Iacoucci. *Symbolisme Psychédélique*. St. Germain des Prés: St GDP 107, 1970.

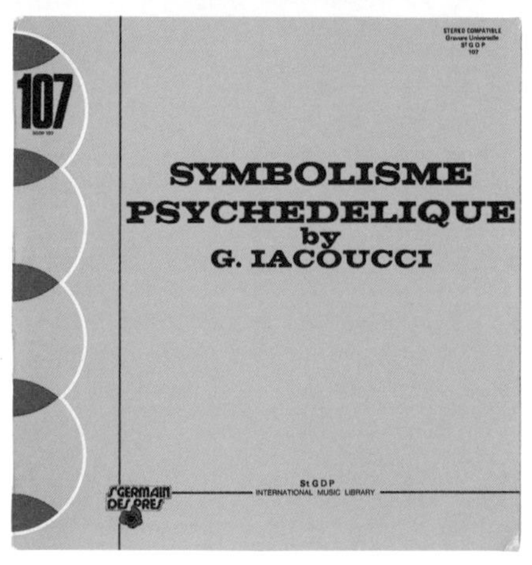

JANKO NILOVIĆ

OPPOSITE TOP

Janko Nilović. *Psyc Impressions*. Éditions Montparnasse 2000 (France): MP 06, 1969.

OPPOSITE BOTTOM LEFT

Janko Nilović. *Vocal Impressions*. Éditions Montparnasse 2000 (France): MP 08, 1971.

OPPOSITE BOTTOM RIGHT

Janko Nilović. *Pop Impressions*. Éditions Montparnasse 2000 (France): MP 11, 1972.

Born in Istanbul to a Yugoslavian-Montenegrin father and a Greek mother, Janko Nilović put his multicultural, pan-lingual background to use when he arrived in Paris at the age of twenty and embarked on a genre-spanning career in music. After becoming a well-known club pianist and arranger for film and pop acts, Nilović was hired in 1969 to create twenty albums of music for the new Montparnasse 2000 library. His discography includes hundreds of credits recorded under several pseudonyms, but he is particularly known for jazz-funk recordings that employed aspects of big band, world music, and psych rock, perhaps best exemplified in the 1974 album *Rythmes contemporains*. Nilović continues to compose and record, and was sampled on the 2009 Jay-Z album *The Blueprint 3* and by Dr. Dre on 2015's *Compton*.

Origins

Janko Nilović: I was born in 1941 in the French embassy in Turkey, because my father worked there in Turkey for thirty-five years, so it was an accident, if I can say that. My father never got back to Montenegro, so we stayed in Turkey. I could speak the language, I had my friends; all the embassies were around the French embassy so I, at six, seven years old, was speaking six languages before going to school. And when I was twenty, I came to Paris.

I started to be a professional pianist in a jazz club in Istanbul—I was sixteen years old... My first instrument was the flute, then pan flute, then I touched all the percussions like vibraphone and drums. And when my father died—I was ten, eleven years old—my great aunt said, "OK, you're very sad; I will buy you a piano, because I have a friend who is a piano teacher." So I started to play the piano

06
MP. 06
PSYC
IMPRESSIONS

08
VOCAL
IMPRESSIONS

11
POP IMPRESSIONS

TOP

Janko Nilović. *Soul Impressions.* Éditions Montparnasse 2000 (France): MP 43, 1975.

BOTTOM

Janko Nilović. *Supra Pop Impressions.* Éditions Montparnasse 2000 (France): MP 16, 1973.

TOP

Janko Nilović. *Un couple dans la ville*. Éditions Montparnasse 2000 (France): MP 50, 1976.

BOTTOM

Janko Nilović. *Un homme dans l'univers*. Éditions Montparnasse 2000 (France): MP 84, 1978.

TOP

Janko Nilović. *Chorus*. Éditions Montparnasse 2000 (France): MP 34, 1974.

BOTTOM

Janko Nilović. *Rythmes contemporains*. Éditions Montparnasse 2000 (France): MP 36, 1974.

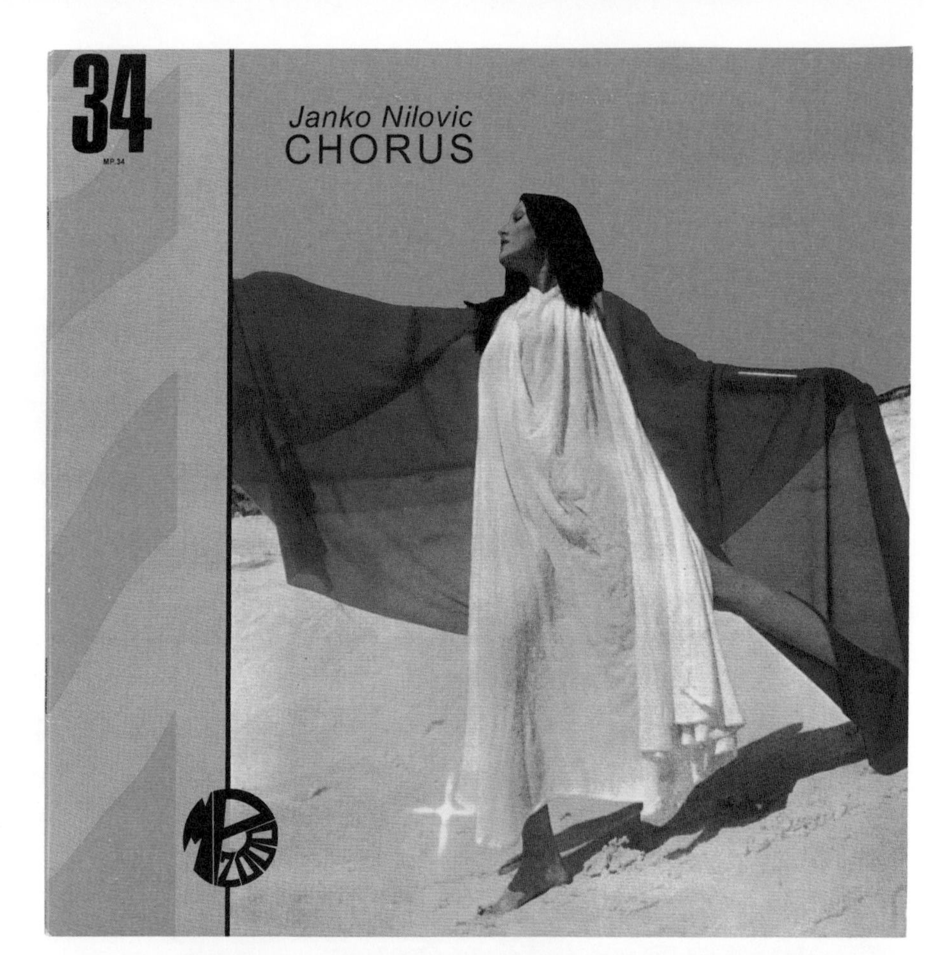

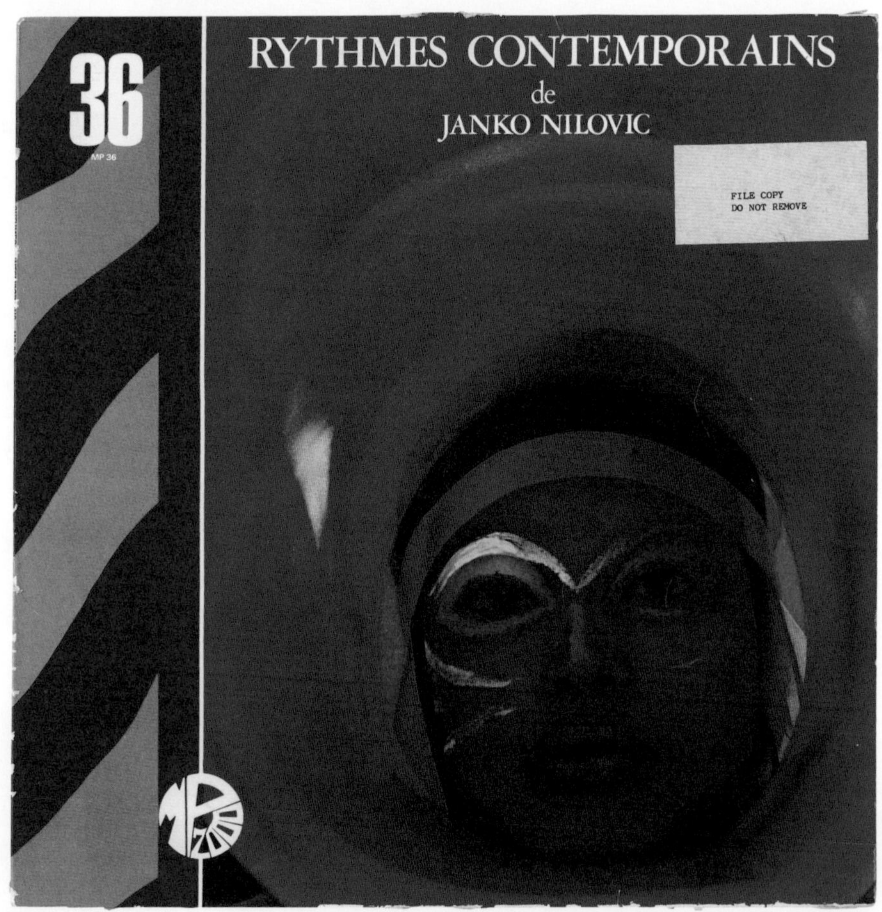

at eleven, twelve years old, I don't remember exactly. And so I learned everything at the piano, and immediately, composition.

[My start in library music] was in '69. First, I worked for Sforzando; it was a small library. And immediately after that, they contacted me from Montparnasse 2000—they liked my music, so we made a contract for twenty records. They loved my arrangements and also the compositions. So I started with *Psyc Impressions*, and then immediately, the second record, the third record, etc. I was very happy. I left everything else; I just composed. Fast and furious (*laughs*).

Before the library music, I was an arranger for different artists and movies, things like that. When I sold this [library] work, I was very happy, because the owner [André Farry] didn't know anything about music. He said, "We'll do a contract for twenty records. And you do what you want." Very rich, you know? "You do what you want. Have a big orchestra, trio, classical, everything." So I love this kind of music. Not for the library especially, but because I composed what I loved to compose, you know? So slowly, slowly, this kind of music was very well-known in France. And with the first record I bought my house. The second one I bought an Italian sports car (*laughs*). So I said, "OK, this business is very good."

Chorus (MP 34, 1974)

Janko Nilović: We had the musical *Hair* in Paris. So I was the organist in *Hair*, and sometime percussionist. And there were very good singers [in the show]. I said "Come and record a few songs on *Chorus*." It's from *Hair* they came, no money, nothing; there were twelve [singers]. And also in *Rythmes contemporains*, you had the same [singers].

"Xenos Cosmos" from *Rythmes contemporains* (MP 36, 1974)

Janko Nilović: My mother was Greek. "Xenos" was made from "outer," "cosmos" is "the world." "Xenos Cosmos." It's in this title, it's typically Greek music and I put it with my big band. I love this space thing, you know? When I'm looking to the clouds, the blue sky... I love space.

Un couple dans la ville (MP 50, 1976)

Janko Nilović: *Un couple dans la ville*, this girl, this guy, they leave the city and they're going to the country, you know? And I had a very good friend, a singer, and I sang with her, in duet—not really text, just ba-da-ba-ba (*sings*), you know, things like that. This girl was fantastic at reading music, and she said "OK, I'll come to sing with you on this record." I love this record. And my wife did the cover, because she's a painter.

TOP

Janko Nilović. *Concerto pour un fou*. Éditions Montparnasse 2000 (France): MP 82, 1976.

BOTTOM

Juan de Dios Muñoz / Michael Gésina. *Guitare classique*. Éditions Montparnasse 2000 (France): MP 69, 1976. Features several compositions by Nilović.

OPPOSITE TOP LEFT

Janko Nilović. *Super America*. Éditions Montparnasse 2000 (France): MP 103, 1978.

OPPOSITE TOP RIGHT

Janko Nilović. *Pop Shopin*. Éditions Montparnasse 2000 (France): MP 71, 1976.

OPPOSITE BOTTOM LEFT

Jerry Mengo / Richard Morand / Janko Nilović. *Black Jack Party*. Éditions Montparnasse 2000 (France): MP 12, 1972.

OPPOSITE BOTTOM RIGHT

Janko Nilović. *Un piano dans l'ouest*. Éditions Montparnasse 2000 (France): MP 86, 1979.

103
MP 103
SUPER AMERICA

71
POP SHOPIN

12
MP 12
BLACK JACK PARTY

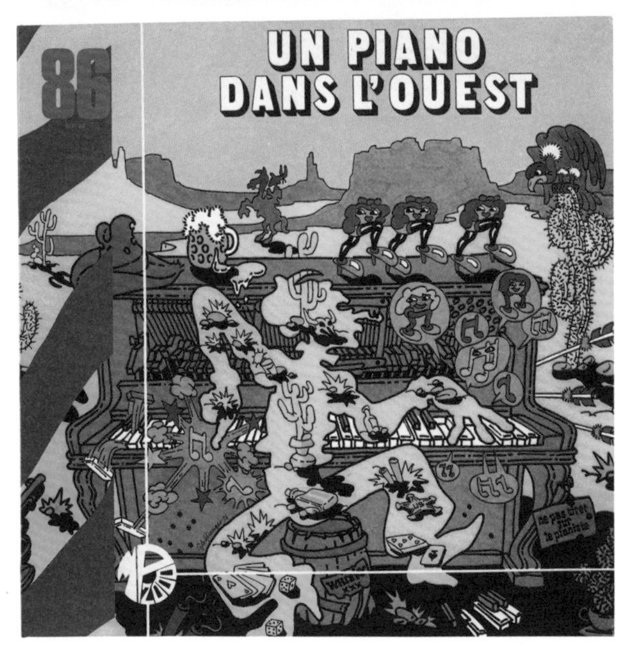
86
UN PIANO
DANS L'OUEST

JEAN-JACQUES PERREY / PAT PRILLY

OPPOSITE TOP

Pat Prilly. *Moog Expressions*. Éditions Montparnasse 2000 (France): MP 26, no date.

OPPOSITE BOTTOM LEFT

Pat Prilly / Harry Breuer. *Moog Is Moog*. Éditions Montparnasse 2000 (France): MP 106, no date.

OPPOSITE BOTTOM RIGHT

Pat Prilly. *Moog Generation*. Éditions Montparnasse 2000 (France): MP 27, no date.

Known for his playful, humorous style of synthesizer composition, Jean-Jacques Perrey became an early advocate for electronic music when he began using the Ondioline, a pre-synth keyboard instrument known for its natural vibrato and its capability to produce a wider range of sounds than any previous electronic instrument. After several years spent demonstrating the Ondioline's capabilities throughout Europe as a sales representative, Perrey immigrated to the United States in 1959 at the age of thirty, leading to a 1960 appearance on the television show *I've Got a Secret*, during which the composer and the host played up the Ondioline's uncanny ability to mimic other instruments. In the ensuing years, Perrey befriended Robert Moog and became one of the earliest adopters of the Moog synthesizer. Perrey also began a fateful collaboration with fellow Moog pioneer Gershon Kingsley, with whom he recorded the landmark 1966 album *The In Sound from Way Out!*—responsible, along with records like Wendy Carlos' 1968 *Switched-On Bach*, for popularizing electronic music outside of the avant-garde.

Following several successful collaborative and solo recordings, Perrey returned to France in 1970 and began to pursue a career in music therapy while simultaneously lending his talents to library labels, then hungry for the electronic sounds Perrey had been playing for nearly two decades. He contributed several records to Montparnasse 2000, often being credited alongside "Pat Prilly"—actually a pseudonym for the composing duo of Perrey and his daughter Patricia Leroy, who had no composing background but would give her father ideas and improvise on his instruments.

After a pioneering career across multiple continents and some six decades, Perrey died in 2016 at the age of eighty-seven.

26
MP 26
MOOG
EXPRESSIONS

106
moog is
moog

27
Fusée dans le Ciel - Bal Campagnard - L'horloge Hantée - Pot-pourri de Rondes Enfantines Internationales - Le Défilé des Moustiques - Pizzicato Polka (d'après Léo Delibes) - Go-Go Scotch - Un Soir à Munich - Glockenspeil Gavotte
Kiyouli le Clown
MOOG GENERATION
by
PAT PRILLY

LES STRUCTURES SONORES LASRY-BASCHET / TEDDY LASRY

BELOW

Structures Sonores Lasry-Baschet. *Musique démesurée*. International Music Label (France): IML 03, 1972.

OPPOSITE

Jacques Lasry. *Chronophagie "The Time Eaters."* Columbia Masterworks (US): MS 7314, 1969.

PAGES 194–195

Frederic Mercier / Teddy Lasry / Claude Perraudin. + *Ou - 8000*. Patchwork (France): MC 28, 1978.

An experimental group created by the union of musicians Jacques and Yvonne Lasry, the sculptor François Baschet, and his engineer brother Bernard, the "Structures Sonores" refers specifically to the "sound sculptures" created by the Baschet brothers: new experimental instruments, often made from steel, aluminum, and glass and played by the Lasrys to eerie, entrancing effect. The exciting sonic qualities of the "structures sonores" combined with their striking appearance made the group an unlikely international hit—they toured successfully, and even performed on *The Ed Sullivan Show*—and led to their use in the avant-garde corners of the production music world. Jacques Lasry would compose his iconic 1969 record *Cronophagie "The Time Eaters"* using the "structures sonores," and the group's music also appeared on the 1972 library record *Musique démesurée*, released on the MP2000 sublabel International Music Label (IML). Les Structures Sonores were so popular as to even be considered to write the theme for the BBC's *Doctor Who*, a job that eventually and fatefully landed with Delia Derbyshire of the BBC Radiophonic Workshop.

The Lasrys' son Teddy, a proficient multi-instrumentalist and composer in his own right, is himself a big name in the library field; he released multiple albums on labels like Sonimage, Patchwork, and the aforementioned IML.

Columbia
Stereo
MS 7314
MASTERWORKS
The hypnotic music of sculptures that sound
Chronophagie
"The Time Eaters"
Music of Jacques Lasry
CHRONOPHAGIE MUSIC OF JACQUES LASRY
played on
Structures Sonores Lasry-Baschet
MUSIC OF OUR TIME

28
patchwork

MC 28

28

+ou–8000

\+ ou – 8 000

face A

1 /SUNRISE (T. Lasry) 6'40

2 /ANNAPURNA (T. Lasry) 2'15

3 /ÉPOPÉE COSMIQUE (F. Mercier) 4'15

4 /NANDA DEVI (T. Lasry) 1'35

5 /ALTITUDE (T. Lasry) 4'40

6 /ASCENSION (T. Lasry) 3'10

\+ ou – 8 000

face B

1 /MOINS 8000 (T. Lasry) 5'05

2 /GROTTE (T. Lasry) 3'25

3 /STALACTITE (T. Lasry) 4'05

4 /CORAUX (T. Lasry) 2'10

5 /TROGLODYTES (C. Perraudin) 3'30

Les Œuvres de ce disque ont été spécialement enregistrées pour l'illustration sonore. Ce disque ne peut être vendu dans le commerce.

YAN TREGGER (TED SCOTTO)

Born in Algeria to French parents, Ted Scotto began his musical life as a trumpet player, but got his foot in the door of production soundtracks when he composed the theme for the 1968 French animated series *Les Shadoks*. Soon taking on the pseudonym Yan Tregger (chosen for its nonspecific, English-sounding connotations), Scotto wrote and recorded more than thirty library records, ranging from funk and R&B tunes to deep dives into the then-prevalent Italo disco sound. He also continued to record commercial music (including two albums with his disco act M.B.T. Soul and the underwater trumpet novelty hit "Bubble Bubble"), and work on film scores, including 1982's *L'Amour à la bouche* and an early film by Jean-Jacques Annaud. In 1973, Scotto released *The Pop World of Yan Tregger* for the IM library, regarded to this day as a classic of the genre.

Ted Scotto: My name is Ted Scotto, and my pseudonym is Yan Tregger. I took on that pseudonym when I began to make music for films and library music. And at the time, it was more interesting to have a name with an American / English consonance, and I took the pseudonym Yan Tregger, and I made many records under that name. And music for films: *L'Amour à la bouche* (1974), and then a film for Jean-Jacques Annaud, the director of *La Guerre du Feu* [*Quest for Fire*].

I created the themes for *Les Shadoks*, and that got my foot in the door with record labels in general. I would propose a project for a record, and they'd say yes or no, and I'd make the recordings. Then, the records were released under different French record companies, like Montparnasse 2000, IM—L'Illustration Musicale—KPM, what else... also, Polygram, Polydor, Phillips, Barclay, RCA, (*laughs*)... close to every record company. Because I made my first record, which was the record for IM, and this record went around to every record company. So everybody asked me, "Can you do this thing," "Can you make a record," and I'd present it and record it. Voilà.

In my work as a musician, I was approached by the director of a company called Mood Music, and he was looking for someone who knew music to be able to lead their musical program and set up their library, their record library. At that time, I was immersed in music—Supertramp, Barry White, Chicago, many others—and it was really the basis for my style. I was imprinted with all the styles between rock, pop music, rhythm and blues that were coming out, all these musical genres.

Pictures (MP 44) and *Stories* (MP 58)

Ted Scotto: I worked with a man named—excuse me, who *was* named, because he passed away, unfortunately—Louis Delacour. And this man also worked in [music] publishing, and he published in collaboration with another owner whose name I don't remember anymore [André Farry]: it was Montparnasse 2000. And one day at the beginning, he called me and said, "I need music. I want very, very, very modern music—can you give me a hand? Can you make a record?" And I did it. The first record, I think it was *Stories*. I made three records in all.

We recorded it very quickly. It was very fast. And so perhaps there's some sloppiness on [some records], but that's what also characterized the style. It's not mistakes, it's sloppiness. It's not the same thing.

Montparnasse 2000 was interesting: It was a company that worked well, that had presence as far as radio and television. [Farry] was pretty businesslike, intelligent businesslike, and when he had a record, he brought it to radio, and when that worked, you heard them all over the radio. It wasn't songs, it wasn't like the hits, but you would hear them as background music, or as bumpers. It was interesting.

44
MP 44
PICTURES

RYTHMIQUES STATIQUES
(Compositeur: YAN TREGGER)
STATIC RHYTHMICS
(Composer: YAN TREGGER)
STATISCHE RHYTMEN
(Komponist: YAN TREGGER)
RITMICAS ESTATICAS
(Compositor: YAN TREGGER)
RITMICA STATICA
(Compositore: YAN TREGGER)
CAM
CmL 130
EDUCATIONAL MATERIAL
Not for sale
MATERIEL EDUCATIF
Vente interdite
CAM
DISCO DI SONORIZZAZIONE
SCORING RECORD
DISCO DE SONORIZACIÒN
DISQUE DE SONORISATION
BESCHALLUNGS PLATTE
DISCO DE SONORIZAÇÃO

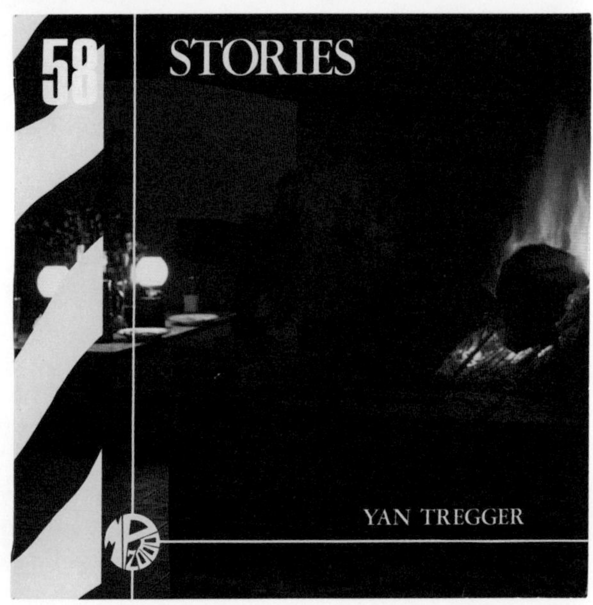
58
STORIES
YAN TREGGER

OPPOSITE TOP

Yan Tregger. *Pictures (Pop Sound)*. Éditions Montparnasse 2000 (France): MP 44, 1975.

OPPOSITE BOTTOM LEFT

Yan Tregger. *Rhythmiques statiques*. CAM (Italy): CmL 130, 1974.

OPPOSITE BOTTOM RIGHT

Yan Tregger. *Stories*. Éditions Montparnasse 2000 (France): MP 58, no date.

Montparnasse 2000 was a company that did library music, but they [also] put [*Pictures*] out on Neuilly (Neuilly MC 8004), because Neuilly was a label for commercial sales. They found at the time that these albums were selling, so it was released with them.

With Montparnasse 2000, I worked with rhythms, violins, brass—[the company] was very rich. Now, you have these synthesizers; most brass you don't have except electronically. But there, I had everything.

The Pop World of Yan Tregger (IM 11, 1973)

Ted Scotto: I made many, many recordings. And I was in sessions all day—in two years I made 1,500 recordings.

Eddie Warner [the director of IM] was a friend... a great man, head of an orchestra, known the world over, because he had an orchestra with a style that was slightly rhumba, samba... I played with his orchestra. It was exactly the same situation as with Louis Delacour; Eddie Warner had become a good friend, and since he knew that I composed, and he'd heard what I'd done, he asked me to do a record. Right away: "Do whatever you want."

At this time we were called the Yan Tregger Group. I had formed a group—it was friends, and they were paid, it was normal. But I had formed a group that knew one another, and since I played and made recordings ceaselessly, every day... (*laughs*) they had a cohesion. I had the best rhythm [section] in France... I had the guitarist and pianist for Johnny Hallyday, the drummer became—I won't say his name, but he's become a big worldwide star now. I had set up that bass and rhythm section that knew how to play together. And that's something exceptional; they were fused together.

"Bubble Bubble" b/w "Sea Love Trumpet" (Major Music MAJ 702, 1974)

Ted Scotto: This is something else (*laughs*). I had gone to see [French radio and TV presenter] Jacques Martin on the radio. He had a secretary who I spoke with. "I'm a trumpet player, I make albums with the trumpet; can you help me? Can Jacques Martin help me?" She said, "I hear trumpet players on every street corner; it's pointless. Go throw it in the Seine—send for journalists and throw the trumpet in the Seine, while playing." Well, OK (*laughs*)!

So I went into the studio, I chose a kind of large transparent tank, and I played the trumpet inside, which created the sound of the "underwater trumpet," which was super-imitated in the world. And I made two or three albums in this style of music, but it was still library music.

Then, there was [TV presenter Philippe] Bouvard. I did programs with Bouvard on the radio... when he saw [the act] he died of laughter. He said "We have to do TV." So I did [a TV segment] with him, I did TV with Maritie and Gilbert Carpentier, I did TV in

bubble

blub

blub

YAN TREGGER

sea love trumpet

OPPOSITE

Yan Tregger. *Bubble Bubble b/w Sea Love Trumpet*. Omega International (Belgium): OM 36.188, 1974.

BELOW

Scotto demonstrating the "underwater trumpet" technique with singer Mick Micheyl.

Switzerland. There, I was onstage, and there was a light in a tank in front of me, and the director said, "When you finish your piece, pull the trumpet out of the water, and show us the water." OK... I pulled my trumpet out of the water, and right then, there was an explosion everywhere, because the water had splashed onto the light and blown it out. It was a farce (*laughs*)...

I have the same story with Maritie and Gilbert Carpentier. It was a gag: They prepared a bathtub, and I was in a black smoking jacket with a bowtie, and I was supposed to get into the bathtub and play the trumpet in the water. And it was a revolving set, so the hosts were talking on one side, they went around to the bathtub, and at the bathtub, [asked] "Mr. Scotto, can you touch the water, is the temperature suitable for you?" Of course, "Yes, yes, very good." And so he pushes the tub around, and there was a thick electrical wire on the ground that blocked off the tub and all the water goes everywhere. The show is about to start—it was live—so everyone runs out with buckets of water to refill the tub. We get there, they say "OK, play the trumpet in the water," and I get in... the water was freezing. It was the middle of winter: it was three or four degrees! It was lethal.

L'ILLUSTRATION MUSICALE

BELOW

Eric Swan / Eddie Warner. *100% Electronic*. L'Illustration Musicale (France): IM 12, 1973.

OPPOSITE

The Yan Tregger Group. *The Pop World of Yan Tregger*. L'Illustration Musicale (France): IM 11, 1973.

Founded and run by German bandleader and composer Eddie Warner (leader of his own Latin music ensemble, Eddie Warner et sa Musique Tropicale, throughout the 1950s), L'Illustration Musicale's library is highly regarded in spite of its small catalog; where other labels pumped out recordings by the hundreds, IM released only twenty-six albums between 1967 and 1978. Still, listed within the library's releases are many undisputed classics of the genre, including seminal recordings by the Yan Tregger Group, Bernard Fèvre, and Jacky Giordano. Warner went on to some success in film scoring until his death in 1982 and is still celebrated as a bandleader in the mold of Xavier Cugat and Pérez Prado, but among library aficionados he is best known for his work at the helm of IM, the self-dubbed "label of modern rhythms."

IMLP 11
im
the label of modern rhythms

TELE MUSIC

BELOW

Bernard Estardy / Alan Feanch. *Electronics*. Tele Music (France): TM 3052, 1975.

Founded in 1966 by Roger Tokarz, a former home appliance salesman, Tele Music began on the budget-conscious fringes of the French production music scene (after Tokarz negotiated a deal with studio owners for free monthly recording sessions), but soon built a sizable and sought-after catalog featuring, in addition to the usual TV cues, many notable soul, funk, and disco recordings. The library is also known for its association with Voyage, the pop group composed of veteran Tele Music session players that scored a string of number one dance hits in the late 1970s. The label continued to operate under Tokarz's direction until 2014, when the eighty-three-year-old founder handed the reins to its current manager, Rémi Agostini.

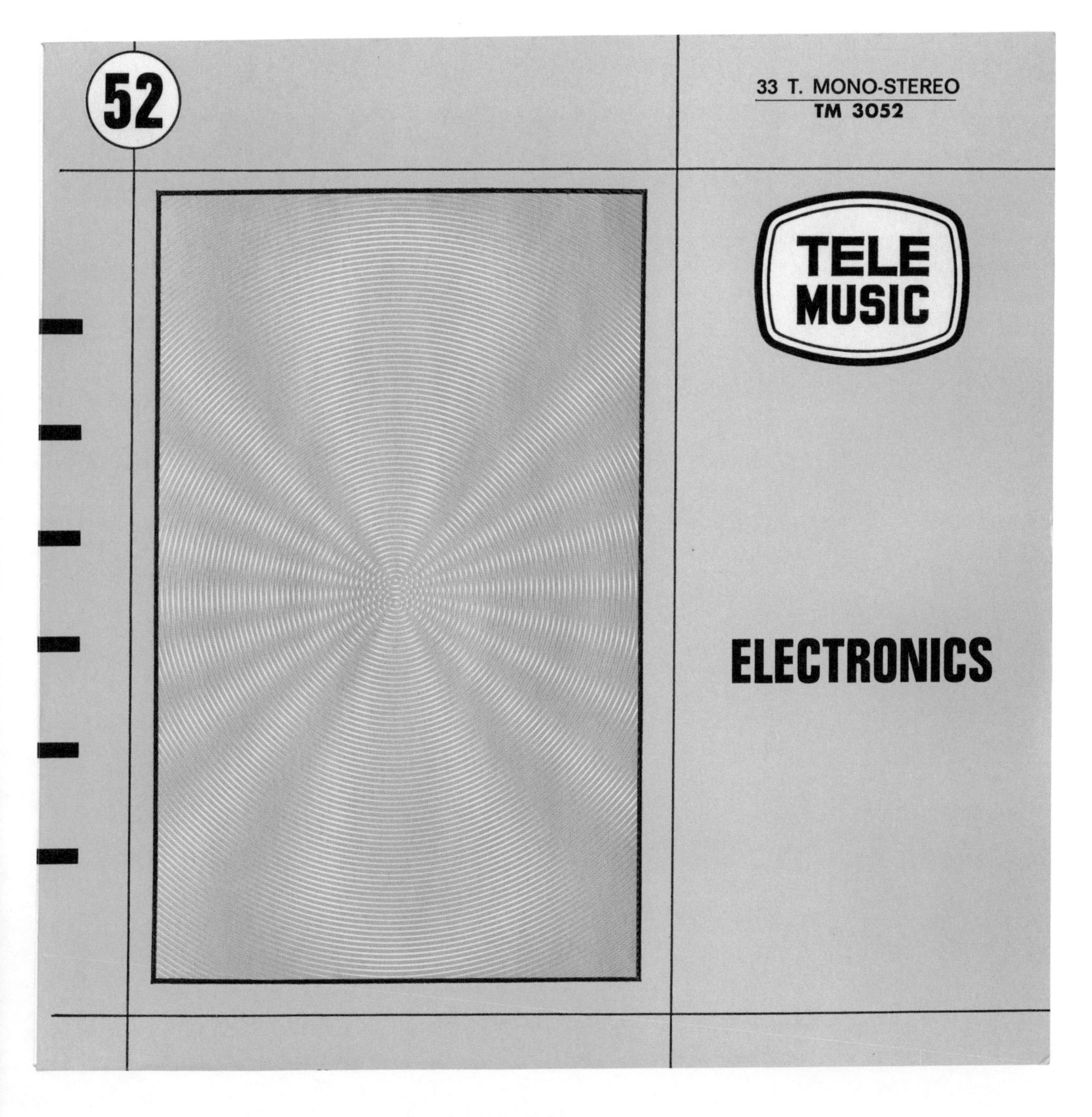

TOP

Sauveur Mallia. *Cosmosynthetic Vol. 2*. Tele Music (France): TM 3084, 1981.

BOTTOM

Marc Chantreau / Pierre-Alain Dahan / Slim Pezin. *Percussions & Company*. Tele Music (France): TM 3086, 1981.

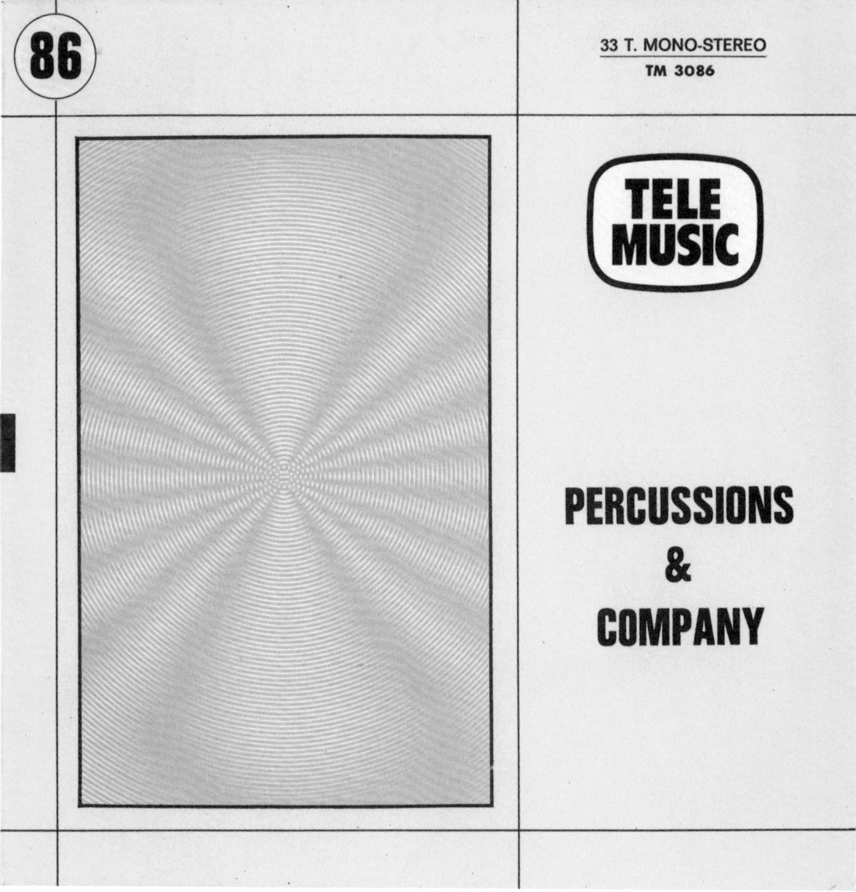

MUSIQUE POUR L'IMAGE

BELOW

Vincent Gémignani. *Modern Pop Percussion*. Concert Hall (France): SPS 1333, 1970.

OPPOSITE

Vladimir Cosma. *Enfance*. Musique pour l'Image (France): MPI / LP 534, 1971.

A large French publisher founded in 1967, Musique pour l'Image was run by the composer Robert Viger, and counted the equally notable PSI library as a sublabel. As had become increasingly common in the late 1960s, many MPI recordings were distributed on multiple platforms, whether internationally—particularly in the UK via the Sylvester label—or through the commercial market (as was the case with Vincent Gémignani's seminal percussive instrumental *Musique pour un voyage extraordinaire* [MPI 535], also issued as *Modern Pop Percussion* on the Concert Hall label). In addition to its unique distribution methods, MPI is noted for its catalog, which included 10" record covers with striking modernist designs (credited to a Robert J. Hilton) and recordings by Viger, Cameroonian saxophonist Manu Dibango, and the prolific Romanian-French composer Vladimir Cosma, among others.

musique
de
Vladimir
cosma
enfance

BERNARD PARMEGIANI

OPPOSITE

Bernard Parmegiani. *Chants magnétiques*. PSI (France): PSI-X 20705, 1974.

PAGE 210

Giampiero Boneschi / Mitridate. *New Times Vol. 3*. Orly (France): SBV 323, no date.

Born in Paris in 1927, the legendary Bernard Parmegiani began his musical education with an early immersion in classical music and piano, but quickly became more fascinated with the new field of musique concrète. After undertaking some sonic experiments in a job as a television engineer, Parmegiani encountered Pierre Schaeffer and soon went to work as part of his Groupe de Recherches Musicales collective ("Musical Research Group," or GRM). The GRM had a specially built electroacoustic music studio in the offices of ORTF, the French public media station, and there the group's composers (who included Pierre Boulez, Karlheinz Stockhausen, Iannis Xenakis, and many other titans of postwar composition) set about pushing the boundaries of sonic expression. Though Parmegiani is largely associated with these developments in electroacoustic and especially "acousmatic music" (wherein the listener hears a sound without being able to identify its source), this period also saw him experiment with traditional composition, free jazz, and electronics, and this all-encompassing freeform approach made him a natural fit for the field of production music. *Chants magnétiques*, released in 1974 for the PSI library, is a prime example of Parmegiani's striking atmospheres and unique musical palette, and it's been a library staple ever since. Parmegiani died in 2013, leaving behind a massively influential legacy and an extraordinary catalog of recordings.

CHANTS MAGNÉTIQUES
Bernard Parmegiani
ΨPSI

new
times
SBV 323
3
Orly
jc trambouze

ITALIAN
LIBRARIES

ROMANO DI BARI

BELOW

A young Romano di Bari outside RCA Italiana's Rome offices.

Born in Rome on November 13, 1936, Romano di Bari parlayed his early career steps in finance and the Italian commercial record industry into an innovative role as the founder of Flipper Srl Edizioni Musicali (now Flippermusic). Soon after its 1968 founding—effectively the ground floor of the Italian library music scene—the company's first label, Canopo, was able to capitalize on di Bari's experience and business savvy, establishing a vast international catalog of music libraries. One of the most notable relationships forged by di Bari was with the seminal French library Montparnasse 2000, which repackaged Flipper recordings in France under its St. Germain des Prés sublabel. Now, after five decades of business, di Bari still helms the independent and family-run Flipper, which presides over some of the most noteworthy and historic Italian library recordings.

Romano di Bari: In my youth, I had some experience in the banks, and then I left the banks, and in 1960 I joined RCA Italiana—at that time, the leading record and publishing company in Italy. RCA Italiana was based in Rome, and they had a very big plant. I joined the company, and my first job was in the royalties department. The music world was completely different: At that time RCA was the leading record company in Italy, with very big, very important artists. They were selling two million 45 rpms each, so you can imagine, it was a really... an incredible world. Very quickly I became a personal assistant of the general manager of the company, and

BOTTOM LEFT

A Canopo-branded promotional glass doorstop, produced by the company in 1973.

BOTTOM RIGHT

An advertisement in a June 1968 copy of *Record Retailer* magazine announces the advent of di Bari's Canopo label.

then I became the number two of the international [division], and was responsible for Italian artists abroad. I was with RCA until 1966 or '67, when a record company in Milan, Ariston Records, offered me the position as a general manager. Then I transferred my life from Rome to Milan. I spent a year and a half in Milan, and then I decided to leave the company, to go back to Rome and to try to launch myself as an independent publisher.

For the first six months, based on the connections that I had in the past, I tried to enter the pop music market: publishing, trying to search for new composers, preparing a demo, and then going around offering demos to the record companies and so on. But after six months, I understood that the competition was too strong, and I decided to enter the library publishing business—because at that time, the library publishing business was ignored by the multinationals. It was really a niche job for a niche market, a niche market that was very rich.

I started with vinyl in 1968. In developing my business, I was applying all the publishing experience that I had in the previous years with RCA, and also the connections I had abroad. I immediately started to export vinyl also, into France mainly.

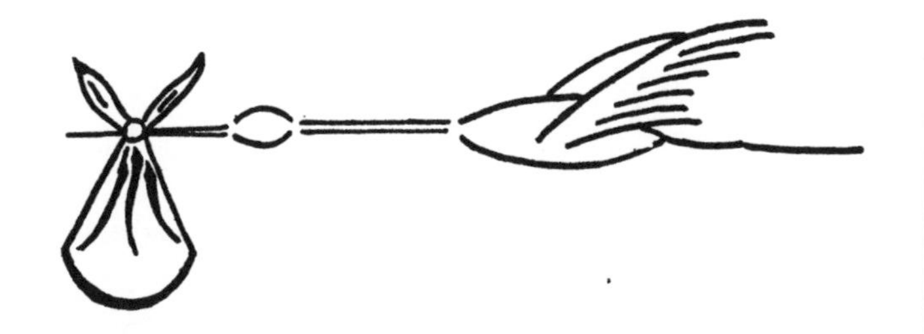

A New Italian "Pubbery" is Born

ROMANO DI BARI

IS PROUD TO ANNOUCE THE BIRTH OF

Canopo Edizioni Musicali SRL

VIALE PASTEUR 70-00144 ROME - Phone 595786

A YOUNG DYNAMIC FIRM AT THE SERVICE OF YOUR MUSIC

Today, we are the number one publishing company in library music in Italy. I'm very proud, too, because we administer more than one hundred foreign catalogs, many of them from the US, and now we have about 400,000 tracks.

Founding Flipper

Until '64, '65, '66, the only music used by Italian television were the library vinyl albums from BBC, because BBC was the first radio station who thought to record library music to be used in their broadcasting. In the first years immediately after the war, when Italian TV started in the '50s, the only music used in the broadcasts was the music coming from the BBC. And I learned all those things because my initial activity as a publisher in pop music failed, because I was not able to make any business with my songs.

When I left RCA, a very well-known Italian composer and pianist called Amedeo Tommasi one day called me and told me, "Romano, listen. A film guy, a director, has asked me to compose some original music for a couple of documentaries that will be broadcast by Italian TV. If we do the music—I am the composer, you are the publisher—you will get some money." I said, "Why not?" And I did it. This was the first album I did. I have [it] in my house in Rome, on the wall: It was Canopo number one, *Flash Internazionale - Servizi Speciali*.

Amedeo Tommasi is a great composer, and he's a great keyboard player. He's really good. He introduced me to the manager of the record archive of Italian TV. His name was Anton Giulio Perugini—he's retired, but still alive—and he explained to me all the mechanisms connected with the choices of the music, and how the music recorded by the BBC was based on categories. So the main rule is that each album should refer to a special subject, in order to make the work of the music supervisor responsible for the selection of the music easier. I got a lot of information from him, and so when I started [releasing] my vinyl, I was using all these ideas that I got. If you check the titles of my vinyl at that time, all the titles refer to one subject or, maximum, two subjects, offering a certain selection of music.

You know, I remember that at that time, before going in the recording studio—or better, before the composer started to write the music—we discussed, one by one, the tracks that would be recorded or written later. We were discussing atmosphere. Let's say one track could be of the scripted music, so you can imagine a landscape with green mountains and then the sun. *What is the feeling?* Because the creation of library music is connected with emotions. With library music, we express emotions to be put together with images. If the effect is really positive, if when you're watching the images you feel the music working inside you, it means that you did a good job.

Recording

At that time, there were small recording studios in Rome... apart from RCA recording studios that were very expensive. Normally,

OPPOSITE TOP

Peymont. *Cibernetica*. Canopo (Italy): CNP 0057, 1971.

OPPOSITE BOTTOM LEFT

Atmo. *Telegiornale*. Octopus Records (Italy): OTP 0287, 1971.

OPPOSITE BOTTOM RIGHT

H. Caiage / Amedeo Tommasi. *Carnet Turistico*. Deneb Records (Italy): DNB 0109, 1971.

at that time, I used to make my recordings in Piero Umiliani's studio. [He] had a very nice studio close to my office. I recorded in his studio because he was, very kindly, giving me time to pay my invoices, because at that time my business [was] without any money. It took time for me to recover, to pay the debt, and finally to start with some fresh money in my pocket. I must still say thanks to all the people who gave me support, like Piero Umiliani.

I recorded several albums there. For some years I was there recording. This was in the early '70s. Then—especially with very good composers like Alessandro Alessandroni and Giuliano Sorgini—they started to have the first well-equipped home studios, and so all the masters were prepared at home. The collections that I did with Alessandro Alessandroni and Giuliano Sorgini [were] wonderful albums, recorded in the home studio of Alessandro Alessandroni.

St. Germain des Prés

Let me tell you the story. Originally, Montparnasse 2000 was owned by a gentleman who had a chain of nightclubs in Paris: three, four nightclubs... André Farry, he is the founder of Montparnasse 2000. And in order to acquire a kind of respectability in front of friends or business friendships, I don't know, he decided to enter the music publishing business, because he preferred to be known as a publisher, although the real money that he was making was coming from nightclubs. We met in Cannes, and we decided that he would represent me in France and I would represent [him] in Italy. Our collaboration started.

In the first period, I was exporting my vinyl to France and he was exporting his vinyl to me, but later on he decided that it was much more convenient for him to press my vinyl in France. Then he started his label, St. Germain des Prés, because his office was in St. Germain des Prés.

CANOPO CNP 0057
CIBERNETICA
7
canopo

OCTOPUS OTP 0287
7
Octopus
MUSICA DI ATMO
TELEGIORNALE

DENEB DNB 0109
DENEB
CARNET TURISTICO
9

TOP

Alessandro Alessandroni. *Il Tempo Dello Spirito*. Flirt Records (Italy): LIR 0431, 1971.

BOTTOM

Joel V.D.B. (Joel Vandroogenbroeck). *L'Immagine del Suono*. Flirt Records (Italy): LIR 0440, 1972.

OPPOSITE

Franco Tamponi. *Un Volto Una Storia*. Flower Records (Italy): LEW 0543, 1972.

FLOWER LEW 0543

3

flower

Musiche di F. TAMPONI

UN VOLTO UNA STORIA

FLIPPER

BELOW

E. Orti. *Underground Session*. Éditions Montparnasse 2000 (France): MP 4100, 1974. A pseudonymous rerelease of Janko Nilović's *Rythmes contemporains* (Orti being an Italian-inflected pseudonym of Nilović's).

Initially founded by Romano di Bari in 1968 after a stint at RCA, Flipper started out as an attempt to create an independent music brand with the international reach of a major label; it was soon established as the publishing company responsible for the licensing of di Bari's many library ventures. By the early 1970s, di Bari had struck publishing deals across Europe (particularly in France via Montparnasse 2000) and handled the rights for labels now regarded as iconic, including Canopo, Deneb, Flirt, Flower, and Octopus. Today, Flipper publishes hundreds of catalogs and houses some of Italian library music's finest recordings.

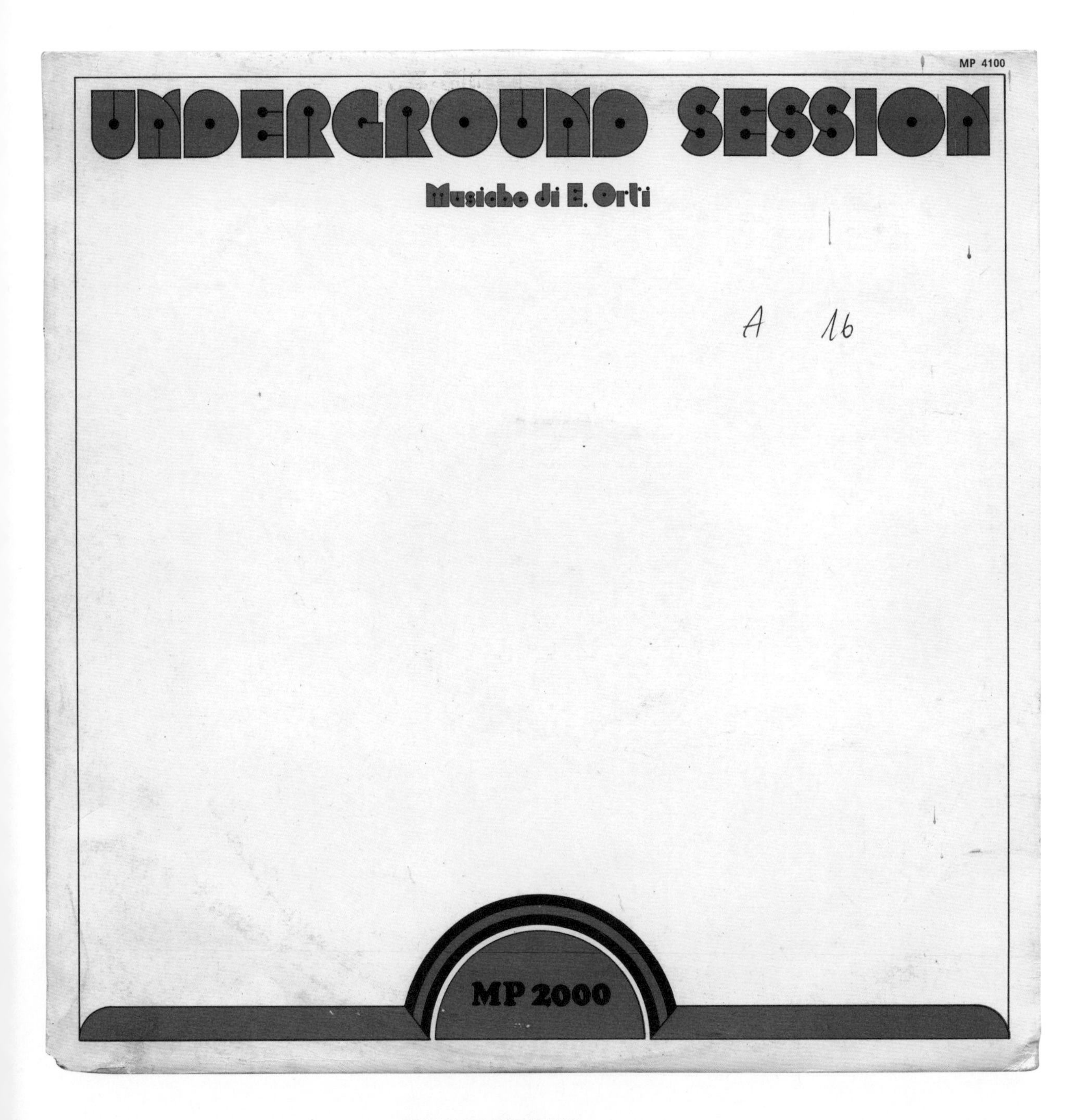

TOP

Daniela Casa. *Ricordi d'Infanzia*. Flirt Records (Italy): LIR 0444, 1975.

BOTTOM

Gruppo Sound. *Dancin'*. Flower (Italy): LEW 0588, 1976.

CAM

TOP LEFT

Aldo Tamborrelli / Massimo Ruocco. *Construction*. CAM (Italy): CmL 215, 1988.

TOP RIGHT

Daniele Patucchi. *Sweet and Sauvage Themes*. CAM (Italy): CmL 212, 1985.

BOTTOM LEFT

Aldo Tamborrelli. *Entertainment Show*. CAM (Italy): CmL 204, 1984.

BOTTOM RIGHT

Alessandro Sbordoni. *Incantation*. CAM (Italy): CmL 208, 1984.

Founded in 1959, Creazioni Artistiche Musicali (Musical Artistic Creations, or CAM) was the brainchild of the Campi brothers, successful publishers of sheet music, radio songbooks, and, starting in 1952, the magazine *TV Sorrisi e canzoni* ("TV Smiles and Songs," Italy's answer to *TV Guide*). As interest grew in the connections between music and popular new media, such as the blossoming Italian film industry, the Campis decided to move into music publishing more actively, and CAM soon became the first Italian label to specialize in film scores and soundtracks: their early catalog contains classic recordings by film music luminaries like Riz Ortolani, Nino Rota, and Ennio Morricone, as well as musicians working actively in the exploitation, spaghetti western, and slasher genres.

In 1971, CAM started a sideline into library music with the advent of the CmL sublabel, which began releasing records for the production market, packaged in uniform sleeves with titles like *Psichedelico - Introspettivo - Flash-Back* and *Classic, Satirical and Insane*. CmL's catalog was founded on repurposed works from its parent company's commercial label—repackaging successful film scores as library records for the production industry. This was the case with the score for *Andrea Doria-74*, a 1970 documentary on the famous sunken ocean liner, written by the master film composer Riz Ortolani. Another example is the soundtrack to the 1974 Spanish police film *Metralleta Stein*, composed of recordings that also appear on CmL library releases by composers including Daniele Patucchi, Mario Molino, and Stelvio Cipriani. Having issued *Metralleta Stein* as a commercial release, CmL's reuse of the recording as production music enabled it to cash in on well-known film placements of its parent company's commissioned material.

TOP LEFT

Vittorio Gelmetti. *Musica Aleatoria - Collage - Memorie*. CAM (Italy): CmL 001, 1971.

TOP RIGHT

Oscar Lindok's Orchestra. *The Rhythm of Life*. CAM (Italy): CrT 001, 1972.

MIDDLE

Pierre Porte. *Le Monde du Music Hall*. CAM (Italy): CmL 119, 1977.

BOTTOM LEFT

Jean-Pierre Decerf, Lawrence Wiffin. *Thèmes Médicaux*. CAM (Italy): CmL 120, 1977.

BOTTOM RIGHT

Alain Leroux / Dominique Tremblay / Rahul Sariputra. *India West - Indies and Quebec*. CAM (Italy): CmL 169, 1977.

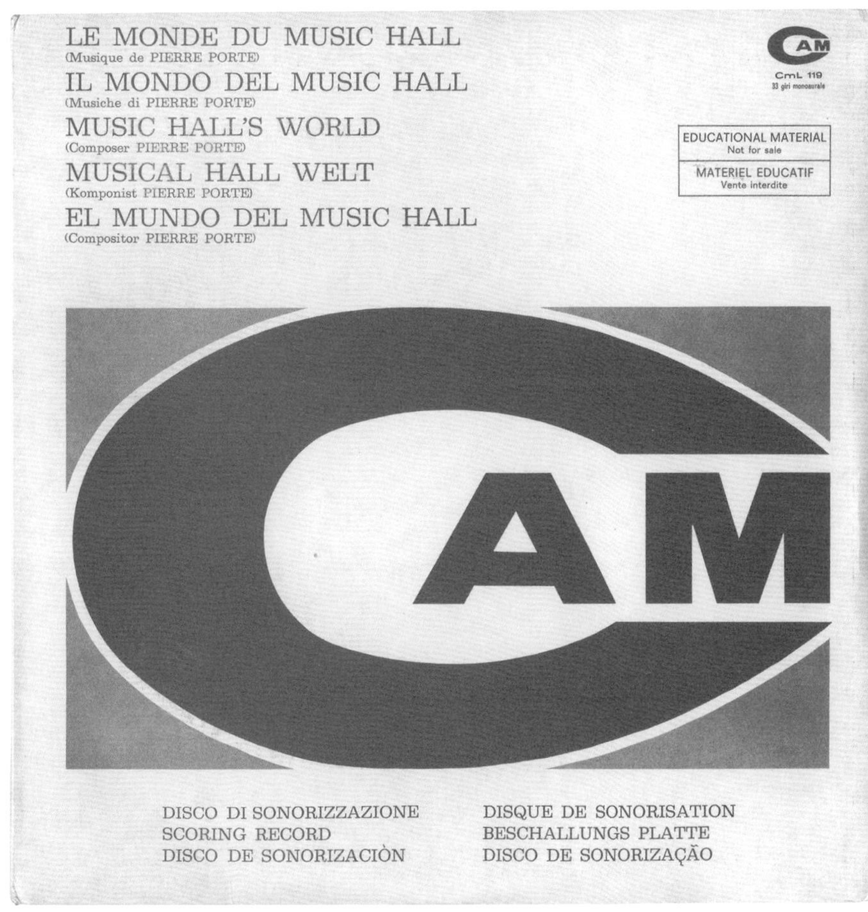

BELOW

Riz Ortolani. *Andrea Doria 74*. CAM (Italy): MAG 10024, 1969.

OPPOSITE TOP

Stelvio Cipriani / Daniele Patucchi / Carlo Rustichelli. *Metralleta Stein*. CAM (Italy): ZDL 17106, 1974.

OPPOSITE BOTTOM LEFT

Mario Molino. *Mario Molino 1*. CAM (Italy): CmL 050, 1974.

OPPOSITE BOTTOM RIGHT

Daniele Patucchi. *Brani Drammatici, Violenti e Suspence*. CAM (Italy): CmL 028, 1973.

But in spite of this business tactic (not to mention a tremendous catalog of iconic composers and recordings), the CmL library never succeeded internationally in the production music field. Still, CAM's overall catalog remains among the best in film music released for the commercial market, a fitting soundtrack to the extraordinary heyday of Italian cinema.

Romano di Bari: The mistake done by CAM was to take the music from the soundtracks and do albums without taking care [with] the classification of the music. They took the music and put it together. With library music, all tracks must have a certain common feeling in order to be closed in a sort of container, where you know that if you listen to that record, you will find that kind of music. For this reason, CAM was not successful, because the music was very good, but it was wrongly classified and so it was impossible to use it. And for this reason they were not successful. It is really a shame, because they had so much music available that you can't imagine.

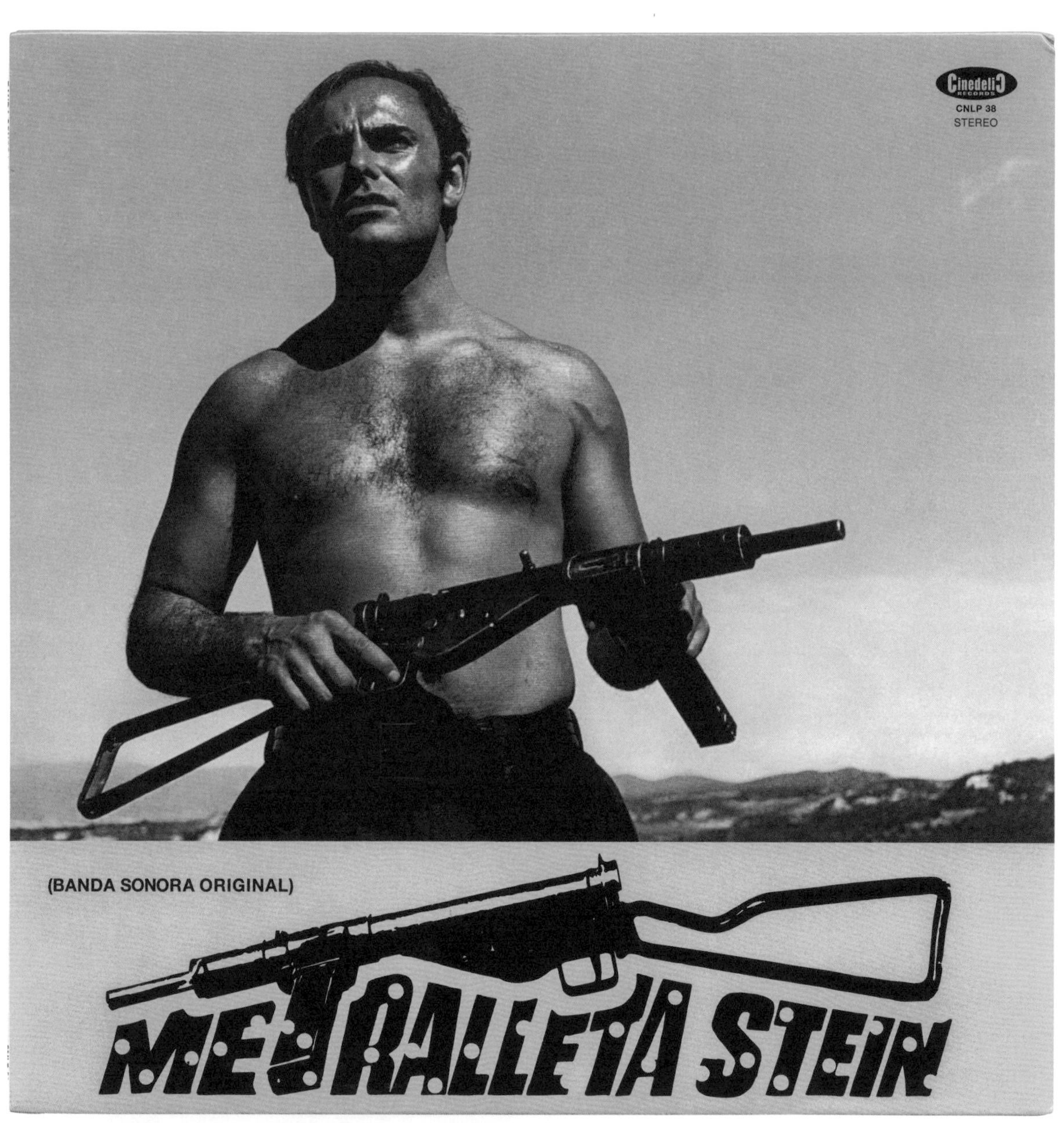
Cinedelic RECORDS
CNLP 38
STEREO
(BANDA SONORA ORIGINAL)
METRALLETA STEIN

CAM
MARIO MOLINO
1
mario molino
mario molino
mario molino
mario molino
mario molino
mario molino
mario molino
mario molino

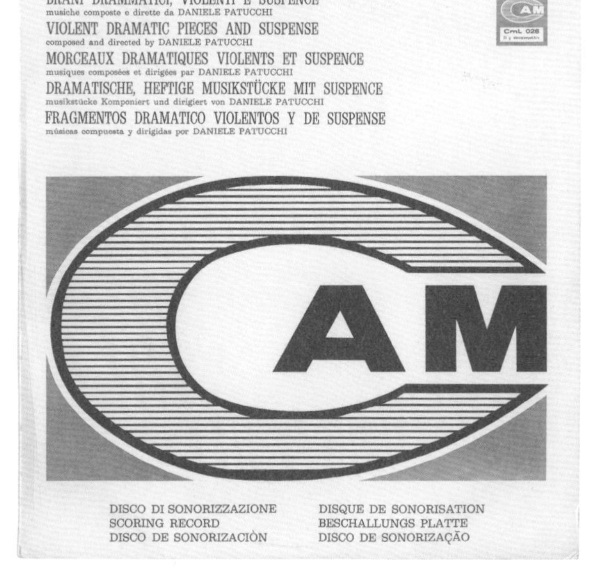
BRANI DRAMMATICI, VIOLENTI E SUSPENCE
musiche composte e dirette da DANIELE PATUCCHI
VIOLENT DRAMATIC PIECES AND SUSPENSE
composed and directed by DANIELE PATUCCHI
MORCEAUX DRAMATIQUES VIOLENTS ET SUSPENCE
musiques composées et dirigées par DANIELE PATUCCHI
DRAMATISCHE, HEFTIGE MUSIKSTÜCKE MIT SUSPENCE
musikstücke Komponiert und dirigiert von DANIELE PATUCCHI
FRAGMENTOS DRAMATICO VIOLENTOS Y DE SUSPENSE
músicas compuesta y dirigidas por DANIELE PATUCCHI
CAM
CmL 028
CAM
DISCO DI SONORIZZAZIONE
SCORING RECORD
DISCO DE SONORIZACIÒN
DISQUE DE SONORISATION
BESCHALLUNGS PLATTE
DISCO DE SONORIZAÇÃO

TOP LEFT

Various. *Do You Like Dancing?* CAM (Italy): CmL 181, 1980.

TOP RIGHT

Luis Bacalov. *Musica Per Commenti Sonori Tratta dal Film «Il Prezzo del Potere»*. CAM (Italy): PRE 8, 1969.

MIDDLE

Vittorio Marino. *Fugue of Light*. CAM (Italy): CmL 173, 1979.

BOTTOM LEFT

Daniele Patucchi. *Temi Conduttori Sentimentali*. CAM (Italy): CmL 030, 1973.

BOTTOM RIGHT

Carlo Maria Cordio, Franco Vinciguerra. *Quips and Cranks*. CAM (Italy): CmL 184, 1980.

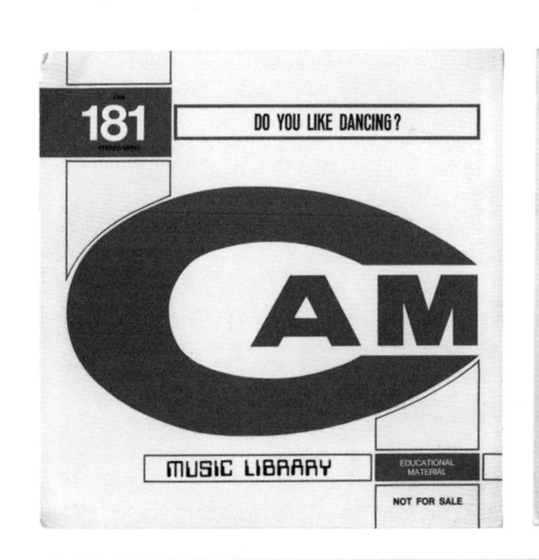

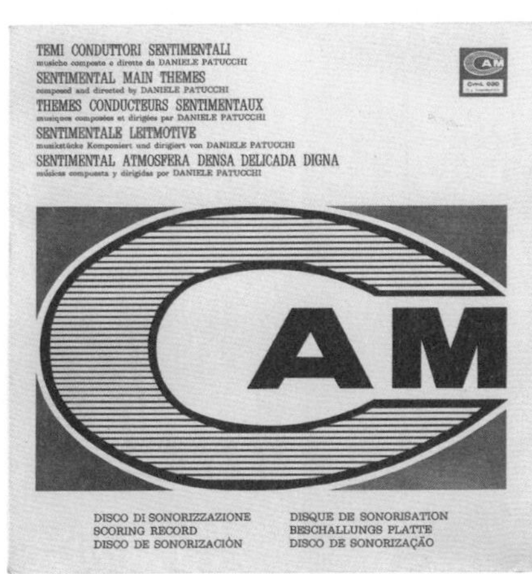

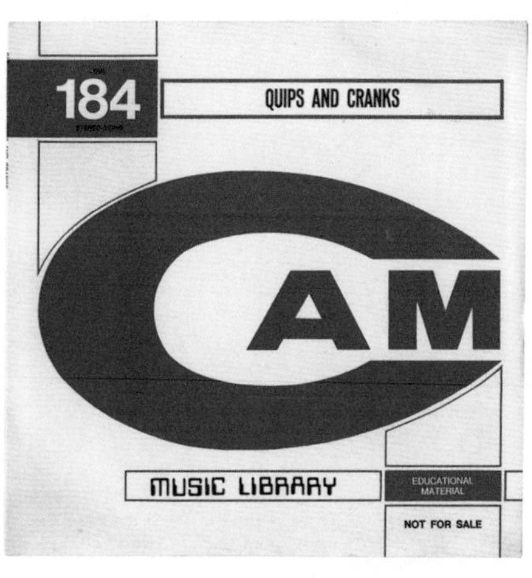

TOP

Various. *Giallo 2 (Suspence - Drammatico)*. CAM (Italy): CmL 023, 1973.

BOTTOM

Ettore de Carolis. *Microdramas*. CAM (Italy): CmL 196, 1982.

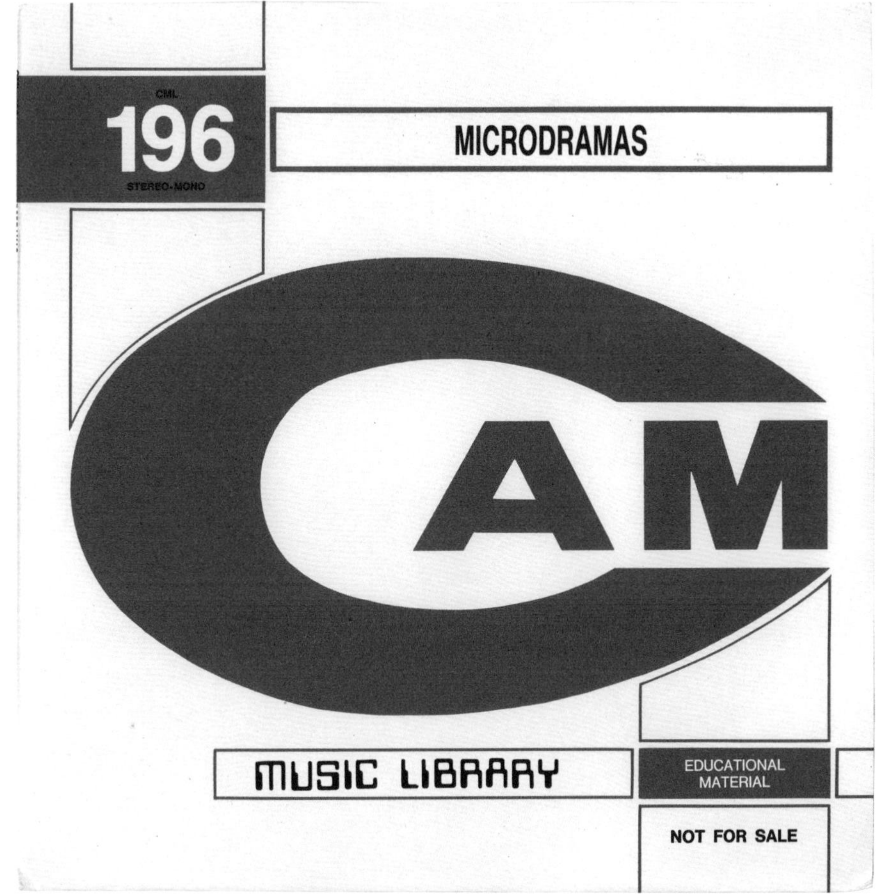

STELVIO CIPRIANI

OPPOSITE TOP

Stelvio Cipriani e La Sua Orchestra. *Antla*. CAM (Italy): SAG 9043, 1972.

OPPOSITE BOTTOM LEFT

Stelvio Cipriani. *Tema Con Variazioni: "Patetico-Tensivo"*. CAM (Italy): CmL 124, 1977.

OPPOSITE BOTTOM RIGHT

Stelvio Cipriani. *Anonimo Veneziano*. CAM (Italy): SAG 9031, 1970.

Born in Rome in 1937, Stelvio Cipriani began studying piano and harmony at the city's Santa Cecilia Conservatory at the age of fourteen before becoming a backing pianist for well-known pop singers such as Rita Pavone. Like many musicians of his generation, Cipriani was tremendously influenced by American jazz, and an opportunity to study with Dave Brubeck in the United States enabled him to incorporate the form into his evolving style. In 1966, CAM released Cipriani's score for the spaghetti western *The Bounty Killer*, after which he became a stalwart composer in their ranks. Cipriani's scores for such films as *The Stranger Returns*, *The Anonymous Venetian*, and *The Great Kidnapping* are considered classics, high-water marks in the already celebrated annals of 1970s Italian film scores.

Romano di Bari: A good friend, and a brilliant composer in the '70s. You know, I did a soundtrack with him, *The Concorde Affair*. In that time, in the '70s, because of my music experience with RCA, I understood since then the importance of having good connections with the people who were producing the images, because they were in need to have my music. So I was visiting and meeting different film producers in Rome and Milan, and one of them was a very important producer called Luciano Martino, who was the king of the Italian comedies in the '70s. I did some films with him with Stelvio Cipriani... The soundtrack, the music, is on a label called Octopus: an old label that I've taken again now and I'm inserting there all the soundtracks that I did in that time and also the soundtracks that I do now.

But in this time, Stelvio Cipriani really had the magic touch in his fingers, because he had this incredible sense of melody. Unfortunately, I was not the publisher of *Anonimo Veneziano* [*The Anonymous Venetian*], his masterpiece.

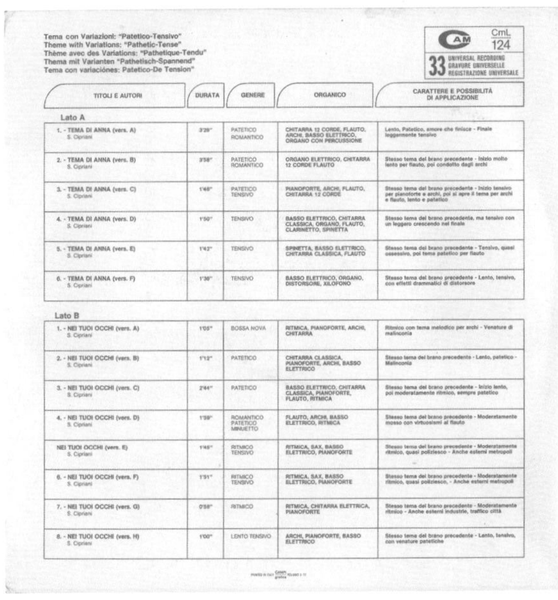

Tema con Variazioni: "Patetico-Tensivo"
Theme with Variations: "Pathetic-Tense"
Thème avec des Variations: "Pathetique-Tendu"
Thema mit Varianten "Pathetisch-Spannend"
Tema con variaciónes: Patetico-De Tension"

CAM CmL 124
33 UNIVERSAL RECORDING GRAVURE UNIVERSELLE REGISTRAZIONE UNIVERSALE

TITOLI E AUTORI	DURATA	GENERE	ORGANICO	CARATTERE E POSSIBILITÀ DI APPLICAZIONE
Lato A				
1. - TEMA DI ANNA (vers. A) S. Cipriani	3'29"	PATETICO ROMANTICO	CHITARRA 12 CORDE, FLAUTO, ARCHI, BASSO ELETTRICO, ORGANO CON PERCUSSIONE	Lento, Patetico, amore che finisce - Finale leggermente tensivo
2. - TEMA DI ANNA (vers. B) S. Cipriani	3'58"	PATETICO ROMANTICO	ORGANO ELETTRICO, CHITARRA 12 CORDE FLAUTO	Stesso tema del brano precedente - Inizio molto lento per flauto, poi condotto dagli archi
3. - TEMA DI ANNA (vers. C) S. Cipriani	1'48"	PATETICO TENSIVO	PIANOFORTE, ARCHI, FLAUTO, CHITARRA 12 CORDE	Stesso tema del brano precedente - Inizio tensivo per pianoforte e archi, poi si apre il tema per archi e flauto, lento e patetico
4. - TEMA DI ANNA (vers. D) S. Cipriani	1'50"	TENSIVO	BASSO ELETTRICO, CHITARRA CLASSICA, ORGANO, FLAUTO, CLARINETTO, SPINETTA	Stesso tema del brano precedente, ma tensivo con un leggero crescendo nel finale
5. - TEMA DI ANNA (vers. E) S. Cipriani	1'42"	TENSIVO	SPINETTA, BASSO ELETTRICO, CHITARRA CLASSICA, FLAUTO	Stesso tema del brano precedente - Tensivo, quasi ossessivo, poi tema patetico per flauto
6. - TEMA DI ANNA (vers. F) S. Cipriani	1'30"	TENSIVO	BASSO ELETTRICO, ORGANO, DISTORSORE, XILOFONO	Stesso tema del brano precedente - Lento, tensivo, con effetti drammatici di distorsore
Lato B				
1. - NEI TUOI OCCHI (vers. A) S. Cipriani	1'05"	BOSSA NOVA	RITMICA, PIANOFORTE, ARCHI, CHITARRA	Ritmico con tema melodico per archi - Venature di malinconia
2. - NEI TUOI OCCHI (vers. B) S. Cipriani	1'12"	PATETICO	CHITARRA CLASSICA, PIANOFORTE, ARCHI, BASSO ELETTRICO	Stesso tema del brano precedente - Lento, patetico - Malinconia
3. - NEI TUOI OCCHI (vers. C) S. Cipriani	2'44"	PATETICO	BASSO ELETTRICO, CHITARRA CLASSICA, PIANOFORTE, FLAUTO, RITMICA	Stesso tema del brano precedente - Inizio lento, poi moderatamente ritmico, sempre patetico
4. - NEI TUOI OCCHI (vers. D) S. Cipriani	1'39"	ROMANTICO PATETICO MINUETTO	FLAUTO, ARCHI, BASSO ELETTRICO, RITMICA	Stesso tema del brano precedente - Moderatamente mosso con virtuosismi al flauto
NEI TUOI OCCHI (vers. E) S. Cipriani	1'45"	RITMICO TENSIVO	RITMICA, SAX, BASSO ELETTRICO, PIANOFORTE	Stesso tema del brano precedente - Moderatamente ritmico, quasi poliziesco - Anche esterni metropoli
6. - NEI TUOI OCCHI (vers. F) S. Cipriani	1'51"	RITMICO TENSIVO	RITMICA, SAX, BASSO ELETTRICO, PIANOFORTE	Stesso tema del brano precedente - Moderatamente ritmico, quasi poliziesco, - Anche esterni metropoli
7. - NEI TUOI OCCHI (vers. G) S. Cipriani	0'58"	RITMICO	RITMICA, CHITARRA ELETTRICA, PIANOFORTE	Stesso tema del brano precedente - Moderatamente ritmico - Anche esterni industrie, traffico città
8. - NEI TUOI OCCHI (vers. H) S. Cipriani	1'00"	LENTO TENSIVO	ARCHI, PIANOFORTE, BASSO ELETTRICO	Stesso tema del brano precedente - Lento, tensivo, con venature patetiche

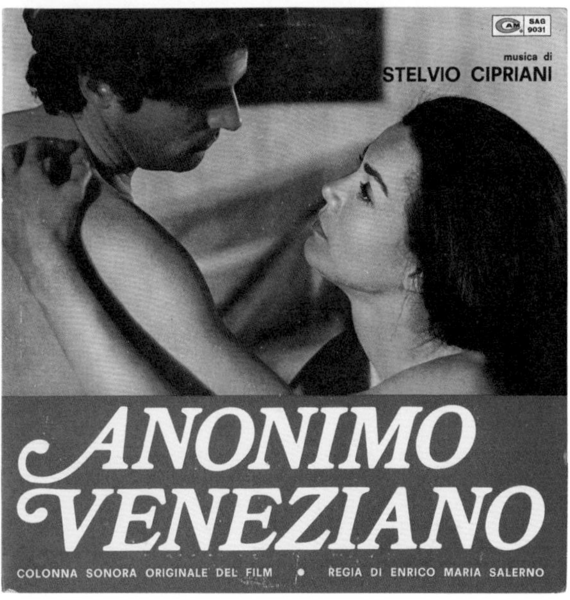

FABIO FRIZZI

BELOW

Fabio Frizzi. *Amore Libero (Free Love)*. Cinevox (Italy): MDF 055, 1974.

Though he worked in genres as diverse as gentle exotica, country-tinged acoustic folk, and high '70s "cop funk," Fabio Frizzi (born in 1951 in Bologna) is most renowned by far for the scores he composed for Lucio Fulci, the seminal Italian horror filmmaker and so-called "Godfather of Gore." After spending the late 1960s and '70s as part of an instrumental trio with Franco Bixio and Vince Tempera (a group also known as Magnetic System, itself responsible for seminal soundtrack work), Frizzi struck out on his own with the score to Fulci's infamous "video nasty" *Zombi 2*, in which he perfected the style of dramatic electronic composition that would become his trademark—incorporating elements as disparate as orchestral classical and Italo disco into an eerie, rhythmic whole. Frizzi has composed for Italian libraries like CAM and Octopus, and his work's influence is plainly evident today in the synth-heavy, arpeggiated soundscapes that populate sci-fi and horror scores for film and TV, in addition to the arenas of modern-day pop and electronic music.

Romano di Bari: I did a couple of soundtracks with him. His father was a very important person in the managing board of a film production company called Cineriz fifty years ago, and the father introduced the son to the soundtrack business. He was mainly inclined for film music [rather than] for library—because between library music and film music there is a difference, obviously. Film music you write [based on] images already existing, but with library music, you are blind. You just work with your imagination.

STEFANO TOROSSI

BELOW

Jay Richford / Gary Stevan (Stefano Torossi / Sandro Brugnolini). *Feelings*. Carosello (Italy): CLN 25041, 1974.

A major figure in the fields of Italian film scoring, commercial, and advertising music, Stefano Torossi is perhaps best known for his library recordings for labels such as CAM, Costanza, and Flipper and its many sublabels. One record in particular has earned Torossi an iconic reputation in the library community: *Feelings*, released in 1974 by Carosello for the commercial market and in 1976 by the UK's Conroy library. Due to legal restrictions of the time and the library market's requirement for semi-anonymity, both releases were pseudonymously credited to "Jay Richford" (a pseudonym for composer Puccio Roelens) and "Gary Stevan" (Giancarlo Gazzini), though the record's actual composers were Torossi and Sandro Brugnolini. In spite of its bizarre release history, *Feelings* has gone down in the annals of library music as a masterpiece of the lavishly arranged orchestral jazz-funk style.

Romano di Bari: Stefano Torossi is my beloved friend. I did my second vinyl album with him in '69, *Il Mondo dei Bambini*, "Children World," where he was composing the music with Amedeo Tommasi. Together they did a wonderful job. It's a masterpiece. Stefano Torossi's still a good friend. I see him nearly every day. We go out now. He's retired, probably because his health is not so brilliant, but until a few years ago he was writing music, he had produced an album, and he's a very nice guy.

GIAMPIERO BONESCHI

Born in Milan in 1927, Giampiero Boneschi studied composition with famed composer and organist Gian Luigi Centemeri and signed his first record deal at eighteen (for solo piano recordings on La Voce del Padrone, the Italian wing of the historic British label His Master's Voice). By the mid-1950s, Boneschi was in high demand—as a composer / arranger for several Italian labels and as a performer in several noted jazz combos. It was starting in the 1970s, however, that Boneschi did the early synthesizer work for which he's most celebrated in library circles, bringing his compositional mastery to the new frontier of electronic music on extraordinary LPs for labels including CAM, Fonit, and Music Scene.

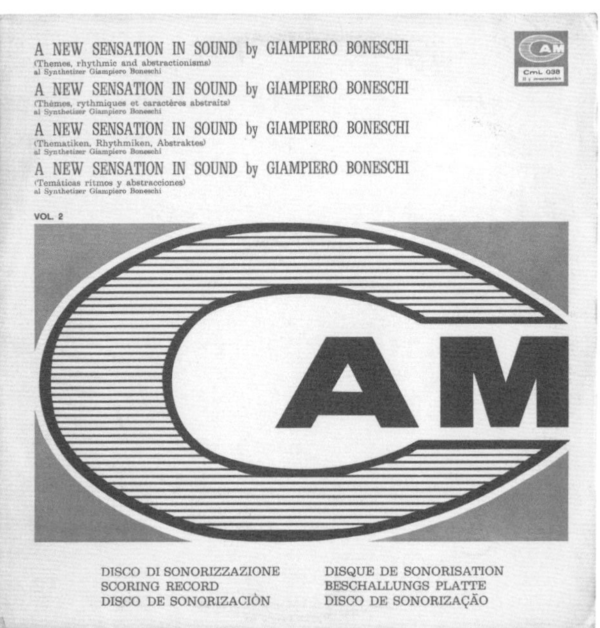

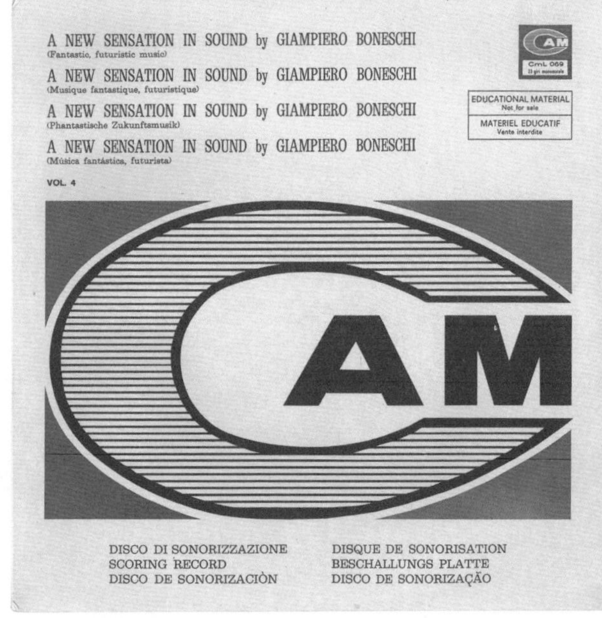

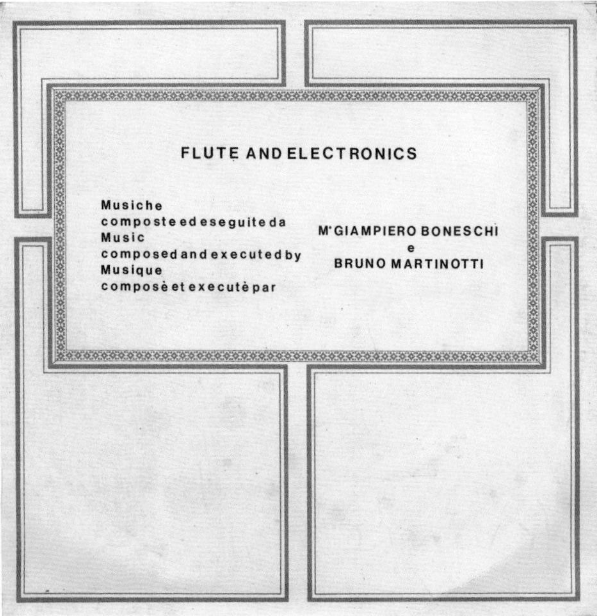

ENNIO MORRICONE

OPPOSITE TOP LEFT

Giampiero Boneschi / Mitridate. *Caratteristici (Temi Romantici E Sentimentali Realizzati Con Apparecchiature Elettroniche)*. Fonit (Italy): C 261, 1970.

OPPOSITE TOP RIGHT

Giampiero Boneschi. *A New Sensation in Sound Vol. 2*. CAM (Italy): CmL 038, 1973.

OPPOSITE BOTTOM LEFT

Giampiero Boneschi. *A New Sensation in Sound Vol. 4*. CAM (Italy): CmL 069, 1973.

OPPOSITE BOTTOM RIGHT

Giampiero Boneschi / Bruno Martinotti. *Flute and Electronics*. Edibi (Italy): MR.021, 1978.

BELOW

Ennio Morricone. *Ideato, Scritto e Diretto da Ennio Morricone*. RCA Italiana (Italy): PSL 10481, 1970.

With more than five hundred scores to his credit, over 70 million records sold and Grammys, BAFTAs, and an Oscar to his name, Ennio Morricone is without a doubt one of the most successful and influential film composers in history. Though his best-known scores are those he composed for Sergio Leone's spaghetti western classics (most notably *The Good, the Bad and the Ugly*), Morricone has worked across genre: from traditional classical to high-'60s psychedelia, from operatic vocal works to sound effects and foley, from *giallo* horror scores to avant-garde experimental composition (as part of the improvisational composers collective Gruppo di Improvvisazione di Nuova Consonanza, aka "Il Gruppo").

Morricone's Leone scores were recorded in collaboration with Alessandro Alessandroni and his vocal group Cantori Moderni, with Alessandroni—a childhood friend of Morricone's—providing the guitar and instantly recognizable whistling components to these now-famous soundtracks. And like Alessandroni's, Morricone's career intersected with the world of library music on several occasions, whether via CAM releases of his film scores, or via recordings for his friend Bruno Nicolai's label Gemelli. Although he is known first and foremost as a master of the film score, Morricone plays no small role in the history of Italian library music.

ALESSANDRO ALESSANDRONI

BELOW

Alessandro Alessandroni. *Biologia Marina*. Rhombus (Italy): RM 1051, 1973.

A composer and multi-instrumentalist of extraordinary talent, Alessandro Alessandroni was born just north of Rome in 1925. After quickly demonstrating a proficiency at guitar, piano, and other string and keyboard instruments (in addition to a natural ability for whistling), Alessandroni began touring as a singer / instrumentalist and arranging for and leading a vocal group modeled on the hit 1950s American band the Four Freshmen. In the early 1960s, however, Alessandroni's career took a definitive turn toward production music when he began collaborating with his boyhood friend Ennio Morricone on the latter's now-iconic western film scores: in addition to providing innovative, surf-influenced guitar work and harmonies via his vocal group, Alessandroni also provided the memorable whistle lines used by Morricone to such famous effect in *A Fistful of Dollars*, *The Good, the Bad and the Ugly*, and many more. After numerous celebrated soundtrack collaborations, Alessandroni branched into his own production music and library recordings, and released dozens of albums through a variety of European libraries, including CAM, Octopus, and Coloursound. Alessandroni died in March 2017.

Romano di Bari: I started to collaborate with [Alessandroni] when I was still with RCA. He had this wonderful choir called Cantori Moderni, and I did the first album when I was independent with Cantori Moderni. This is still a masterpiece today.

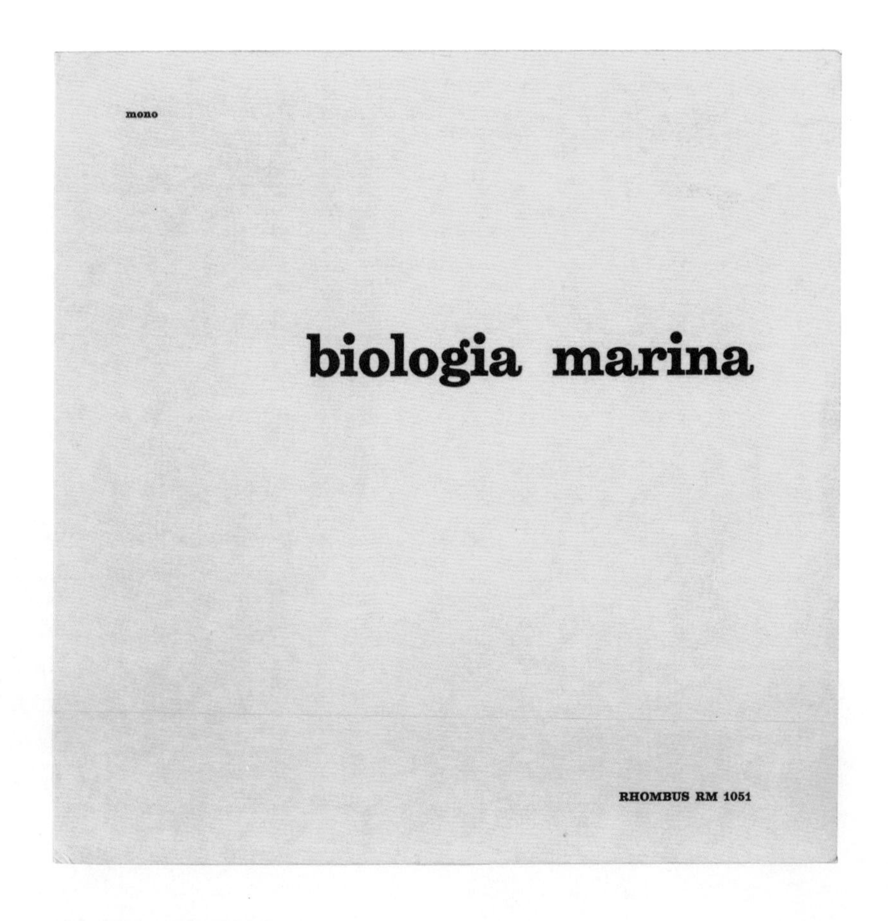

TOP

Alessandro Alessandroni. *Industriale*. Octopus Records (Italy): OTP 0295, 1976.

BOTTOM

Alessandro Alessandroni. *Light and Heavy Industry*. Colloursound Library (Germany): CS 6, 1982.

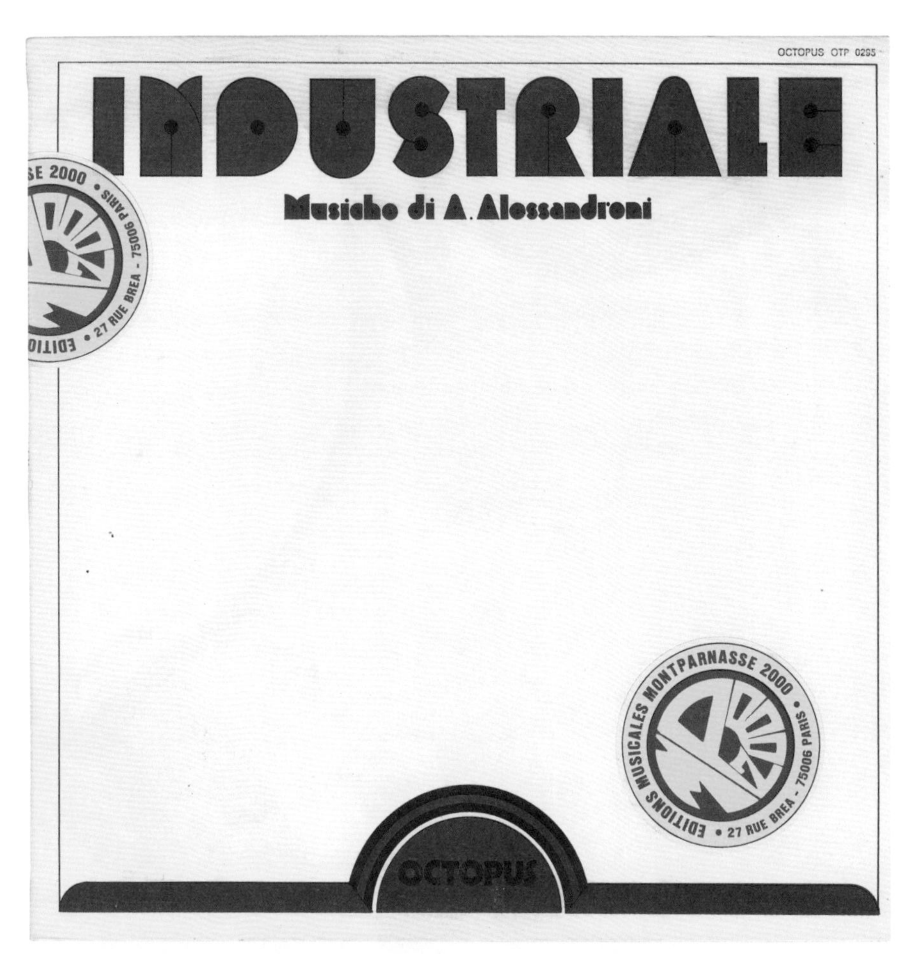

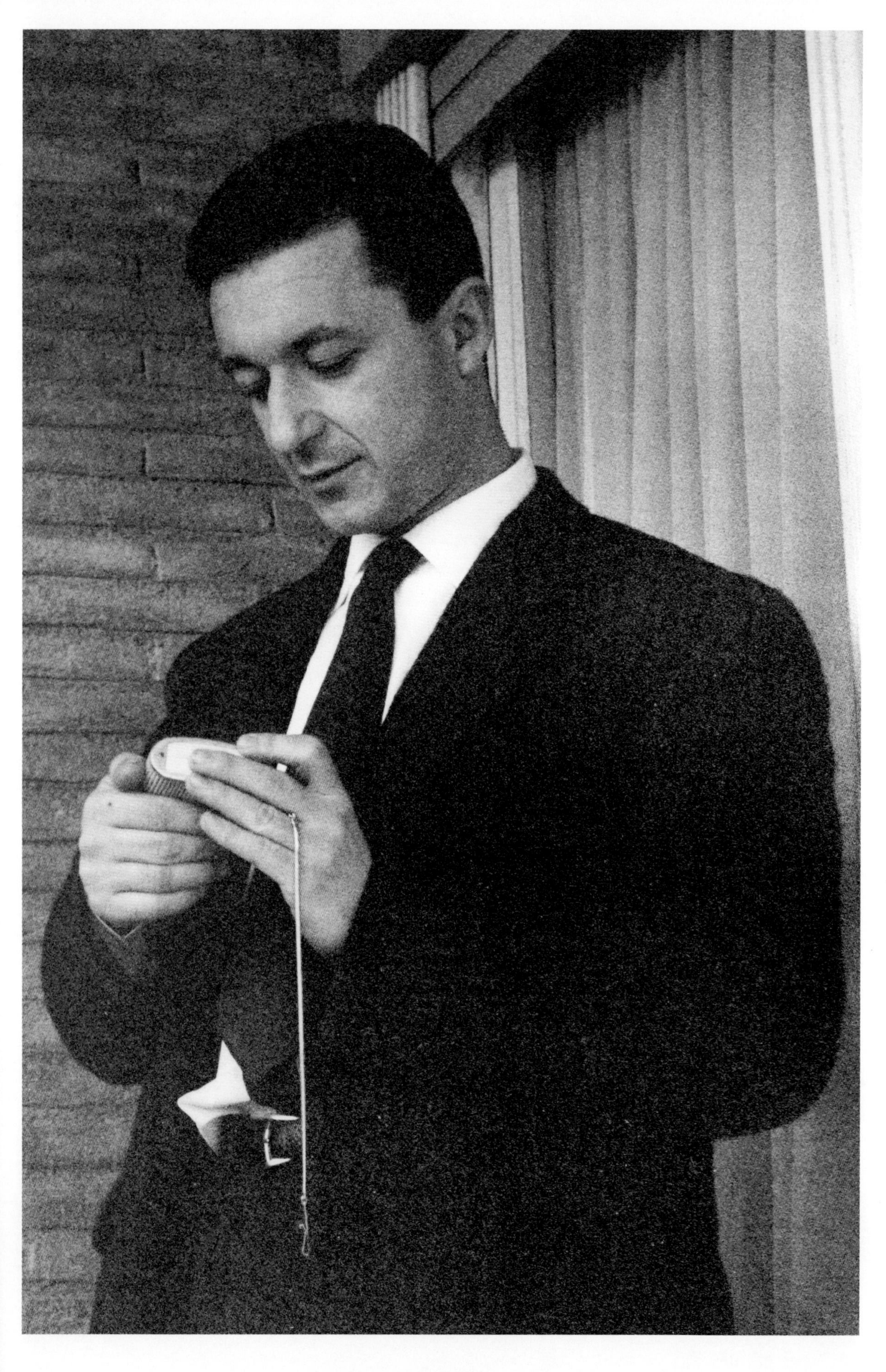

PIERO UMILIANI

BELOW

Umiliani at work with the seminal EMS VCS3 synthesizer.

A native of Florence who came of age during World War II, Piero Umiliani parlayed an early talent for music into a conservatory degree and a regular gig playing piano in the jazz clubs frequented by American GIs. Combining his background in classical composition with his passion for new musical forms, Umiliani created some of the earliest recordings to integrate jazz rhythms and bebop with Italian standards, and a bustling career in film soundtracks followed. From the late 1950s into the '80s, he scored dozens of films—largely of the gangster, comedy, horror, and spaghetti western varieties—and wrote enormously popular TV themes (including "Mah Nà Mah Nà," originally recorded for the 1968 Italian mondo exploitation flick *Sweden: Heaven and Hell* but later immortalized on the first episode of *The Muppets*). Above and beyond his best-known credits, Umiliani is equally well represented in the field of library music, where he registered hundreds of recordings for the CAM library as well as his own Omicron and Liuto labels. After a long and storied career, Umiliani died in 2001.

L'UOMO NELLO SPAZIO
PIERO UMILIANI AL MOOG
Omicron
LPS 0026 STEREO

OMICRON

OPPOSITE

Piero Umiliani. *L'Uomo Nello Spazio*. Omicron (Italy): LPS 0026, 1972.

BELOW

Piero Umiliani. *Angeli Bianchi... Angeli Neri*. Omicron (Italy): LPS 0017, 1969.

With origins stretching back to its founder Piero Umiliani's youth, Omicron was established as the successor to Omega, the label established by Umiliani's mother to protect her then-eighteen-year-old son's first copyrights. As Umiliani's success in film scoring grew, he founded the Omicron label in 1964 as a clearinghouse for his compositions and a library adaptable to the growing production requirements of Italian television. Soon Umiliani expanded Omicron to include several independent sublabels run out of the Sound Work Shop, the innovative home studio he built in 1968. Omicron and its sublabels (Liuto, Sound Work Shop, Videovoice, and Telesound) continued producing records throughout the 1970s, and their catalogs are regarded today as key documents in the history of the European library music industry.

TOP LEFT

Piero Umiliani. *Panorama Italiano*. Sound Work Shop (Italy): SWS 128, 1979.

TOP RIGHT

Piero Umiliani. *Paesi Balcanici*. Omicron (Italy): LPS 0029, 1972.

MIDDLE

Rovi (Piero Umiliani). *Storia e Preistoria*. Omicron (Italy): LPS 0030, 1972.

BOTTOM LEFT

Rovi (Piero Umiliani). *Piano Fender Blues*. Omicron (Italy): LPS 0031, 1975.

BOTTOM RIGHT

Moggi (Piero Umiliani). *Tra Scienza e Fantascienza*. Omicron (Italy): LPM 0040, 1980.

TOP

Johnny Moggi Quintet. *Hard Rhythms and Soft Melodys*. Omicron (Italy): LPM 0038, 1975.

BOTTOM

Piero Umiliani. *Atmospheres*. Omicron (Italy): LPM 0036, 1975.

TOP

Moggi (Piero Umiliani). *News! News! News!* Sound Work Shop (Italy): SWS 124, 1979.

BOTTOM

Piero Umiliani. *Chitarra Classica*. Liuto Records (Italy): LRS 0060, 1976.

TOP

Rovi (Piero Umiliani).
Motivi Allegri e Distensivi.
Sound Work Shop (Italy):
SWS 120, 1978.

BOTTOM

Moggi (Piero Umiliani).
Tensione. Sound Work Shop
(Italy): SWS 123, 1979.

TOP

Tusco (Piero Umiliani). *Suspence Elettronica*. Telesound (Italy): 112, 1983.

BOTTOM

Zalla (Piero Umiliani). *Paesaggi*. Ciak Record (Italy): CKRC 0040, 1980.

OPPOSITE TOP

Catamo (Piero Umiliani). *Fascismo e Dintorni*. Videovoice (Italy): VDVC 114, 1981.

OPPOSITE BOTTOM LEFT

Piero Umiliani. *L'Uomo e La Città*. Liuto Records (Italy): LRS 0059, 1976.

OPPOSITE BOTTOM RIGHT

Moggi (Piero Umiliani). *Double Face*. Videovoice (Italy): VDVC 116, 1981.

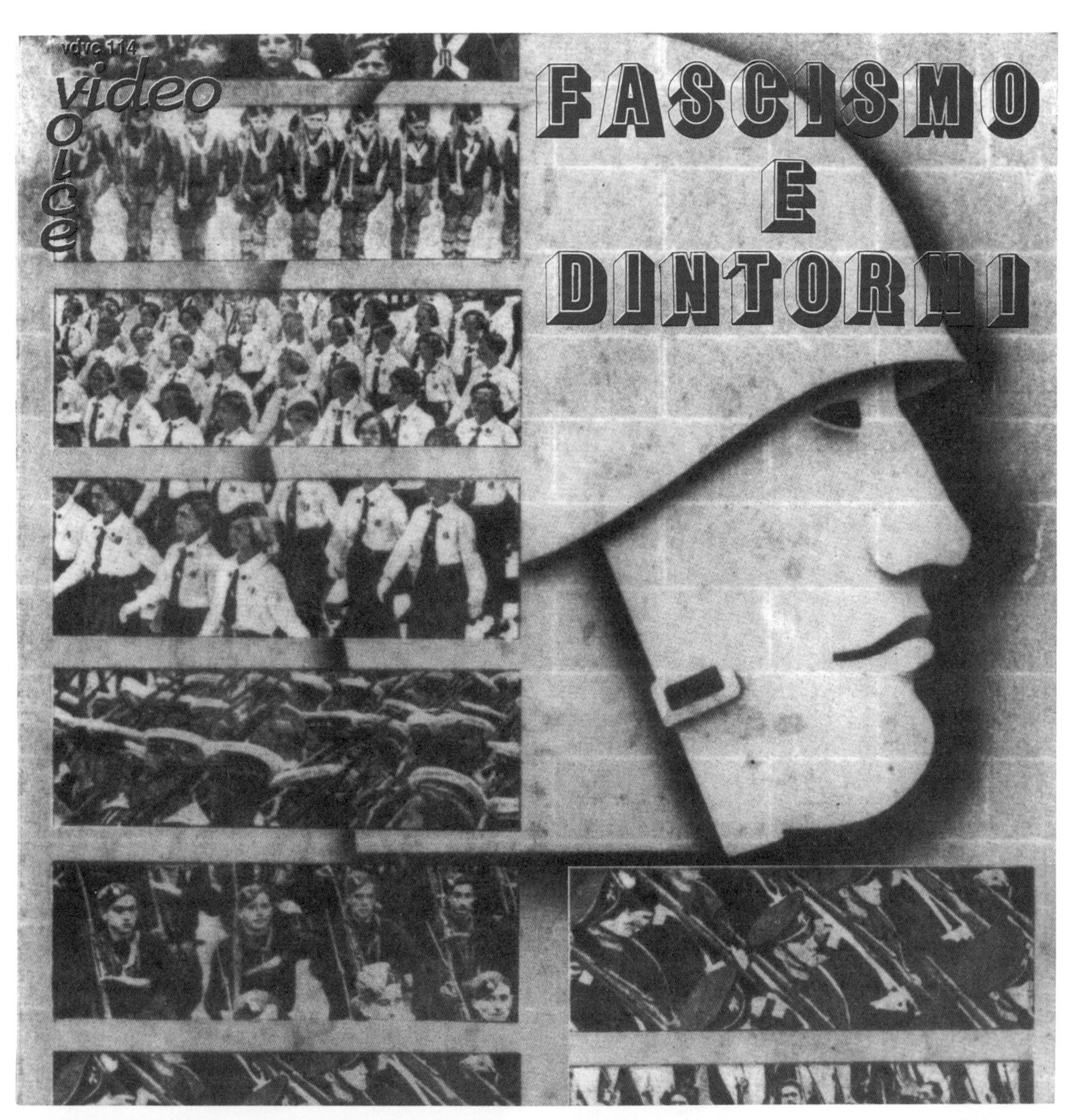
vdvc 114
video
voice
FASCISMO
E
DINTORNI

L'UOMO E LA CITTA'
LIUTO RECORDS
LRS 0059

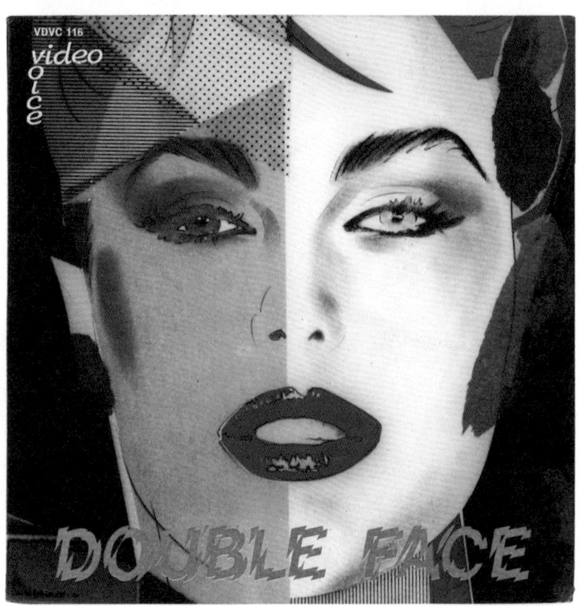
VDVC 116
video
voice
DOUBLE FACE

TOP

Piero Umiliani. *Guerre et Destruction 1*. Éditions Montparnasse 2000 (France): MP 108, 1972.

BOTTOM

Piero Umiliani. *Guerre et Destruction 2*. Éditions Montparnasse 2000 (France): MP 109, 1972.

OPPOSITE

Piero Umiliani. *Sweden: Heaven and Hell* (Original Motion Picture Soundtrack). Ariel Records (US): ARS 15000, 1969.

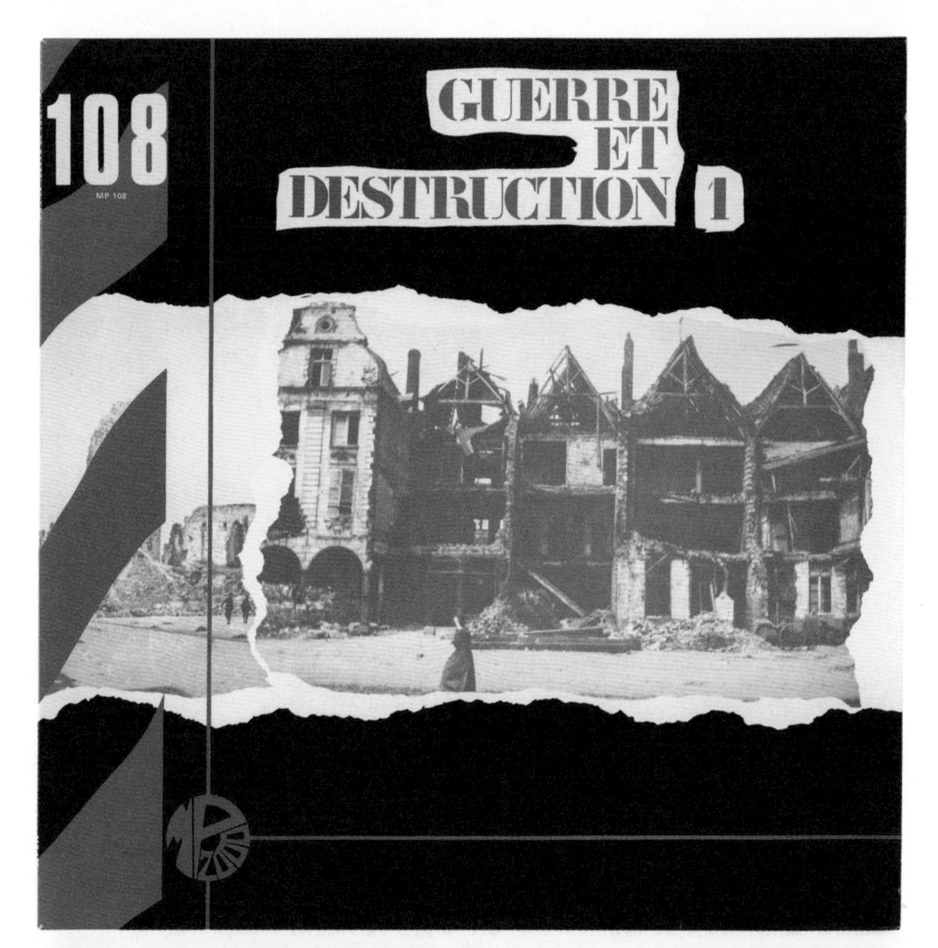

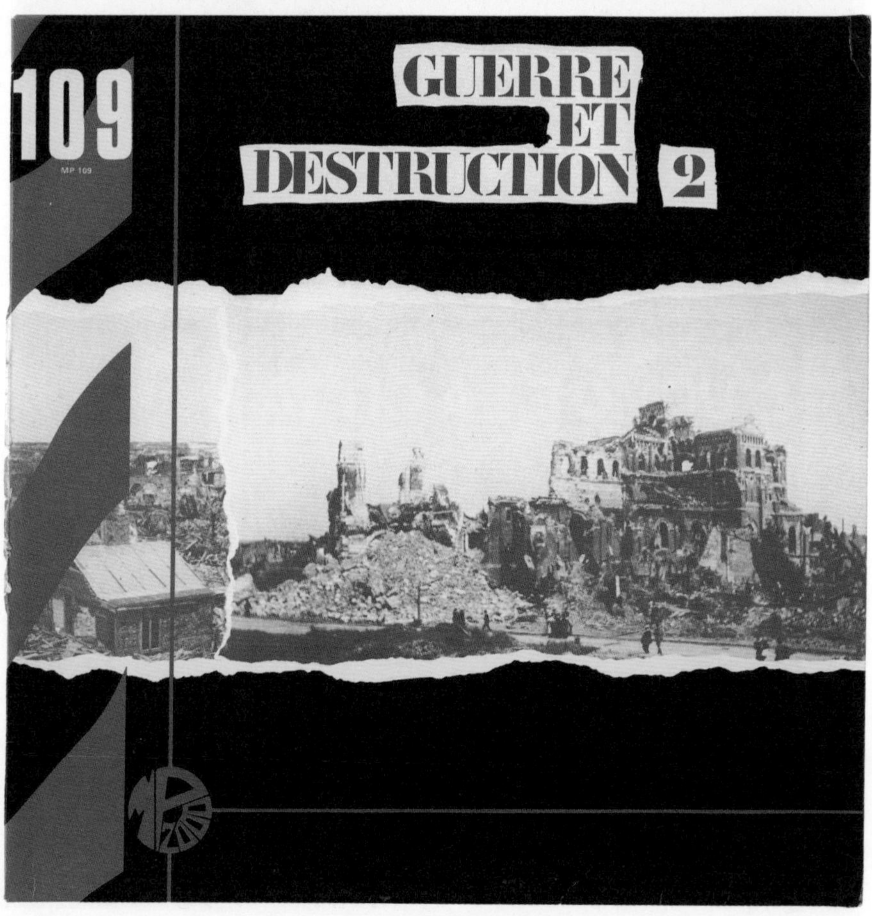

FEATURING THE HIT SINGLE MAH-NÀ-MAH-NÀ
ORIGINAL MOTION PICTURE SOUNDTRACK
AVCO EMBASSY PICTURES presents
Sweden
HEAVEN AND HELL
STEREO
COLUMBIA
ARS 15000
SWEDEN ...Where The Facts Of Life Are Stranger Than Fiction!
THE MOST REVOLUTIONARY MOST PERMISSIVE LIFE-STATE IN THE WORLD!
SEE: "The Love Cruise"! A training trip for turned-on teens!
SEE: "The Bachelorette Party"! A bride-to-be's last fling!
SEE: "Moonlighting Nudes"! Meter- maids by day —models at night!
SEE: "The Swap Shop"! A trade-in deal for married couples only!
X PERSONS UNDER 17 NOT ADMITTED
Written and Directed by LUIGI SCATTINI • Photographed by CLAUDIO RACCA • Music by PIERO UMILIANI • Narrated by EDMUND PURDOM
ARIEL RECORDS

C 262
FONIT
SERIE USIGNOLO

FONIT: SERIE USIGNOLO

OPPOSITE

Giampiero Boneschi / Mitridate. *Caratteristici*. Fonit (Italy): C 262, 1970.

BELOW

Orchestra Ollamar / Orchestra R. de Filippi. *Atmosfere*. Fonit-Cetra International Hi Fi (Italy): 7001, 1971.

A library series published under the umbrella of the venerable Italian label Fonit and the publisher Usignolo, the "Serie Usignolo" exemplifies much of what made the era's library scene so unique: Fonit, founded in 1911 to cater to the brand-new market for 78-rpm records, had by the 1970s become a primary purveyor of music for the Italian public television station Rai TV, and the records released under the Usignolo series reflected the vast experimental possibilities offered, improbably, by such commercial arrangements. With record sleeves featuring only catalog numbers on otherwise totally abstracted designs, the series put anonymity front and center while publishing hugely innovative records ranging from classical Italian music to orchestral pop excursions to the avant-leaning work of various electronic pioneers.

GEMELLI

BELOW

Zanagoria. *Insight Modulation*. Gemelli (Italy): GG.ST. 10.011, 1972.

Founded by noted film music composer and orchestra director Bruno Nicolai in the late 1960s, Gemelli initially featured work by Nicolai and his film scoring compatriots (chief among them his longtime friend Ennio Morricone) and operated as a commercial label and a production library simultaneously. It soon distinguished itself, however, by providing a haven for the left-of-center, stranger side of the Italian musical scene, publishing bizarre avant-garde compositions by electronic pioneer Vittorio Gelmetti and jarringly dissonant collaborations between Morricone and the free-improv outfit Gruppo di Improvvisazione di Nuova Consonanza. Amid a soundtrack scene characterized largely by orchestral swells and instrumental melodrama, Gemelli made a niche for itself at the vanguard of modern composition.

JUMP

BELOW

Giancarlo Barigozzi / Oscar Rocchi. *Rock Scene*. Music Scene (Italy): MSE 130, no date.

An Italian publisher based in Milan, Jump Edizioni Musicali (and its two primary sublabels, Jump Records and Music Scene) released records from across the spectrum of the country's musical world beginning in the 1960s. Among the hundreds of records in its catalog, Jump published works by notable Italian composers and bandleaders like Giampiero Boneschi, Carlo Savina, and Fabio Fabor—many of whom were also active in the soundtrack and library field on larger Italian labels like CAM. Jump's releases also ran the gamut musically, from smooth jazz easy listening to traditional folk, and from electronic experimentation to orchestral grandeur.

TOP

Various. *International Parade*. Jump Records (Italy): J-0136, 1983.

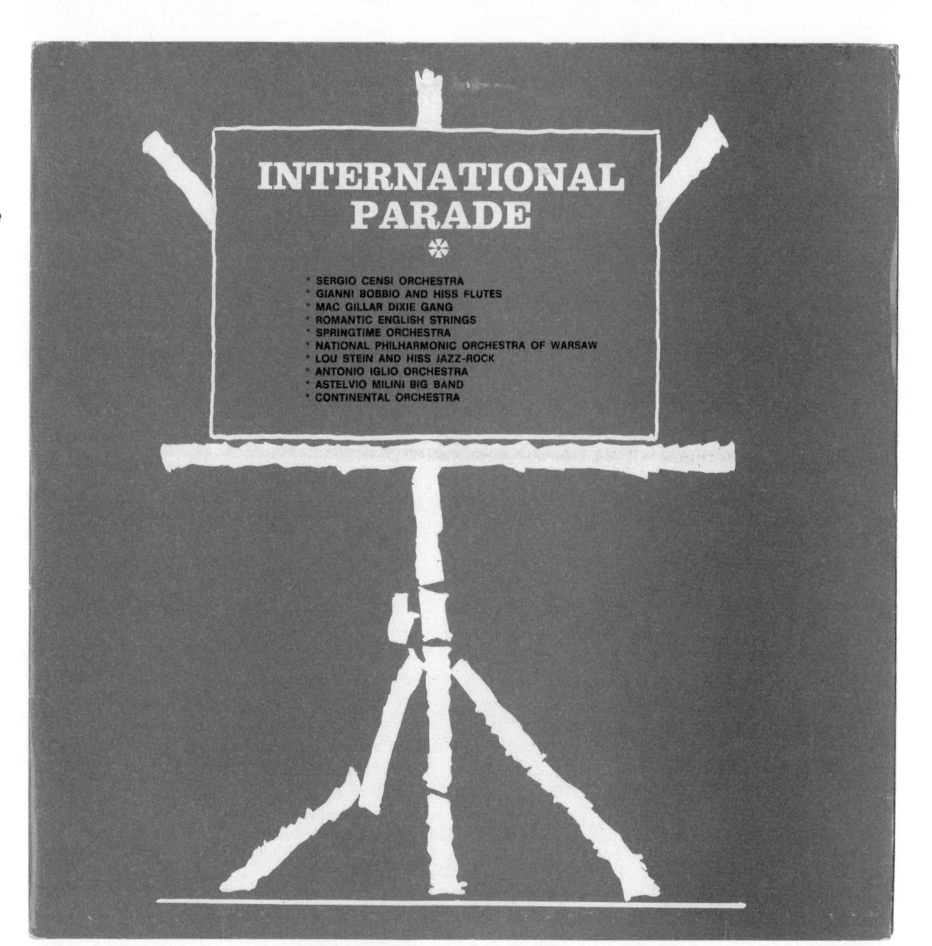

BOTTOM

Giampiero Boneschi, Sergio Farina. *Western 'n' Country Scene - Children's Land*. Music Scene (Italy): MSE 147, no date.

TOP

Space Craft's Men. *Adventures*. Music Scene (Italy): MSE 160, 1983.

BOTTOM

Sound Games Orchestra. *Games Power*. Music Scene (Italy): MSE 161, 1984.

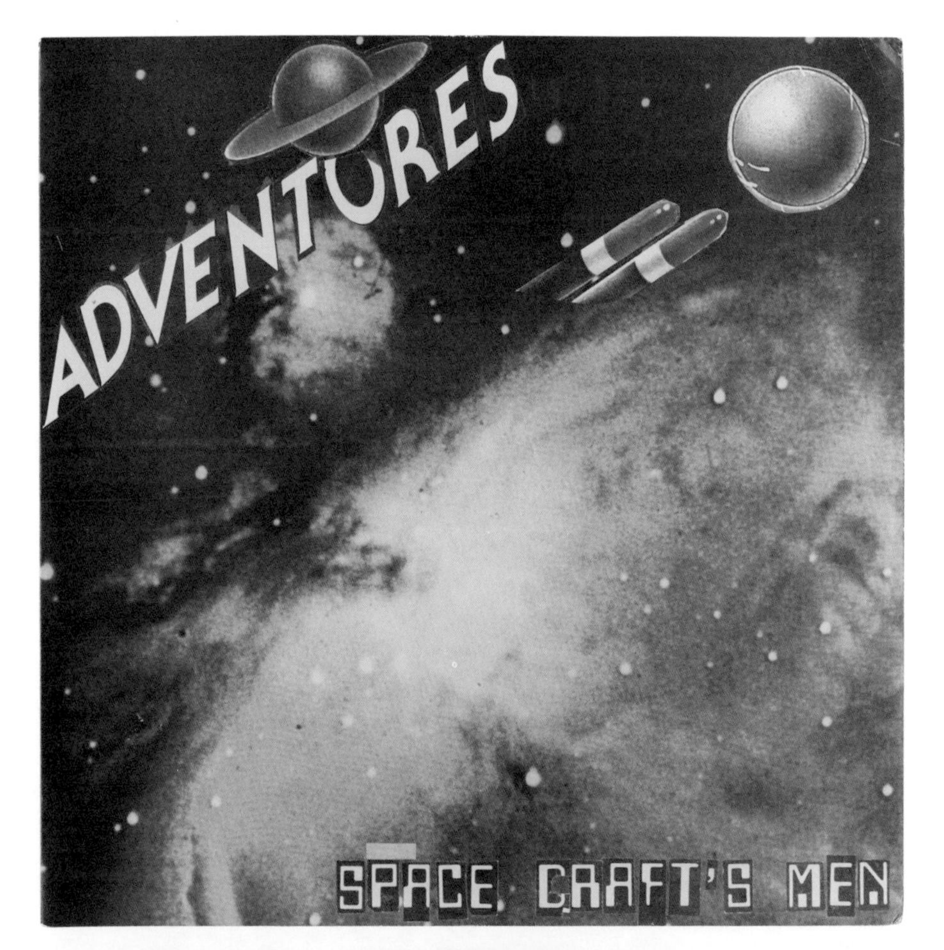

LATIN FRIENDS
Los Minus Hernandez

OPPOSITE

Los Minus Hernandez. *Latin Friends*. Music Scene (Italy): MSE 162, 1984.

TOP

Italian Fantasy Orchestra. *Music for Relax*. Music Scene (Italy): MSE 166, no date.

BOTTOM

Gianni Safred & His Electronic Instruments. *Futuribile (The Life to Come)*. Music Scene (Italy): MSE 146, 1978.

RISOLUZIONI SONORE

LEONARDI

OPPOSITE

Gian Paolo Chiti / Sergio Montori. *Risoluzioni Sonore*. Lupus (Italy): LUS 226, 1971.

BELOW

Ugo Fusco / Stefano Torossi. *Beat in Ampex*. Dischi Montecarlo (Italy): SM 5009, 1972.

Having been founded in 1927, Leonardi Edizioni SRL was an early publishing contributor to the Italian music industry, decades old by the time the country's library heyday hit in the 1960s. And yet as the parent company of notable libraries such as Dischi Montecarlo, Grand Prix, Leo, and Lupus Records, Leonardi was responsible for releasing many classic records of the era. As a commercial label, it put out major releases for the Italian market featuring foreign stars as varied as Petula Clark and Pérez Prado, but it was its sublabels which made the company's reputation in the library world, releasing works by many big names in the Italian scene—composers like Alessandro Alessandroni, Giuliano Sorgini, Oronzo de Filippi, and Daniela Casa.

TOP

Antonio Ricardo Luciani. *Jazz in Libertà*. Lupus (Italy): LUS 228, 1976.

BOTTOM

Blue Sharks. *It Became Crystal*. Leonardi Records (Italy): SL 27, 1972.

OPPOSITE TOP LEFT

Oronzo de Filippi. *Meccanizzazione*. Leo Records: LR 15, 1969.

OPPOSITE TOP RIGHT

Remigio Ducros. *T.S.T. '73 Cronaca*. Leonardi Records (Italy): SL 30, 1974.

OPPOSITE BOTTOM LEFT

Paolo Renosto. *Medioevo & Rinascimento*. Leo Records (Italy): LR 14, no date.

OPPOSITE BOTTOM RIGHT

Carlo Esposito / Nunzio Pellegrino / Giuliano Sorgini / Carlo Zoffoli. *Natura e Musica N. 7*. Grand Prix (Italy): G.P. 128, no date.

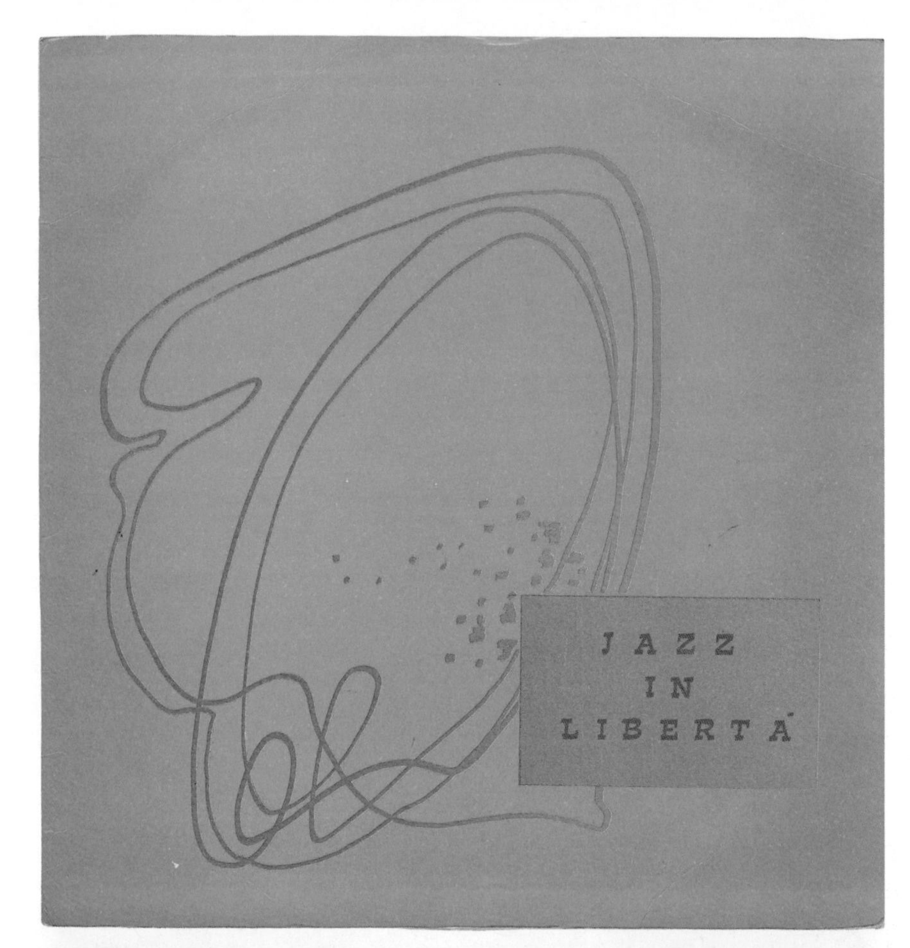

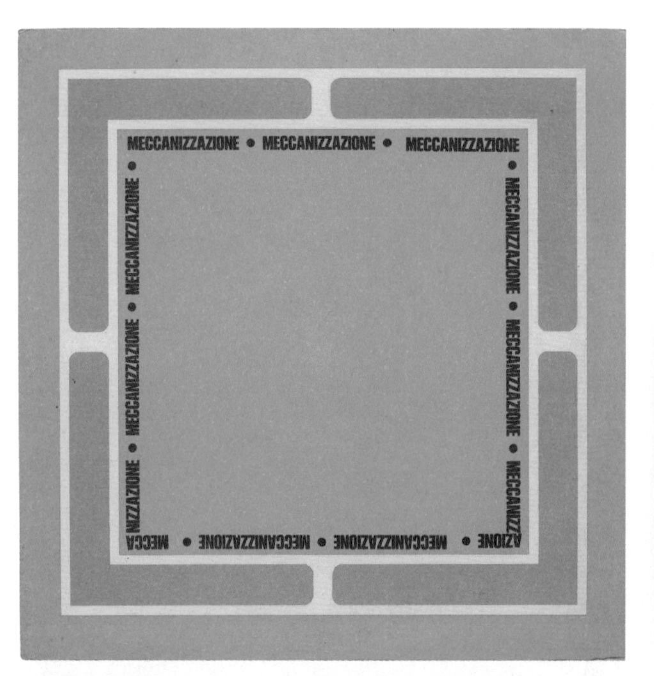
MECCANIZZAZIONE • MECCANIZZAZIONE • MECCANIZZAZIONE
• MECCANIZZAZIONE • MECCANIZZAZIONE • MECCANIZZ
AZIONE • MECCANIZZAZIONE • MECCANIZZAZIONE • MECCA
NIZZAZIONE • MECCANIZZAZIONE • MECCANIZZAZIONE •

T.S.T. '73
CRONACA

Medioevo
&
Rinascimento
LEO records lr 14 mono

Natura e musica n. 7
STEREO COMPATIBILE MONO
Side A
1 BRIM - G.Sorgini 2,30
2 BARCAROLA - Nelabi 3,12
3 SERENATA VENEZIANA - Nelabi 3,48
4 MONOTONIA - G. Sorgini 2,10
5 STELLE LUCENTI - C. Zoffoli 2,28
1 - 4 Complesso diretto da Giuliano Sorgini
2 - 3 Orchestra diretta da Carlo Esposito
5 - Complesso diretto da Carlo Zoffoli
Side B
1 BURLESCA - Giacchino 1,55
2 ALBUM BLATT - Giacchino 2,17
3 TETE A TETE - Giacchino 2,47
4 MATTUTINO - Giacchino 1,35
5 SHAME - G. Sorgini 1,33
6 TORPEDO - G. Sorgini 2,21
1 - 2 - 3 - 4 Complesso diretto da Nunzio Pellegrino
5 - 6 Complesso diretto da Giuliano Sorgini
GRAND PRIX
G.P. 128

TELEMUSICA
N. 3

OPPOSITE

Paride Miglioli. *Telemusica N. 3*. Metropole Records (Italy): SM 7013, no date.

TOP

Massimo Catalano. *Telemusica N. 2*. Metropole Records (Italy): SM 7009, no date.

BOTTOM

Enrico Cortese / Eliaron / Ugo Fusco. *Video Musica N. 2*. Dischi Montecarlo (Italy): SM 5004, 1970.

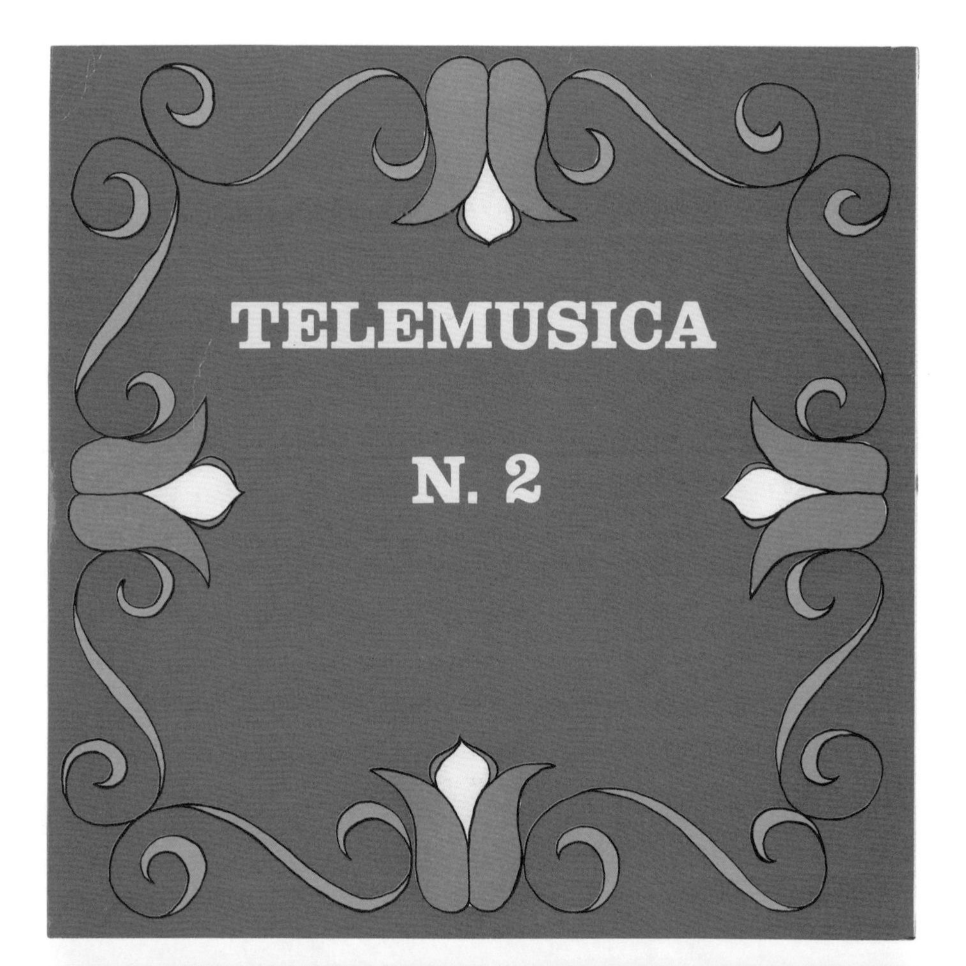

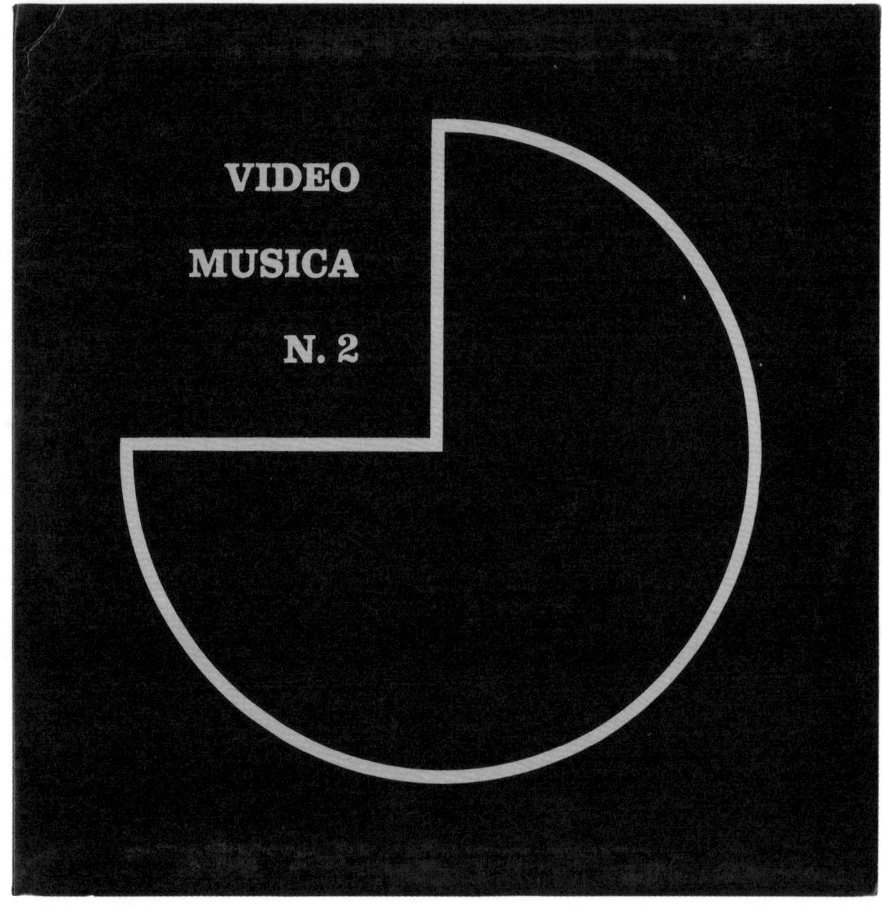

AMERICA GIOVANE

DANIELA CASA

OPPOSITE

Remigio Ducros. *America Giovane*. Leo Records (Italy): LR 25, 1972.

BELOW

Daniela Casa. *America Giovane N.2*. Leo Records (Italy): LR 27, 1972

Born in Rome in 1944, Daniela Casa came to music early—despite being the daughter of a builder of motorboats, she attended art school, where she studied singing and guitar. In 1963, at the age of nineteen, Casa was signed to the Fonit label, and was soon active as a performer in the covers duo Dany & Gepy (a collaboration with Giampiero Scalamogna aka "Gepy & Gepy," the deep-voiced Italo disco performer known as the "Italian Barry White"). Casa, however, was destined for more than minor chart success, and in the early 1970s became an active, versatile, and highly successful composer contributing to the Italian production music field.

Casa's library compositions ranged from more typical guitar folk, exotic pop, and jazz-funk excursions to the nationally tinged genre exercises then prevalent in the field—as in her contribution to the multivolume *America Giovane* ("Young America") on Leo Records, which featured USA-themed tracks with titles like "N.Y.C. 42nd" and "Kentucky Fried Chicken." Casa distinguished herself, however, with subtle keyboard and electronic scores of a darker, more experimental bent—as in 1975's *Società Malata* ("Sick Society") on Romano di Bari's Deneb label, which took on the uncharacteristically bleak theme of civilizational decay via ambient soundscapes and avant-garde electronics.

Casa died in 1986 at only forty-two, and though her legacy was overshadowed for years by her better-known male contemporaries in the Italian library scene, recent reissues have brought long-overdue attention back to her unique oeuvre. Today Casa is increasingly recognized as a visionary of the production music field.

TOP LEFT

The BRF Studio Group. *Musical Fantasy No. 1*. Broadway International (Italy): BW 13084, no date.

TOP RIGHT

Virgilio Braconi, Peymont. *Videomusic N. 1*. Le Monde (Italy): LMR 1250, 1972.

MIDDLE

Quintetto Record TV. *Serie Jazz*. Record TV Discografica (Italy): RT 10, no date.

BOTTOM LEFT

Various. *Mixed Grill*. New Tape (Italy): NWT 2001, 1972.

BOTTOM RIGHT

Various. *Ostinazione (Piccola Serie Ritmica)*. Ediphon (Italy): E9-70, no date.

OPPOSITE TOP

Alberto Baldan Bembo. *Sound Orchestra*. Star Track (Italy): ST.LP.TR1982, no date.

OPPOSITE BOTTOM LEFT

Enrico Cortese. *Antica Grecia*. Grifo Records (Italy): GR 515, no date.

OPPOSITE BOTTOM RIGHT

Complesso I Pazzi Virtuosi. *Musica Per Bambini*. Fontana (Italy): 6830 122, 1972.

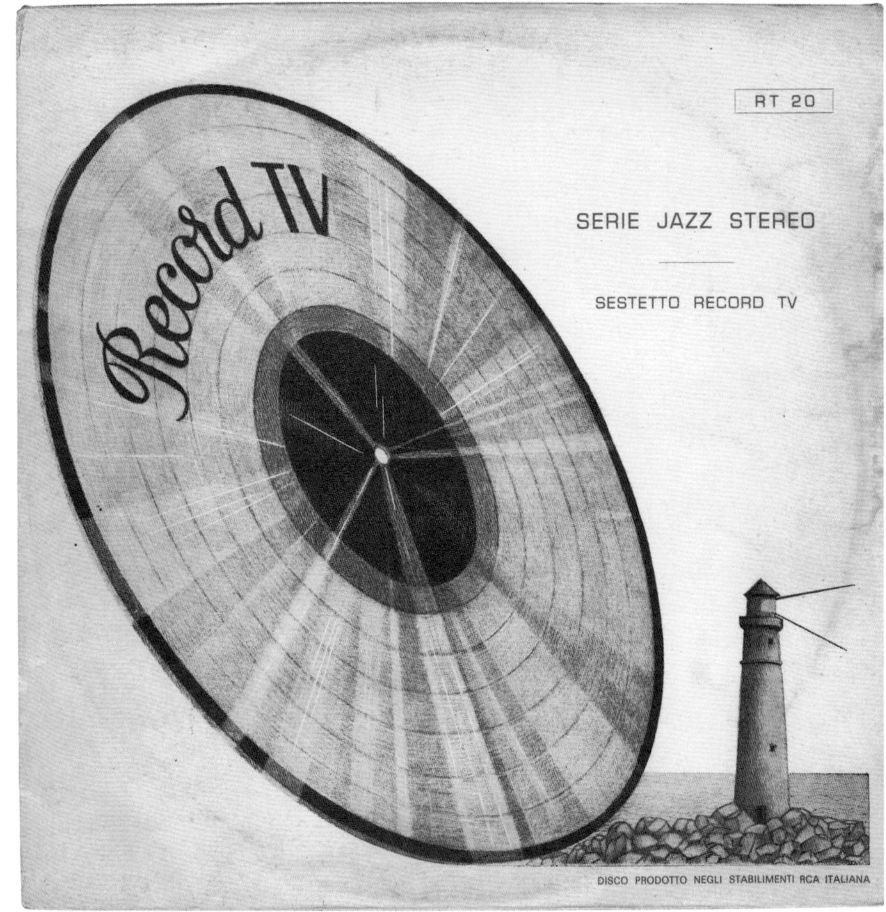

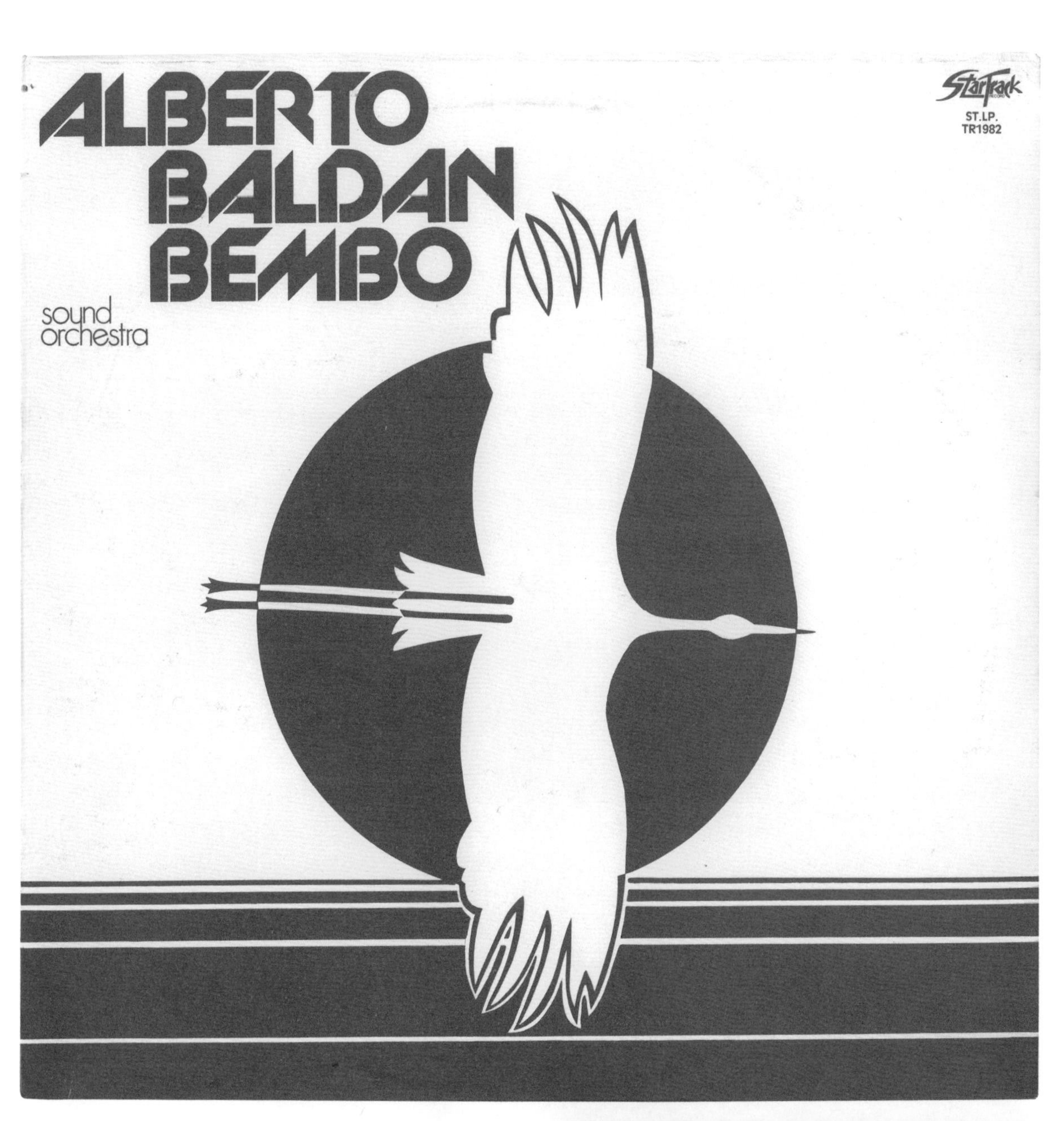
ALBERTO
BALDAN
BEMBO
sound
orchestra
ST.LP.
TR1982

GRIFO records gr 515mono
antica
grecia

MUSICA PER BAMBINI
(da 1 a 99 anni)
fontana
Sottofondi
musicali

i gres
GLOBEVISION
GV-002

OPPOSITE

I Gres. *I Gres Vol. lll*. Globevision (Italy): GV 002, 1975.

TOP

Cardius and Bordoni. *Sonor*. Dany Records (Italy): no CAT number, no date.

BOTTOM

Franco Bonfanti / Arnaldo Graziosi. *Registrazioni Effettuate Per Commento Musicale Radio - Televisione - Film*. Dany Record (Italy): DR 03, 1975.

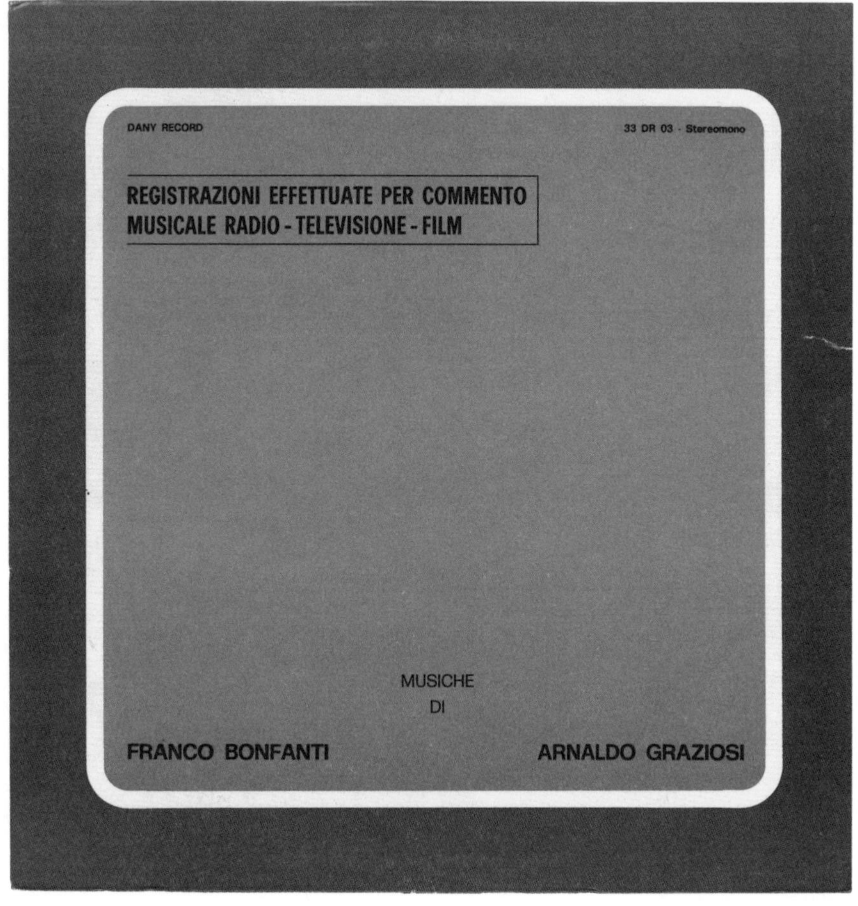

TOP

Cicci Santucci, Enzo Scoppa. *Looking Around*. Fly Record (Italy): AS55, 1971.

BOTTOM

Renato Serio. *Impressioni*. Pony (Italy): no CAT number, 1972.

OPPOSITE

Complesso Strumentale I Panamera. *Rebus N. 4*. CGO Records (Italy): FC 1016, 1972.

TOP

Mirot. *Apprendista Hitchcock*. Titian Records (Italy): TRL 5016, no date.

BOTTOM

Enzo Minuti. *Themes for Flutes*. Black Rock Records (Italy): ECR 111, no date.

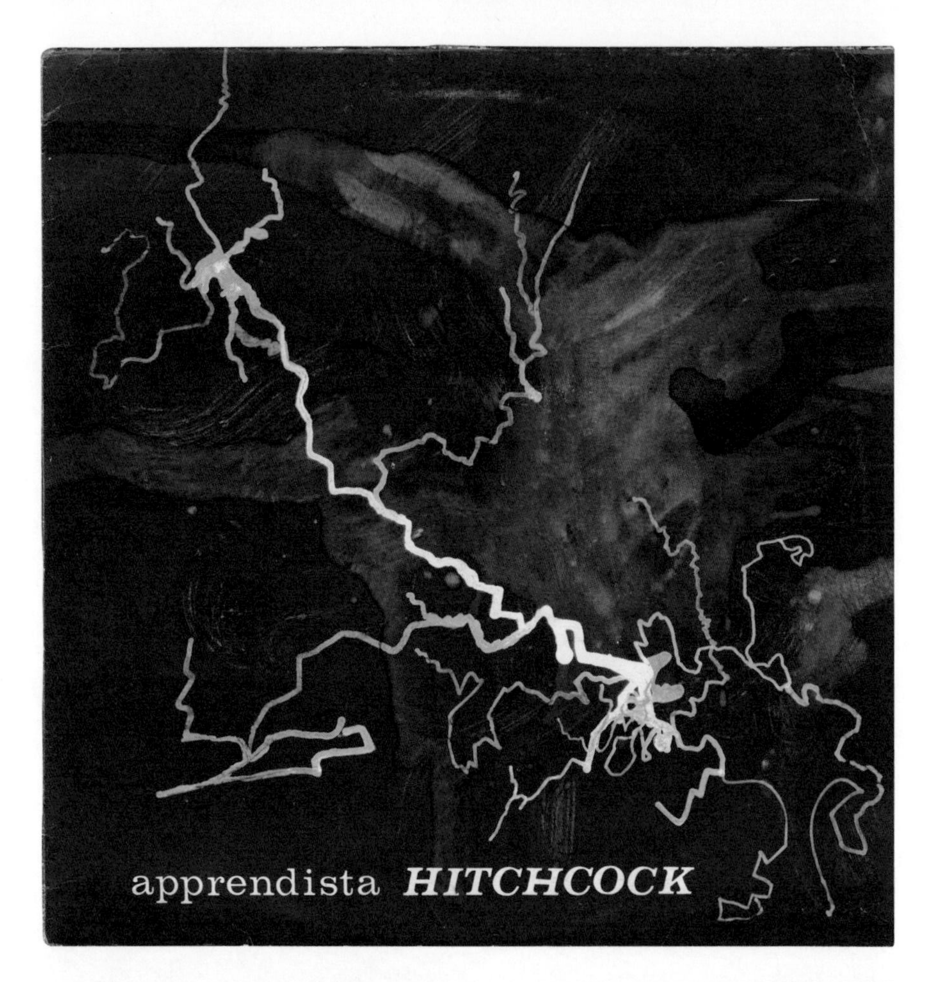

TOP

No artist. *Caleidoscope*. Melodie (Italy): M/011, no date.

BOTTOM

Leonardo Marietta. *Percussioni ed Effetti*. Cenacolo (Italy): M 715, 1983.

TOP

Enzo Scoppa. *Traffico*. Roman Record Company (Italy): AG 110, 1972.

BOTTOM

Rino de Fillippi. *Tema: Amore*. Nazionalmusic (Italy): 1023, 1972.

OPPOSITE TOP

Fabio Fabor. *Pape Satan*. Hard: HLP 200, 1980.

OPPOSITE BOTTOM LEFT

King Zerand. *Improvvisi Musicale*. Edizioni Bang Bang (Italy): BB.LP. 8462, no date.

OPPOSITE BOTTOM RIGHT

Guido Manusardi. *Electronic-Dance*. Edizioni Bang Bang (Italy): BB.LP. 8692, no date.

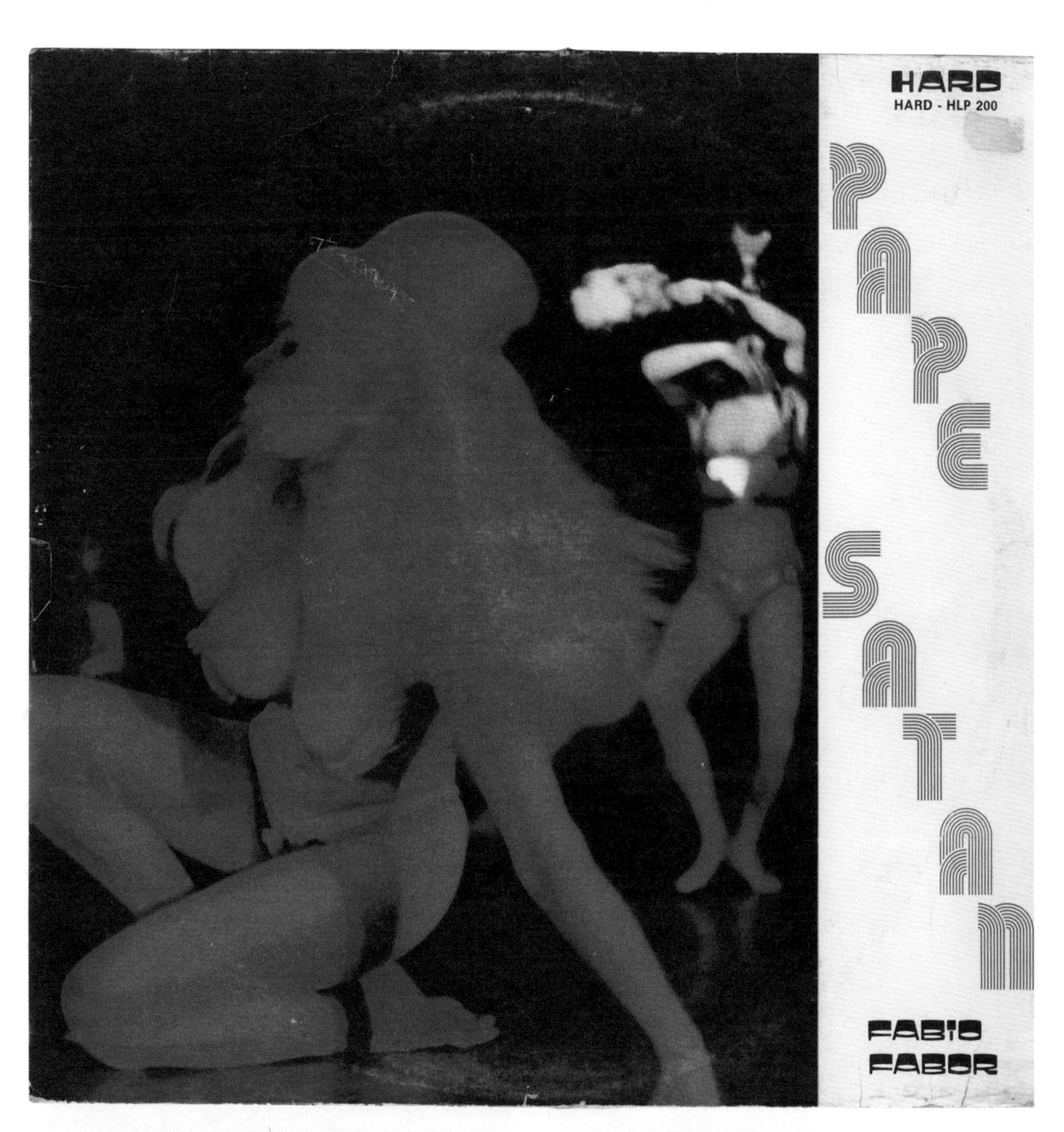
HARD
HARD - HLP 200
PAPE SATAN
FABIO
FABOR

BB.LP. 8482
KING ZERAND
IMPROVVISI MUSICALI

BB.LP. 8692
GUIDO MANUSARDI
ELECTRONIC-DANCE
Side A
ORIZZONTI (G. Manusardi - A. Olivieri) 3,24
SPAZI (G. Manusardi - A. Olivieri) 3,29
CREPUSCOLARE SEI (G. Manusardi - A. Olivieri) 3,02
GRANDI SPAZI (G. Manusardi - A. Olivieri) 3,22
DIXI (G. Manusardi - A. Olivieri) 3,22
ROMANTICA (G. Manusardi - A. Olivieri) 2,22

TOP

Franco Delfino. *Astrattismo*.
Edizioni Bang Bang (Italy):
BG LP 2016, no date.

BOTTOM

Hingross. *Record for Murder*.
Horse Shoe Records (Italy):
HSIR 3224, no date.

NORTH
AMERICAN
LIBRARIES

PARRY MUSIC LIBRARY

BELOW

Various. *Moods for Drama*. Parry Music Library (Canada): PML 04, 1977.

Based out of Toronto, Parry Music Library was founded in 1974 by a former Chappell library manager and a music consultant, and constitutes the primary '70s music library from Canada. Now a subsidiary of BMG Production Music, Parry's early catalog largely consisted of the era's popular library styles (funk, disco, early electronic music), all packaged in the brand's standardized, maple-leaf-adorned sleeves.

EMIL ASCHER LIBRARY

BELOW

Edgar Redmond / Bill Loose. *Soul / Action / Activity*. Emil Ascher Inc. (US): EA 010, no date.

OPPOSITE TOP LEFT

Seymour Rubenstein, Betty Byers. *Orchestral Shades*. Emil Ascher Inc. (US): EA 2005, 1984.

OPPOSITE TOP RIGHT

Craig Palmer. *American Panorama*. Emil Ascher Inc. (US): EA 2007, 1984.

OPPOSITE BOTTOM

Larry Owens. *Dynamic Impressions*. Emil Ascher Inc. (US): EA 2006, 1984.

The second production music imprint of the longstanding American publisher Emil Ascher Inc. (the first was Video Moods, which produced recordings from 1955 to 1961), Emil Ascher Library published library records in the mid-1970s, including several compositions by Doug Wood, who would go on to form the Omnimusic library label.

ORCHESTRAL
SHADES

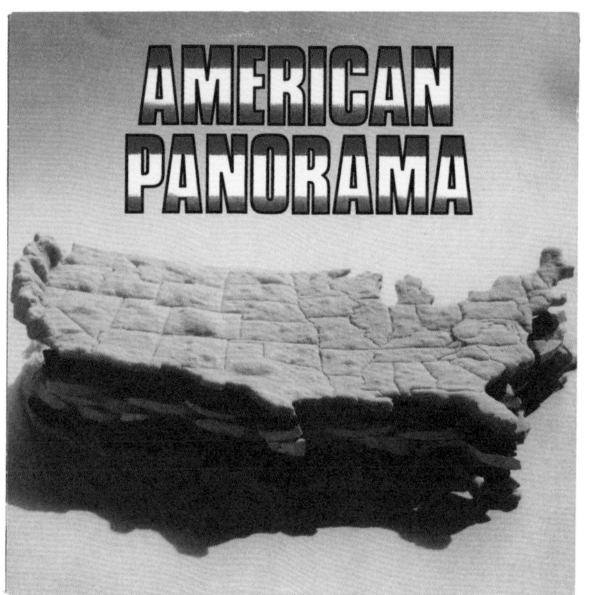
AMERICAN
PANORAMA

DYNAMIC
IMPRESSIONS

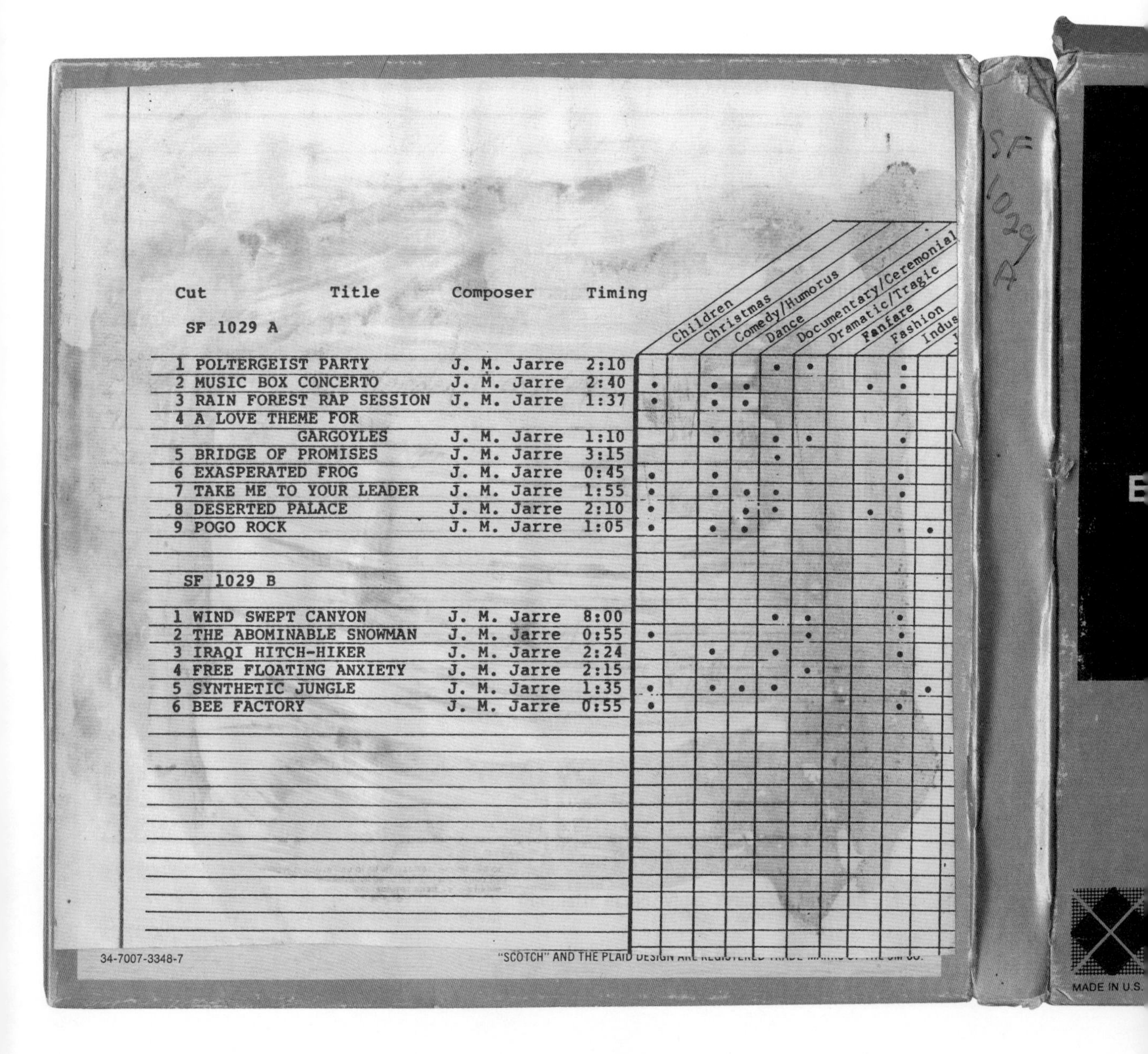

Cut	Title	Composer	Timing	Children	Christmas	Comedy/Humorus	Dance	Documentary/Ceremonial	Dramatic/Tragic	Fanfare	Fashion	Indus	
SF 1029 A													
1	POLTERGEIST PARTY	J. M. Jarre	2:10					•	•			•	
2	MUSIC BOX CONCERTO	J. M. Jarre	2:40	•		•	•				•	•	
3	RAIN FOREST RAP SESSION	J. M. Jarre	1:37	•		•	•						
4	A LOVE THEME FOR GARGOYLES	J. M. Jarre	1:10			•		•	•			•	
5	BRIDGE OF PROMISES	J. M. Jarre	3:15					•					
6	EXASPERATED FROG	J. M. Jarre	0:45	•		•						•	
7	TAKE ME TO YOUR LEADER	J. M. Jarre	1:55	•		•	•	•				•	
8	DESERTED PALACE	J. M. Jarre	2:10	•			•	•			•		
9	POGO ROCK	J. M. Jarre	1:05	•		•	•						•
SF 1029 B													
1	WIND SWEPT CANYON	J. M. Jarre	8:00					•	•			•	
2	THE ABOMINABLE SNOWMAN	J. M. Jarre	0:55	•					•			•	
3	IRAQI HITCH-HIKER	J. M. Jarre	2:24			•		•				•	
4	FREE FLOATING ANXIETY	J. M. Jarre	2:15						•				
5	SYNTHETIC JUNGLE	J. M. Jarre	1:35	•		•	•	•					•
6	BEE FACTORY	J. M. Jarre	0:55	•								•	

JEAN-MICHEL JARRE

OPPOSITE AND BELOW

Tape master and case for Jean-Michel Jarre's' *Deserted Palace*. A Sam Fox Production (US): SF 1029, 1973.

A onetime staunch avant-gardist and electronic music pioneer who is in the rare position of also being an internationally known platinum-selling musician, Jean-Michel Jarre embodies much of the library field's paradoxical relationship between mainstream music and the fringe. No surprise, then, that his first solo album, *Deserted Palace*, was a library record: Jarre produced it in 1973 for Sam Fox Productions, a US production music label. The record, while containing much of the melodic synth workouts for which Jarre would soon become famous, also features abstract soundscapes and experimental touches, a possible reflection of the composer's time spent in Pierre Schaeffer's seminal Groupe de Recherches Musicales. Three years later, Jarre would break out, both in his native France and worldwide, with the 15-million-selling album *Oxygène*, but *Deserted Palace* remains a fascinating moment in the musician's career, and a telling artifact in the history of library music.

EBONITE

BELOW

Various. *Persuasive Jazz / Album 1*. Ebonite (US): E 104, 1977.

OPPOSITE TOP

Various. *Intimate Disco / Album 8*. Ebonite (US): E 141, 1977.

OPPOSITE BOTTOM LEFT

Various. *Moods / Album 8*. Ebonite (US): E 222, 1977.

OPPOSITE BOTTOM RIGHT

Various. *Rock & Roll / Album 26*. Ebonite (US): E 254, 1977.

An imprint of the independent label President Records, Ebonite is perhaps best known in library circles for its "album series"—lines of numbered recordings in striking geometric sleeves, organized by genre (*Intimate Disco*, *Persuasive Jazz*, and more). Featuring bought and repurposed compositions by established commercial artists like Herbie Hancock and Stevie Wonder among the anonymous works, these records have become popular items of speculation and crate-digger interest.

Intimate Disco
Album 8
Ebonite E141

Moods
Album 8
Ebonite
Rock & Roll
Album 26
Ebonite

STEREO
Capitol
Media
Music
RELEASE NO. 12

STEREO
from the sound Capitol of the world...
Media
Music
RELEASE NO. 6

STEREO
Capitol
Media
Music
RELEASE NO.10

OPPOSITE TOP

Jan Kimberly. *Release No.12 - Musical Weather Report*. Media Music / Capitol Records (US): MEOS-3, no date.

OPPOSITE BOTTOM LEFT

Henrik Nielsen. *Release No. 6 - Beat Patterns*. Media Music / Capitol Records (US): MECS-9, no date.

OPPOSITE BOTTOM RIGHT

Robert Ascot. *Release No. 10 - Commercial Life Styles / Moog*. Media Music (US): MEKS-4, no date.

RIGHT

Front and back covers of David McAllister and Joe Alter's *Fireball / The Barbershop*. Omnimusic (US): OM 105, 1978.

PAGE 286 TOP

Sam Spence. *All Systems Go / The Coming Conflict*. NFL Music Library (US): NFL 118, 1983.

PAGE 286 BOTTOM LEFT

Various. *Finally... A Production Music Library That Sounds Great!* Network Production Music (US): DEMO-85, 1982.

PAGE 286 BOTTOM RIGHT

Stock cover for the US library Network Production Music.

OMNIMUSIC

OM 105

Stereo playable Mono

Side One: FIREBALL

Rock, jazz and disco

1. TAKE OFF	2:00	Pounding percussion and electric guitars
2. FOXEY	2:24	Funky beat with guitar and organ solos
3. FIREBALL	1:52	Driving percussion with synthesizer solo
4. ALTERMAGIC	2:33	Disco beat with saxophone melody
5. HOW HIGH?	0:55	Jazz combo with blues saxophone solo
6. CRAZY 'BOUT YOU	1:31	Cocktail jazz group sound with piano solo
7. A CHILD'S WORLD	1:31	Light rhythmic jazz piano and vibes duet
8. SANTA CRUZ ROCKIN'	2:30	Rock feel with electric guitar solos

COMPOSERS: 1, 5-8 D.Mcallister
2-4 D. McAllister/J. Alter

Side Two: THE BARBERSHOP

Nostalgia, comedy, and location music in a variety of styles

1. AT THE RACES	1:37	Old fashioned banjo duet
2. THE BARBERSHOP	1:50	Nostalgic banjo and honkey-tonk piano duet
3. THE SET UP	2:12	Vaudeville melody with mute trumpet and flute
4. THE HOUSE ON THE HILL	1:36	Haunted house theme with woodwinds and brass
5. COMEDY SKETCH #1	1:10	Lighthearted piece with clarinet and flute
6. COMEDY SKETCH #2	1:14	Alternate version of above
7. THE VILLAIN	1:10	Silent movie chase music
8. JOIN THE PARADE	1:20	Old fashioned marching band sound
9. PROGRESS MARCH	1:15	Energetic brass band march

COMPOSER: D. McAllister

All music published by Franklin-Douglas (ASCAP). The compositions and recordings contained in this record are protected throughout the world by Copyright. These recordings may not be synchronized with any visual, or re-recorded in any other medium, without written authorization from OMNIMUSIC. License applications for use are available from OMNIMUSIC and their worldwide agents.

OMNIMUSIC 52 MAIN ST. PORT WASHINGTON NEW YORK 11050

COPYRIGHT © 1978 W. FRANKLIN JOYCE & ASSOCIATES INC.

NFL
MUSIC LIBRARY

network
Finally…
a production
music library
that sounds
great!

network

FILM AND
TELEVISION

TOP

Bullet. *The Hanged Man*. Contour (UK): 2870 437, 1975. Features library music by Alan Tew.

BOTTOM

The Simon Park Orchestra. *Eye Level*. Studio 2 Stereo (UK): TWOX 1009, 1973. A soundtrack to the television show *Van Der Valk* featuring the unlikely De Wolfe number one hit "Eye Level."

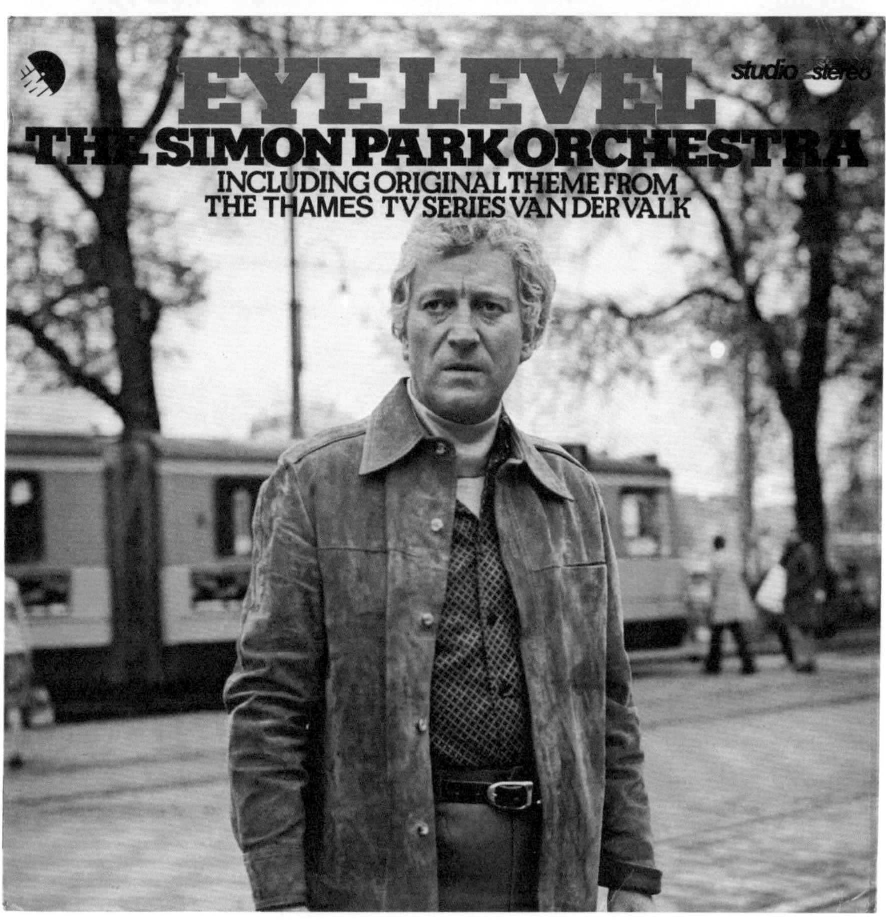

BELOW

A 1972 NFL Monday Night Football Media Guide, published by the Savings and Loan Foundation, Inc.

OPPOSITE

Croatian-language movie poster for the 1981 Italian-Spanish comedy *There Is a Ghost in My Bed*. Dir: Claudio de Molinis (Claudio Giorgi). Music: Piero Umiliani.

PAGE 292

Poster for the 1968 exploitation classic *Sweden: Heaven and Hell*, which famously featured the first appearance of Piero Umiliani's "Ma Nàh Ma Nàh." Dir: Luigi Scattini. Music: Piero Umiliani.

PAGE 293 TOP

Sweden: Heaven and Hell lobby card, 1968.

PAGE 293 BOTTOM

Poster for 1966's *War Italian Style*. Dir: Luigi Scattini. Music: Piero Umiliani.

ITALIJANSKA LJUBAVNA KOMEDIJA
DISTRIBUCIONI – DISTRIBUCIJA
Kosovafilm
PRISHTINË – PRIŠTINA
IMAM DUHA
U KREVETU
LILLI CARATI RENZO MONTAGNANI
VINCENZO CROCITTI LUCIANA TURINA
REŽIJA: CLAUDIO DE MOLINIS
«Rilindja»

SWEDEN...
Where The Facts Of Life Are Stranger Than Fiction!

SEE: "The Love Cruise"! A training trip for turned-on teens! **SEE:** "The Bachelorette Party"! A bride-to-be's last fling! **SEE:** "The Public Library Of Private Thrills"! Government erotica! **SEE:** "Moonlighting Nudes"! Meter-maids by day—models at night! **SEE:** "The Swap Shop"! A trade-in deal for married couples only! **SEE:** "The Polar Bare Club"! The world's most beautiful snow-girls! **SEE:** "Stockholm Strip"! A Haven For Hippies, Where Everything Is Free! **SEE:** "Communal For Survival"! The radiation-proof city beneath a city! **SEE:** "The Eden Of Sweden"! Where Adam finds Eve in naked innocence! **SEE:** "Stockholm's Students"! A love generation that practices what it preaches!

69/252

Herres
KAPP-AHL
Hatts
TOALETT
SHH-13
Copyright ©1969, Avco Embassy Pictures Corp. All rights reserved. Permission granted for Newspaper and Magazine reproduction. Made in U.S.A.
SWEDEN – HEAVEN AND HELL
An Avco Embassy Release
IN COLOR
"Property of National Screen Service Corp. Licensed for display in connection with the exhibition of this picture at your theatre. Must be returned immediately thereafter."
69/252

THE KING OF KOMEDY HAS ANZIO IN HIS PANZERS
BUSTER KEATON
Kommands the
Kookiest Kampaign
that ever
fractured
North Laffrica!
AMERICAN INTERNATIONAL presents
WAR
italian
Style
IN TECHNICOLOR® AND TECHNISCOPE
STARRING
BUSTER KEATON · FRANCO & CICCIO · MARTHA HYER · AND SPECIAL GUEST STAR FRED CLARK
produced by FULVIO LUCISANO · directed by LUIGI SCATTINI · AN AMERICAN INTERNATIONAL RELEASE
COPYRIGHT © 1966 AMERICAN INTERNATIONAL PICTURES
All Rights Reserved Printed in U.S.A.
66/390

BELOW

VHS copy of 1977's *Barbara Broadcast*. Dir: Radley Metzger. Music: Various (includes Madeline Bell, Brian Bennett, Alan Hawkshaw, Keith Mansfield, Alan Tew, Stefano Torossi).

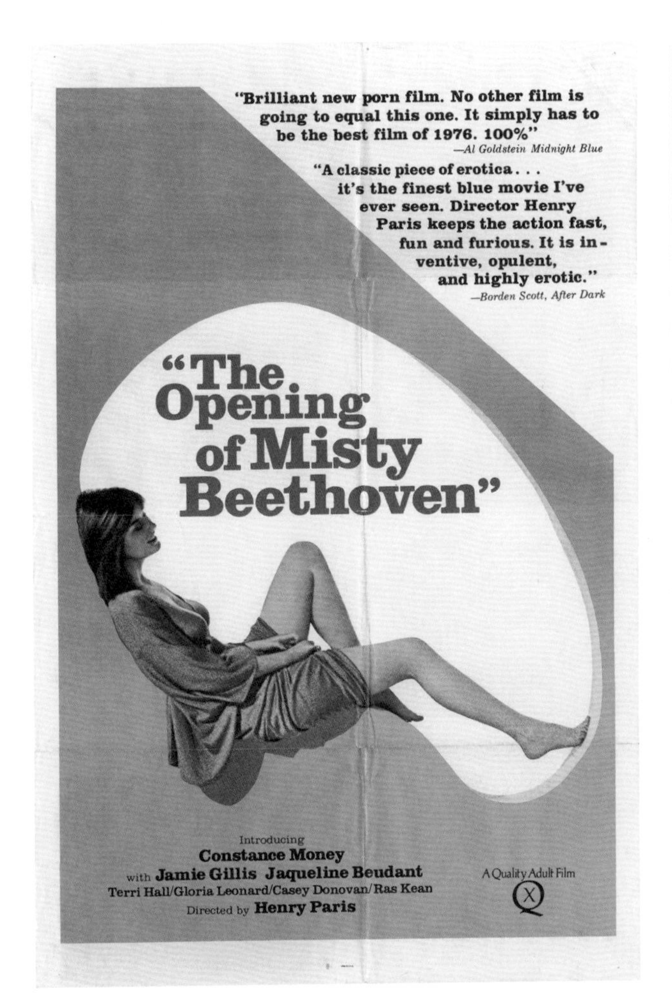

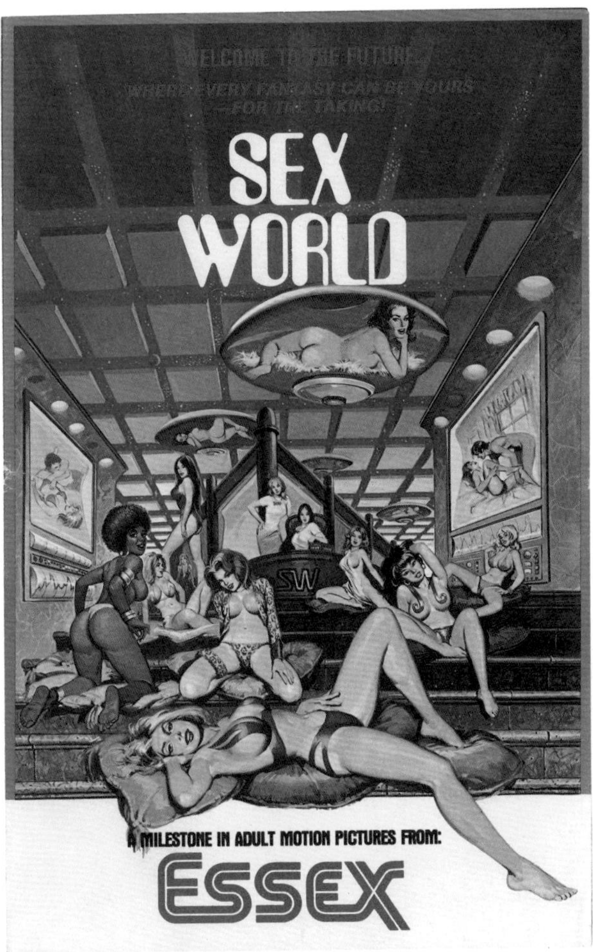

ABOVE LEFT

Poster for 1976's *The Opening of Misty Beethoven*. Dir: Radley Metzger. Music: Various (includes John Cameron, Brian Bennett, and Alessandro Alessandroni).

ABOVE RIGHT

Press kit cover for 1978's *Sex World*. Dir: Anthony Spinelli. Music: Berry Lipman (and numerous library selections).

SUPERSTAR INTERNATIONAL presenta
SEXOMANIA
con ANNETTE HAVEN · LESLIE BOVEE · SHARON THORPE · DESIREE WEST · AMBER HUNT
JOHN LESLIE · JACK WRIGHT · KENT HALL · SUZETTE HOLLAND · CAROLE TONG · JOEY CIVERA
prodotto da BILLY THORNBERG · diretto da ANTHONY SPINELLI · musiche di BERRY LIPMAN · EASTMANCOLOR

OPPOSITE

Sexomania movie poster. Italy, 1974. Dir: Dimitris Papakonstadis, Mario Regi (Marios Retsilas). Music: Berry Lipman.

BELOW

Orgasmo movie poster. Italy, 1969. Dir: Umberto Lenzi. Music: Piero Umiliani.

PAGE 296

Poster for the Shaw Brother's 1978 classic *Handlock*. Kung fu films of the decade (along with Italian giallo horror, US blaxploitation, and pornographic “blue movies”) were among the most prominent film clients of the library music industry. Dir: Ho Meng Hua. Music: Pierre Arvay, Frankie Chan, Ivor Slaney.

PAGE 297

Poster for the Shaw Brothers' 1979 *The Kung Fu Instructor*. Dir: Sun Cheung. Music: Ronald Marquisee, Jack Trombey, Eddie Wang.

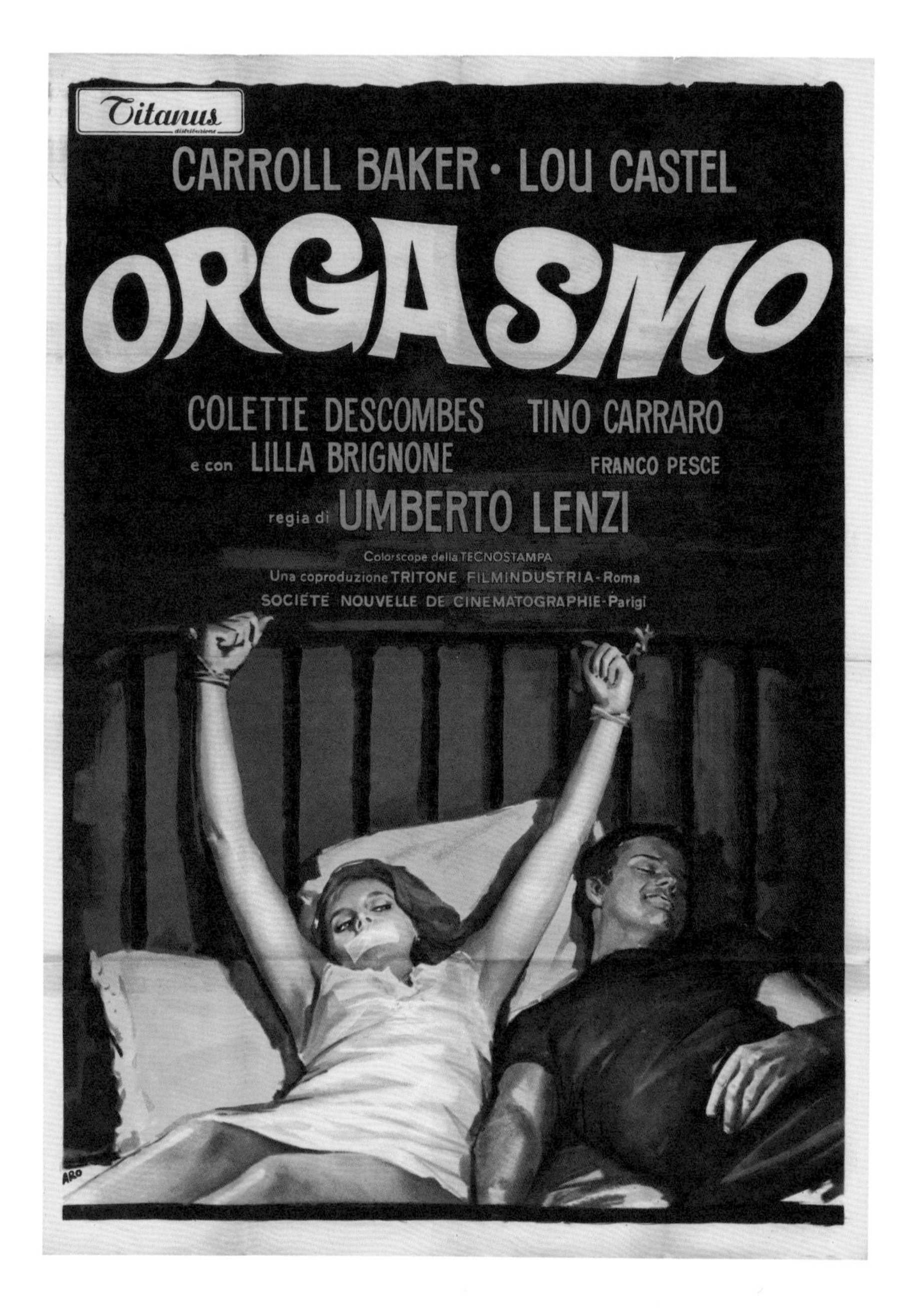

THE WHEELS OF DEATH ARE IN MOTION!

HANDLOCK

A SHAW BROTHERS PRESENTATION

Starring LI CHENG-YING • LING HAO • LI PAI

Directed by HO MENG-HUA • Produced by SIR RUN RUN SHAW

A WRLD NORTHAL FILM

DESIGN • CINEMA HORIZONS / NEW YORK

IF YOU LEARN WELL...
YOU STAY ALIVE!
The Final Test
"THE CIRCLE OF DEATH"
Starring
TI LING &
WANG YU
THE KUNG FU
INSTRUCTOR
A SHAW BROTHERS PRESENTATION
R NO ONE UNDER 17 ADMITTED WITHOUT PARENT OR GUARDIAN
A WORLD NORTHAL FILM
COPYRIGHT 1983 WORLD NORTHAL CORPORATION—ALL RIGHTS RESERVED

YOU HAVE'NT LIVED UNTIL
YOU'VE FOUGHT-
DIRTY HO
...AND THEN YOU'RE DEAD!
A SHAW BROTHERS
PRESENTATION
Starring GORDON LIU
THE MASTER KILLER
A WORLD NORTHAL FILM
R RESTRICTED
Under 17 requires accompanying Parent or Adult Guardian
COPYRIGHT 1981 WORLD NORTHAL CORPORATION
ALL RIGHTS RESERVED
DESIGN BY CINEMA HORIZONS • NEW YORK
A DIVISION OF SHORLANE-BENET ADVERTISING
DIRTY HO

OPPOSITE

Dirty Ho movie poster, 1976. Dir: Chia-Liang Liu. Music: Reg Tilsley, Eddie Wang.

BELOW LEFT

Thai-language poster for the 1978 Shaw Brothers film *Buddha's Palm*. Dir: Taylor Wong. Music: Sam Spence.

BELOW RIGHT

The Unbeatable Dragon movie poster, 1978. Dir: Chang Cheh. Music: Eric Towren.

TOP

Promotional photo from the US television series *In Search Of...* featuring star Leonard Nimoy, 1982. Music: Michael W. Lewis, Laurin Rinder.

BOTTOM

Poster for the UK television series *Space: 1999*, 1975. Music: Vic Elms, Barry Gray, Big Jim Sullivan, Derek Wadsworth.

OPPOSITE

The 1978 Fan Club Annual for the German sci-fi television series *Star Maidens*. Music: Berry Lipman.

PAGES 304-305

Interior spread from the 1978 *Star Maidens* annual.

STAR MAIDENS

filmax
WILLIAM BERGER · IRA FÜRSTENBERG
EDWIGE FENECH · HOWARD ROSS
5 MUÑECAS
PARA LA
LUNA DE AGOSTO
DIRECTOR
MARIO BAVA
EASTMANCOLOR
DEPOSITO LEGAL B.26155-1972
GRAFICAS BOBES, S. A. - Paris, 159 - BARCELONA

OPPOSITE

Spanish-language poster for Mario Bava's 1970 *giallo* horror film *5 Dolls for an August Moon*. Music: Piero Umiliani.

BELOW

Italian-language movie poster for 1972's *Tales from the Crypt*. Dir: Freddie Francis. Music: Douglas Gamley, Nicolas Kynaston.

RIGHT

American poster for Freddie Francis' *Tales from the Crypt*.

OPPOSITE PAGE AND FOLLOWING SPREAD

Tales from the Crypt lobby cards.

3
COPYRIGHT ©1972 CINERAMA RELEASING
LITHO. IN U.S.A.
TALES FROM THE CRYPT
72/80

4
COPYRIGHT ©1972 CINERAMA RELEASING
LITHO. IN U.S.A.
TALES FROM THE CRYPT
72/80

7
COPYRIGHT ©1972 CINERAMA RELEASING
LITHO. IN U.S.A.
TALES FROM THE CRYPT
72/80

5
COPYRIGHT ©1972 CINERAMA RELEASING
LITHO. IN U.S.A.
TALES FROM THE CRYPT
Property of National Screen Service Corporation Licensed for use only in connection with the exhibition of this picture at the theatre licensing this material. Licensee agrees not to trade, sell or give it away, or permit others to use it, nor shall licensee be entitled to any credit upon return of this material. This material either must be returned or destroyed immediately after use.
72/80

ACKNOWLEDGMENTS

The author and editors wish to thank:

Alex Black, Amy Buckley, John Cameron, Song Chong, Chris Clarke, Peter Cox, Suzanne Desrocher, Romano di Bari, Fabio di Bari, Brian DiGenti, Jesper Eklow, Sarah Evans, Lorenzo Fabrizi, Cory Feierman, Ron Geesin, Chris Gibbons, Matthew Gutknecht, Alan Hawkshaw, Adrian Kerridge, Jennifer Lane, Maggie Linn, Keith Mansfield, Luke Moldof, Katie Murphy, Gerhard and Heidi Narholz, Allison Nichols, Janko Nilović, Felix Occhinero, Elisabeth Oei, Daylon Orr, Alan Parker, Brian Reitzell, George A. Romero, Beth Rudig, Paul Sandell, Ted Scotto, Colin Sheen, Wesley Stokes, Ben Swift, Adam Taylor, Sophia Tintori, Andre Torres, Edwina Travis-Chin, Alex Tults, Elisabetta Umiliani, Graham Walker, Adrian Younge.

In memory of George A. Romero and Adrian Kerridge.

INDEX

Pages numbers in *italics* refer to illustrations.

Activity/Travel/Dramatic (album), *129*
Agostini, Rémi, 204
Alan Tew Orchestra, 26
Alessandroni, Alessandro, 216, 233, 234, 257, *295*
Biologia Marina, 234
Il Tempo Dello Spirito, 218
Industriale, 235
Light and Heavy Industry, 235
Alex Bradford Singers, 109
Allen, Eric, *Sketches of Africa, 89*
Alter, Joe, *Fireball/The Barbershop, 285*
Amphonic Music, 72, *72,* 119, *119*
Annaud, Jean-Jacques, 196, 197
APM (Associated Production Music), 75
Argento, Dario, 15
Ariel Records, *246*
Ariola Studios, 37, 38
Ariston Records, 214
Arling, Arthur E., 8
Art Blakely and the Jazz Messengers, *Moonin',* 87
Arvay, Pierre, *297*
Ascher, Emil, 21
Ascot, Robert, *Release No. 10—Commercial Life Styles/Moog, 285*
Asher, James, *Flash Music, 64*
Aspel, Michael, 83
Atking, Ted, *Scoop, 141*
Atlantics, 121
Atmo, *Telegiornale, 216*
Austin, Derek, *Sound Stage 6: Pop-Jazz Fusion, 119*

Bacalov, Luis, *Musica Per Commenti Sonori Tratta dal Film "Il Prezzo del Potere", 226*
Baratas, Maxi, *Romantico, 181*
Barclay, 197
Barigozzi, Giancarlo, *Rock Scene, 251*
Barrett, Stan, *42*
Barrie Moore Combo, *Gemini, 122*
Baschet, Bernard, 192
Baschet, François, 192
Bass, Saul, 11
Bastow, Geoff, *Music to Varnish Owls By, 129*
Bastow, Trevor:
Kinetics/Vision, 83
Suspensions/Galaxy, 91
Bava, Mario, *307*
Baxter, Les, 99
Bugaloo in Brazil (aka *African Blue*), 24, 99, *99*
"Girl from Uganda," 99
"Johannesburg Blues," 99
BBC Coded Music Scheme, *129*
BBC Radiophonic Workshop, 100, *100,* 192
Beatles, 57, 78
Bee Gees, 121
Bell, Madeline, 108, 109, *294*
The Voice of Soul, 24, 103, 107, 108, *109*
"You've Got What It Takes," 18, 20
Bembo, Alberto Baldan, *Sound Orchestra, 264*
Bencker, Laszlo, *Robot Couture - Underscores 1, 143*
Bennett, Brian, 24, 27, 37, 45, 93, *294, 295*
Counterpoint, 93
Fantasia (aka *Voyage [A Journey into Discoid Funk]*), 24, *93*
Synthesizer and Percussion, 105
Benson, Simon:
String Tension, 65
Underworld, 83

Bernstein, Elmer, 42
Berry Music, 133, 137, 150
Birkin, Jane, 27
Bixio, Franco, 230
Black Rock Records, *270*
Bloch, Augustyn:
Unusual Sounds Vol. 1 - Reflections, 153
Unusual Sounds Vol. 2 - The Brain, 153
Blue Sharks, *It Became Crystal, 258*
BMG Production Music, 277
Bolling, Claude, *22*
Boneschi, Giampiero, 20, 21, 232, 251
Caratteristici, 232, 249
Flute and Electronics, 232
A New Sensation in Sound, 22
A New Sensation in Sound Vol. 2, 232
A New Sensation in Sound Vol. 4, 232
New Times Vol. 3, 208
Western 'n' Country Scene - Children's Land, 252
Boneschi Electronic Combo, *Sounds Electronic, 131*
Bonfanti, Franco, *Registrazioni Effettuate Per Commento Musicale Radio-Televisione - Film, 267*
Boosey & Hawkes, 24, 100, 126
Borreani, Gaston, *Rêve abyssal, 177*
Botkin, Perry, 91
Bouchéty, Jean, *Survival, 89*
Boulez, Pierre, 208
Bouvard, Philippe, 201
Braconi, Virgilio, *Videomusic N. 1, 264*
Brainticket, 24, 156, 159
Breuer, Harry, *Moog Is Moog, 190*
BRF Studio Group, *Musical Fantasy No 1, 264*
Broadway International, *264*
Brubeck, Dave, 228
Brugnolini, Sandro, *Feelings*, 231, *231*
Bruton Music, 24, 26, 27, 33, 55, 61, *61, 63, 64, 65*, 76, *77, 83, 84, 87, 89, 91*, 93, *93*
Bullet, *The Hanged Man, 289*
Byers, Betty, *Orchestral Shades, 278*

Cage, John, 126
Caiage, H., *Carnet Turistico, 216*
Caleidoscope (album), *271*
CAM (Creazioni Artistiche Musicali; Musical Artistic Creations), 21, *22*, 23, *199*, 222–24, *222, 223, 224, 226, 227*, 228, *228*, 230, 231, 232, 233, 234, 237, 251
Cameron, John, 24, 33, 37, 50, 52, 55–56, 86–91, *295*
Afro Rock, 24, 86, 91, 107
Atmospheric Chorale, 91
Badlands, 87
Explorer, 91
"49th Street Shakedown," 87
"Half-Forgotten Daydreams," 50, 87
Hot Doughnuts, 64
Jazzrock, 86, 87
Little Creatures, 63
Odyssey, 84
Sketches of Africa, 89
Survival, 89
Suspensions/Galaxy, 91
"Swamp Fever," 91
Voices in Harmony, 86, 87, 91
Candler, Norman, *see* Narholz, Gerhard
Canopo, *214*, 215, *216*, 220
Canopo Vintage, 30

Cantori Moderni, 233, 234
Capitol Hi-Q library, 14
Capitol Records, *285*
Cardius and Bordoni, *Sonor, 267*
Carlos, Wendy, *Switched-On Bach,* 190
Carosello, 231, *231*
Carpentier, Gilbert, 201
Carpentier, Maritie, 201
Casa, Daniela, 257, 263
America Giovane N. 2, 263, *263*
"Kentucky Fried Chicken," 263
"N.Y.C. 42nd," 263
Ricordi d'Infanzia, 221
Società Malata ("Sick Society"), 263
Catalano, Massimo, *Telemusica N. 2, 261*
Catamo, *see* Umiliani, Piero
Cavini, Victor, *Japan, 165*
CBS Records Australia, 121
Ceccarelli, André, *Rythmes, 113*
Cenacolo, *271*
Centemeri, Gian Luigi, 232
CGO Records, *268*
Chameleon, *Superdoop, 116*
Chan, Frankie, *297*
Chang Cheh, *301*
Chantreau, Marc, *Percussions & Company, 205*
Chappell Recorded Music Library, *131,* 277
Checkmates, 78, 79
Chia-Liang Liu, *301*
Chicago, 197
Chiti, Gian Paolo, *Risoluzioni Sonore, 257*
Ciak Records, *244*
Cinemaphonic: Electro Soul (album), 7
Cineriz, 230
Cinevox, *230*
Cipriani, Stelvio, 23, 222, 228
Anonimo Veneziano, 228
Anonimo Veneziano (*The Anonymous Venetian*), 228, *228*
Antla, 228
Metralleta Stein, 224
Tema Con Variazioni: "Patetico - Tensivo," 228
Clark, Petula, 257
Clarke, Charles G., 8
Clarke, James, 24
Televisual, 83, *84*
Classic, Satirical and Insane (album), 222
Claudric, Jean:
Escapade, 181
Génériquement votre, 180
CmL library, 23, 222, *222, 223, 224, 226, 227, 228*
Collective Consciousness Society (CCS), 86, 87
Coloursound, 20, 23, 24, 29, 156, *156, 159, 160, 161,* 163, *163,* 234, *235*
Coltrane, John, 86
Columbia Masterworks, *192*
Columbia Records, 114
Comedy (album), *84*
Complesso I Pazzi Virtuosi, *Musica Per Bambini, 264*
Complesso Strumentale I Panamera, *Rebus N. 4, 268*
Concert Hall, 206, *206*
Concert Pop Orchestra, *Melody All the Way, 119*
Conroy Recorded Music Library, *18,* 20, 23, *132,* 133, *133, 134,* 150, 231
Cordio, Carlo Maria, *Quips and Cranks, 226*
Cortese, Enrico:

Antica Grecia, 264
Video Musica N. 2, 261
Cosma, Vladimir, 206
Enfance, 206
Costanza, 231
Cox, Mike, *New Blood, 103*
Cox, Peter, 33, 34, 37, 38, *38,* 41, 42, 45–46, 50, *50,* 52–53, 57, 67–68, 72, 79, 83, 86, 87, 93, 94, 96, 98, 107, 108
Crea Sound Ltd., 173
Creazioni Artistiche Musicali, *see* CAM
Creeps (album), *114*
Cugat, Xavier, 202

Dahan, Pierre-Alain, *Percussions & Company, 205*
Dale, Sydney, 34, 42, 119
Inversions/Melody in Percussion, 124
Moodsetter, 119
Danger Mouse, 67
Dankworth, Johnny, *41*
Dany & Gepy, 263
Dany Records, *267*
Dave Clark Five, 58
Debray, Alain, *Variations on a Theme, 129*
de Carolis, Ettore, *Microdramas, 227*
Decca, 37, 71
Decerf, Jean-Pierre, *Thèmes Médicaux, 223*
de Filippi, Oronzo, 257
Meccanizzazione, 258
de Fillippi, Rino, *Tema: Amore, 272*
Delacour, Louis, 173, 197
Delfino, Franco, *Astrattismo, 274*
de Molinis, Claudio (Claudio Giorgi), *290*
Deneb Records, *216,* 220, 263
Deneuve, Catherine, 27
Derbyshire, Delia, 100, *100,* 126, 192
Electrosonic, 100
de Wolfe, Meyer, 112, *112*
de Wolfe, Rosalind, 112
Dibango, Manu, 206
di Bari, Fabio, 30
di Bari, Romano, 23, 30, 213–16, *213, 214,* 220, 224, 228, 230, 231, 234, 263
Dios Muñoz, Juan de, *Guitare classique, 188*
Dischi Montecarlo, 257, *257, 261*
DJM Records, *93*
Dockstader, Tod, 126
Eight Electronic Pieces, 126
Electronic series, 126, *126*
Recorded Music for Film, Radio & Television: Electronic Vol. 1, 126
Donovan, 86
Do You Like Dancing? (album), *226*
Dr. Dre, *Compton,* 182
Ducros, Remigio:
America Giovane, 263
T.S.T. '73 Cronaca, 258
Dwight, Reg, *see* John, Elton

Eastman, Marilyn, 14
Eastwood, Clint, 84
Ebonite, 282, *282*
Eddie Warner et sa musique tropicale, 202
Edibi, *232*
Ediphon, *264*
Éditions Montparnasse 2000, *see* Montparnasse 2000

Edizioni Bang Bang, *272, 274*
Elen, Richard, *Contact, 75*
Eliaron, *Video Musica N. 2, 261*
Elms, Vic, *302*
EMI Hamburg, 7, 23–24
Emil Ascher Inc., 278, *278*
Emil Ascher Library, 278
Emile Ford and the Checkmates, 78, 79
EMI Music, 7, *18,* 20, 23, 53, 55, 103, 137, 150
EMI Production Music, 20, 24, 165
Engel, Claude, *More Creative Pop, 179*
Epping, John:
  New Waves Underscores-Flow, 147
  Testimony to the Past Vol. 2, 146
Erwin Lehn Big Band, 163
Esposito, Carlo, *Natura e Musica N. 7, 258*
Estardy, Bernard, *Electronics, 204*

Fabor, Fabio, 251
  Pape Satan, 272
Farina, Sergio, *Western 'n' Country Scene - Children's Land, 252*
Farran, W. Merrick, *Cartoon Capers - Typical Cartoon and Animation Set, 44*
Farry, André, 173, 187, 197, 216
Fast (Motion and Dramatic Movements) (album), *143*
Feanch, Alan:
  Scoop, 141
  Electronics, 204
Fellini, Federico, 21, 126
Fèvre, Bernard, 202
Fiddy, J. *Industrial - Themes and Underscores Vol. 2, 147*
Finally... A Production Music Library That Sounds Great! (album), *285*
Flat, Gil, *Action Tracks, 156*
Fletcher, Guy, 79, 80
Flipper (Flipper Srl Edizioni Musicali; Flippermusic), 23, 213, 215–16, 220, 231
Flirt Records, *218,* 220, *221*
Flower Records, *218,* 220, *221*
Flowers, Herbie, *Bass Guitar and Percussion Volume 2, 44*
Fly Records, *268*
Folk, Robert, *Survival, 89*
Fonior Studios, 37, 93
Fonit, 232, 249, *249,* 263
Fonit-Cetra International Hi Fi, *249*
Fonit: Serie Usignolo, 249
Fontana, *264*
Four Freshmen, 234
Framond, Eric:
  Palpitations, 174
  Univers 2000, 174
Francis, Freddie, *307, 308*
Franko, Mladen, *Amazing Space Vol. 1, 139*
Friedkin, William, 15
Frizzi, Fabio, 230
  Amore Libero (Free Love), 230
Fulci, Lucio, 230
Fusco, Ugo:
  Beat in Ampex, 257
  Video Musica N. 2, 261

Gainsbourg, Serge, 27
Gallo, Gerard, *Suspense, 177*
Gamley, Douglas, *307*

Garfunkel, Art, 57, 91
Gazzini, Giancarlo, *Feelings,* 231, *231*
Geesin, Ron, 46, 94–98
The Electro-Composer, 95–96
Electrosound Volumes 1 and 2, 42, *44,* 94, 96–98, *96*
"Frenzy," 98
Music from 'The Body', 94, 96
"Song of the Wire," 98
"Syncopot," 96–97
Geldard, Bill, *Light and Shade, 129*
Gelmetti, Vittorio, 250
Musica Aleatoria-Collage-Memorie, 223
Gemelli, 233, 250, *250*
Gémignani, Vincent:
Modern Pop Percussion, 206, *206*
Musique pour un voyage extraordinaire, 206
Gentry, Bobbie, 87
"Ode to Billy Joe," 91
Gepy & Gepy, 263
Gésina, Michael, *Guitare classique, 188*
Giallo 2 (Suspence-Drammatico) (album), *227*
Gianni Safred & His Electronic Instruments, *Futuribile (The Life to Come), 255*
Giger, H. R., 156
Gilliam, Terry, 45
Giordano, Jacky, 23, 202
Pop-In... Devil's Train, 177
Giorgi, Claudio (Claudio de Molonis), *290*
Globevision, *267*
GNP Crescendo, 99, *99*
Goblin, 15
"God Rest Ye Merry Gentlemen" (song), 80
Golden Ring, *169*
Gotham Recording Studios, 126
Grandi, Eugenio:
String Tension, 65
Underworld, 83
Grand Prix, 257, *258*
Gray, Barry, *302*
Gray, Steve, 37, 38
Moodsetter, 119
Survival, 89
Televisual, 83, *84*
Graziosi, Arnaldo, *Registrazioni Effettuate Per Commento Musicale Radio - Televisione - Film, 267*
Greffenius, Gunter, 156
Gregor, Max, 26
Gregory, Johnny, 80
Grifo Records, *264*
Groupe de Recherches Musicales (Musical Research Group; GRM), 208, 281
Gruppo di Improvvisazione di Nuova Consonanza (Il Gruppo), 233, 250
Gruppo Sound, *Dancin', 221*
Guaraldi, Vince, 76

Haldenby, Ralph, *Wide World, 169*
Hall, Carlton, *Counterpont, 93*
Hallyday, Johnny, 199
Hancock, Herbie, 282
Hardman, Karl, 14, 15
Hardman and Associates, 14
Harper, Don, 45, 96
Harrison, John, 14–15
Harry, Aaron, 34, 46

Haskell, Jimmy, 87, 91
Have a Nice Day (album), *65*
Hawkshaw, Alan, 24, 26, 27, 33, 34, 41, 42, 50, 55, 78–84, *78,* 93, 122, *294*
Alan Hawkshaw's Universal Bulletin, 84
Beat Incidental, 71–72, *71*
"Beat Me 'Til I'm Blue," 79, 80
"Best Endeavors," 83–84
The Big Beat, 24, *75,* 79
"The Champ," 78, 80
"Chicken Man," 80, 83
"Countdown," 83
Friendly Faces, 79
"Girl in a Sports Car," 79
Kinetics/Vision, 83
"Love De-Luxe and Hawkshaw's Discophonia," 78
New Blood, 103
Odyssey, 84
The Rock Machine, 103
"Rocky Mountain Roundabout," 80
"Senior Thump," 79, 80
Synthesizer and Percussion, 105
Televisual, 83, *84*
Terrestrial Journey, 83
Underworld, 83
Henry, Pierre, 126, 133
Herrmann, Bernard, 14
"Hey Jude" (song), 18
Hicks, Clive, 37
"Highway Patrol" (song), 20
Hilton, Robert J., 206
Hingross, *Record for Murder, 274*
His Master's Voice, 232
Hodgson, Brian, 100
Electrosonic, 100
Hollander, David, 17–30
Holloway, Laurie, 80
Ho Meng Hua, *297*
Horse Shoe Records, *274*
Howgill, Patrick, 33
Humair, Daniel, *Drumo Vocalo, 180*
Hurdle, Les, 26
Hypnose (album), *179*
Hypothese (album), *179*

Iacoucci, Gerardo, *Symbolisme Psychédélique, 181*
I Gres, *I Gres Vol III, 267*
Illustration Musicale (IM), 23, 196, 197, 199, 202, *202*
IML (International Music Label), *see* International Music Label
Impress, 124, *124*
International Music Label (IML), 173, *179, 180, 181,* 192, *192*
International Parade (album), *252*
International Studio Orchestra, *Double or Quits,* 114, *114*
Intersound, *169*
Intimate Disco/Album 8 (album), *282*
Iota Music, *Background Music Library - Atmospheric Electronic, 129*
Iota Records, *129*
Island Records, 100
Italian Fantasy Orchestra, *Music for Relax, 255*

James, Dick, 57
Jarre, Jean-Michel, 281
Deserted Palace, 281, *281*
Oxygène, 281

Jay-Z, *The Blueprint 3,* 182
Jazzopators, 163
Jingles (album), *105*
Joel V.D.B., *see* Vandroogenbroeck, Joel
John, Elton, 57, 109
John Cacavas and His Orchestra:
  Music for Drama, 131
  Wild Side, 131
Johnny Moggi Quintet, *Hard Rhythms and Soft Melodys, 241*
Jones, Quincy, 46, 86
Jones, Terry, 45
Josef Weinberger, 24, 124
Jump Edizioni Musicali, 251
Jump Records, 251, *252*
JW Media Music, 124
JW Music Library, *124*
JW Theme Music, *124*

Kalma, Ariel, *Interfrequence, 174*
Keith, Robert, 33
Keith-Prowse-Maurice library, *see* KPM
Keith-Prowse Music, 33
Kerridge, Adrian, 33, 34, 37, 38, 41–42, 45, 53, 55, 56, 58, *58,* 93
Kimberly, Jan, *Release No. 12–Musical Weather Report, 285*
Kingsland, Paddy, *Moogerama,* 119
Kingsley, Gershon, *The In Sound from Way Out!,* 190
Klaus Doldinger Quartet, 163
KPM, 24, 26, 27, 30, 33–53, *34, 38, 41, 42, 44, 46, 49, 50,* 55, 57, *58,* 61, 67, 68, *69,* 71, *71,* 72, 75, *75,* 76, 78, 79, 80, 86, 87, 91, 93, 94, 96, *96,* 98, 99, 100, 103, 107, 108, 119, 165, 197
KPM 1000 (album), 24
KPM 1000 series, 20, 24, 27, 33, 37, *37,* 41–42, *44,* 58, 61, 100
KPM All-Stars, 24, 72, *78*
KPM Brownsleeves series, 20
Kubrick, Stanley, 15
Kynaston, Nicolas, *307*

Lai, Francis, 87
Lamont, Duncan, 52
  The Magic of Life, 77
Larry Robbins' Dynamic Drums Plus, *Larry Robbins' Dynamic Drums Plus, 132*
Larson, Claude, 165
  Digital Patterns, 144
  Far East Impressions Vol. 1, 144
  Middle East Impressions Vol. 1, 144
  Soundscapes Vol. 2, 144
Lasry, Jacques, 21, 192
  Chronophagie "The Time Eaters", 192, *192*
Lasry, Teddy, 23, 192
  More Creative Pop, 179
  + Ou-8000, 192
Lasry, Yvonne, 192
Latent Image, 14
Laurence, Zack, *Televisual,* 83, *84*
La Voce del Padrone, 232
Led Zeppelin, 86
Le Monde, *264*
Len Turner Band, 110
Leonardi Edizioni SRL, 257
Leonardi Records, 257, *258*
Leone, Sergio, 233
Leo Records, 257, *258,* 263, *263*

Leroux, Alain, *India West - Indies and Quebec, 223*
Les Structures Sonores Lasry-Baschet, 192
Musique démesurée, 192, *192*
Leuter, Cecil, 27
Pop Electronique: Les sons électroniques de Cecil Leuter, 20, *29*
Lewis, Michael W., *302*
Libaek, Sven, 121, 122
My Thing, 121
Solar Flares, 29, 121
Light Activity (album), *104*
Lipman, Berry, *295, 297, 302*
Liuto Records, 237, 239, *242, 244*
Loach, Ken, 86
Loore, Andy, *Water Show, 177*
Loose, Bill, *Soul/Action/Activity, 278*
Los Minus Hernandez, *Latin Friends, 255*
Lubat, Bernard, *More Creative Pop, 179*
Luciani, Antonio Ricardo, *Jazz in Libertà, 258*
Lupus Records, 257, *257, 258*

McAllister, David, *Fireball/The Barbershop, 285*
Madlib, 67
Madonne, Jean-Claude, *Beautiful World, 146*
Magnetic System, 230
Major Music, 199
Major Records Production Library, 7
Mallia, Sauveur, *Cosmosynthetic Vol. 2, 205*
Mansfield, Keith, 24, 33, 38, *38,* 41, 42, *42,* 45, 46, 49–50, *49, 50,* 52, 53, 55, 67–75, *69,* 107, *294*
Beat Incidental, 71–72, *71*
The Big Beat, 24, *75,* 79
"The Big Match," 45
Contact, 75
"Funky Fanfare," 71–72
"Grandstand," 72
"International Athletics," 45
"Light and Tuneful," 24
Night Bird, 72, *72*
Olympiad 2000, 49
"US Open Tennis," 45
Voices in Harmony, 86, 87, 91
Manusardi, Guido, *Electronic-Dance, 272*
Marietta, Leonardo, *Percussioni ed Effetti, 271*
Marino, Vittorio, *Fugue of Light, 226*
Marquisee, Ronald, *297*
Martin, Jacques, 199
Martin, Paul, *Little Creatures, 63*
Martino, Luciano, 228
Martinotti, Bruno, *Flute and Electronics, 232*
Mason, Derrick, *Technical Standpoint/Spice of Life, 44*
M.B.T. Soul, 196
Media Music, *285*
Meek, Joe, 58
Melodie, *271*
Mengo, Jerry, *Black Jack Party, 188*
Mercier, Frederic, *+ Ou-8000, 192*
Metropole Records, *261*
Metzger, Radley, *294, 295*
Micalizzi, Franco, 23
Miglioli, Paride, *Telemusica N. 3, 261*
Minuti, Enzo, *Themes for Flutes, 270*
Mirot, *Apprendista Hitchcock, 270*
Misraki, Paul, 22
Mitridate:

Caratteristici, 232, 249
New Times Vol. 3, 208
Mixed Grill (album), *264*
Modern Africa (album), *89*
Moggi, *see* Umiliani, Piero
Mohawks, 78
The Champ, 27, 80, *80*
Molino, Mario, 222
Mario Molino 1, 224
Montori, Sergio, *Risoluzioni Sonore, 257*
Montparnasse 2000, 20, 23, *24,* 29, 173, *173, 174, 177, 179,* 182, *182, 184, 185, 186,* 187, *188,* 190, *190,* 192, 197, *199,* 213, 216, 220, *246*
Montparnasse 2000 vous présente un échantillon de son catalogue (album), *173*
Mood Music, 197
Moods/Album 8 (album), *282*
Moods for Drama (album), *277*
Moog, Robert, 190
Moorehouse, Alan, 53
Moran, Mike, 26
Morand, Richard, *Black Jack Party, 188*
Morgan, Art, *Go-Go-Go!/Rhythm-Rhythm-Rhythm!, 124*
Morgan, Barry, 26
Bass Guitar and Percussion Volume 2, 44
Morgan Studios, 108
Morricone, Ennio, 23, 222, 233, 250
Ideato, Scritto e Diretto da Ennio Morricone, 233
Most, Mickie, 56
Musical Wildfire, A-Vol. 1: Pastoral (album), *141*
Music De Wolfe, 24, 112–14, *113,* 114, *114, 289*
Music Scene, 232, 251, *251, 252, 253, 255*
Musik Mosaik (album), *169*
Musikverlag Octave, *169*
Musique pour l'Image (MPI), 23, 206, *206*

Nanssen, Wolf, *New Waves Underscores - Flow, 147*
Nardini, Nino, 27, 122
Circus Parade, 174
Narholz, Gerhard, 27, 29, 133, 137, 149–54, *153, 154,* 156, 163
Biology, 148
Mini Takes Vol. 1, 144
Mini Takes Vol. 2, 144
Pollution, 148
Underwater Vol. 1, 140, 151
Underwater Vol. 2, 140, 151
The Walt Rockman Moog Moods, 134
Narholz, Robert, *148*
Narholz, Rotheide "Heidi," 137, 149, 151, *154*
Nascimbene, Mario, 7
Nazionalmusic, *272*
Neel, Agathe, *Romantico, 181*
Nelson, Oliver, 86
Network Production Music, *285*
Netzle, Klaus, *see* Larson, Claude
Neuilly, 20, 23, *29,* 173
Newman, Alfred, 8, 14
Newman, Jeff, *Impact Vol. 2, 143*
Newman, Tony, 71
New Southern Library, *84,* 122
New Tape, *264*
NFL Music Library, *285*
Nicolai, Bruno, *22,* 23, 233, 250
Nielsen, Henrik, *Release No. 6 - Beat Patterns, 285*
Nilović, Janko, 173, 182–87

Black Jack Party, 188
Chorus, 23, *186,* 187
Concerto pour un fou, 188
Pop Impressions, 182
Pop Shopin, 188
Psyc Impressions, 182, 187
Rythmes Contemporains, 23, *186,* 187, *220*
Soul Impressions, 184
Super America, 188
Supra Pop Impressions, 184
Un couple dans la ville, 185, 187
Underground Session, 220
Un homme dans l'univers, 185
Un piano dans l'ouest, 188
Vocal Impressions, 182
"Xenos Cosmos," 187
Nilsson, Harry, 91
Nimoy, Leonard, *302*
Northern Songs, 57

Octopus Records, *216,* 220, 228, 230, 234, *235*
Olympic Sound Studios, 80
Omega, 239
Omega International, *201*
Omicron, 237, 239, *239, 240, 241*
Omnimusic, 278, *285*
Oram, Daphne, 100
Orchestra Ollamar, *Atmosfere, 249*
Orchestra R. de Filippi, *Atmosfere, 249*
Orly, *208*
ORTF, 208
Orti, E., *see* Nilović, Janko
Ortolani, Riz, 222
Andrea Doria 74, 224
Oscar Lindok's Orchestra, *The Rhythm of Life, 223*
Ostinazione (Piccola Serie Ritmica) (album), *264*
"Overture" (song), 12
Owens, Larry, *Dynamic Impressions, 278*

Paige, Patti, 12
Palmer, Craig, *American Panorama, 278*
Pama Records, 78, 80, *80*
Papakonstadis, Dimitris, *297*
Papworth, Keith, *Hard Hitter, 114*
Paris, Henry, 20
Parker, Alan, 24, 38, 45, 46, 49, 50, 52, 56, 79, 103, 107-8, 109, 119
Afro Rock, 24, 86, 91, 107
New Blood, 103
The Rock Machine, 103
The Sound of Soul, 103, *107,* 108
The Voice of Soul, 24, 103, 107, 108, *109*
"You've Got What It Takes," 108
Parmegiani, Bernard, 23, 208
Chants Magnétiques, 208, *208*
Parry Music Library, 277, *277*
Patchwork, 23, 192, *192*
Patucchi, Daniele, 222
Bani Drammatici, Violenti e Suspence, 224
Metralleta Stein, 224
Sweet and Sauvage Themes, 222
Temi Conduttori Sentimentali, 226
Pavone, Rita, 228
Pearson, Johnny, 34, 38, 50, 52, 53, 76
"Cast Your Fate to the Wind," 53

Cottage Industry/Safari Rally, 77
"Heavy Action," 45, 76
The Magic of Life, 77
Pedersen, Guy, *Suspense, 177*
Peer, Ralph S., 122
Peer International Library Limited, *121,* 122, *122*
Peermusic, 21, 29, 121, 122
Pellegrino, Nunzio, *Natura e Musica N. 7, 258*
Pépé Luiz y su Orquesta Hispana, 173
Perrey, Jean-Jacques, 20, 173, 190
The In-Sound from Way Out!, 190
see also Prilly, Pat
Perrey, Patricia Leroy, 190
see also Prilly, Pat
Persuasive Jazz/Album 1 (album), *282*
Perugini, Anton Giulio, 215
Peter Maurice Publishing, 33
Peters, Jean, 8
Peymont:
Cibernetica, 216
Videomusic N. 1, 264
Pezin, Slim, *Percussions & Company, 205*
Phillips, 197
Phillips, Jimmy, 34, 55, 83, 87, 96
Phillips, Peter, 34
Phillips, Robin, 33, 34, 38, 42, 45, 46, 50, 52, 53, 55–56, 57, 58, *58,* 61, *61,* 71, 72, 79, 80, 83, 93, 96, 107-8
Pink Floyd, 94, 98
Atom Heart Mother, 94
Polydor, 197
Polygram, 197
Pony, *268*
Porte, Pierre, *Le Monde du Music Hall, 223*
Powell, Michael, 11
Power, Tyrone, 8, 13
Prado, Pérez, 202, 257
Preminger, Otto, 11
President Records, 282
Price, Ronnie, 80
Prilly, Pat, 20, 190
Moog Expressions, 190
Moog Generation, 190
Moog Is Moog, 190
Prindy, Mac, *New Waves Underscores - Flow, 147*
"Prison Escape" (song), 12
Programme Music, *129*
Pro Viva Productions, 150
Prowse, William, 33
Psichedelico - Introspettivo - Flash-Back (album), 222
PSI library, 206, *208*
Pye Records, 24, 53

Quintetto Record TV, *Serie Jazz, 264*

Rathbone, Basil, 8
RCA, 21, 23, 197, 213, 215, 216, 220, 228, 234
RCA Italiana, 213–14, *213,* 215, 228, *233,* 234
Record TV Discografica, *264*
Redmond, Edgar, *Soul/Action/Activity, 278*
Rees, Gordon, 34
Reflections (album), *83*
Regi, Mario (Marios Retsilas), *297*
Renosto, Paolo, *Medioevo & Rinascimento, 258*
Retsilas, Marios (Mario Reg), *297*
Rhombus, *234*

Rhythmic Underscores - Solo Instruments (album), *132*
Richard, Cliff, 27
Richardson, Joe, 34
Richardson, Neil, 37
  "Approaching Menace," 46
Richford, Jay, *see* Roelens, Puccio
Richmond, Dave, 37
Ricotti, Frank, 26
Ridley, Judith, 14
Rinder, Laurin, *302*
Robbins, Larry, *Larry Robbins' Dynamic Drums Plus, 132*
Robert, Marie-Claude, *Supranatural, 177*
Rocchi, Oscar, *Rock Scene, 251*
Rock & Roll/Album 26 (album), *282*
Rock Comedy (album), 80
Rockman, Walt, *see* Narholz, Gerhard
Roelens, Puccio, 231
  Feelings, 231, *231*
Roger, Roger, 7
  Circus Parade, 174
Roger Spell Ensemble, *Untitled, 129*
Rolling Stones, 78, 79
  "You Can't Always Get What You Want," 109
Roman Record Company, *272*
Romantic Wood, The (album), *104*
Romero, Anne Dvorsky, 8, 12
Romero, Cesar, 8
Romero, George A., 7–16, *11,* 24, 112
Rota, Nino, 21, 222
Roubaix, François de, 22, *23*
Rouge Music, 112, *116*
Rovi, *see* Umiliani, Piero
Royal Artillery Band and Orchestra, 76
Rozsa, Miklos, 11
Rubba, *Some Shufflin', 116*
Rubenstein, Seymour, *Orchestral Shades, 278*
Rubinstein, Donald, 14–15
Ruocco, Massimo, *Construction, 222*
Russell, Ray, *Master Format, 124*
Rustichelli, Carlo, 23
  Metralleta Stein, 224

St. Germain des Prés, 23, 173, *181,* 213, 216
St. Paul, Stephen, *Atmospheric Chorale, 91*
Sam Fox Productions, 281, *281*
Sammy Burdson Group, *Space Fiction, 139*
Sander, Peter, *Technical Standpoint/Spice of Life, 44*
Santucci, Cicci, *Looking Around, 268*
Sariputra, Rahul, *India West-Indies and Quebec, 223*
Sauvage, Camille, 23, 173
  Circus Parade, 174
  Fantasmagories, 24
Savina, Carlo, 251
Sax, Sidney, *42*
Sbordoni, Alessandro, *Incantation, 222*
Scalamogna, Giampiero, 263
Scattini, Luigi, *290*
Scenesetters-Fanfares and Punctuations (album), *44*
Schaeffer, Pierre, 133, 208, 281
Schmidt, Willy, 150
Scoppa, Enzo:
  Looking Around, 268
  Traffico, 272
  Untitled, 129
Scoring House, 57

Scott, John, 38
"Gathering Clouds," 45
Scotto, Ted, *see* Tregger, Yan
Screen International, 52
Selected Sound, 20, 23, 163, 165, *165*
Serio, Renato, *Impressioni, 268*
Sex Pistols, 34
Sforzando, 187
Shadows, 27, 93
Shaw Brothers, 112, *297, 301*
Shepherds Bush Library Music, *129*
Simon, Paul, 57
Simon and Garfunkel, 91
"59th Street Bridge Song," 91
Simon Park Orchestra, 114
Eye Level, 289
Siroul, Jacques, *Midway, 181*
Slaney, Ivor, *297*
Slow (Motion and Movement) (album), *143*
Smith, Jimmy, 79
Snell, David:
Cottage Industry/Safari Rally, 77
On the Side of the Angels, 129
String Tension, 65
Underworld, 83
Soft Moods for Romantic Sequences (album), *156*
Solid Gold (album), 72
Sonimage, 192
Sonopress, 37
Sonoton, 7, 23, 27, 133, *134,* 137, *137, 139, 140, 141, 143, 144, 146, 147, 148,* 149, 150, *153,* 156, 163, *163*
Sonoton Authentic Series (SAS), 27
Sonoton SON series, 27, 29
Sony/ATV Music Publishing, 33
Sorgini, Giuliano, 216, 257
Natura e Musica N. 7, 258
Souffriau, Arsène, 133
Sound Games Orchestra, *Games Power, 253*
Sounds Orchestral, 76
Sound Work Shop, 239, *240, 242, 243*
Southern Library of Recorded Music, 122, *122*
Southern Music Publishing Company, 24, 29, 121, 122
see also Peermusic
Space Craft's Men, *Adventures, 253*
Spence, Sam, 5, *301*
All Systems Go/The Coming Conflict, 285
Spinelli, Anthony, *295*
Spinning Wheel, *Lorry Load, 113*
Spots (album), *169*
Springfield, Dusty, 109
Standard Music Library, 100, *129*
Star Track, *264*
Stelvio Cipriani e La Sua Orchestra, *Antla, 228*
Stereo Tape AG, *165*
Stevan, Gary, *see* Gazzini, Giancarlo
Stockhausen, Karlheinz, 126, 208
Stoeckart, Jan, *see* Trombey, Jack
Strauss, Johann, 124
Stringtronics, *Mind Bender,* 21, *122*
Studio 2 Stereo, *289*
Studio M, 26
Studio One, 133, 150
Stylissimo (album), *174*
Sugar Hill Gang, "Rapper's Delight," 78
Sullivan, Big Jim, 107, *302*

Sun Cheung, *297*
Supertramp, 197
Sven Libaek and His Orchestra, *121*
  see also Libaek, Sven
Swan, Eric, *100% Electronic, 202*
Syd Dale Orchestra, *Where the Action Is, 119*
Sylvester, 206

Tamborrelli, Aldo:
  Construction, 222
  Entertainment Show, 222
Tamponi, Franco, *Un Volto Una Storia, 218*
Tape, Tony, *see* Narholz, Gerhard
Tele Music, 204, *204, 205*
Telesound, 239, *244*
Tempera, Vince, 230
Tew, Alan, 18, 26, 110, *289, 294*
  "The Big One," 110
  Drama Suite volumes 1 and 2, 26, 110, *110*
Themes International Music, 20, 24, 26, 29–30, 76, 103, *103, 104, 105,* 107, *107,* 108, *109, 110,* 119
Thomas, Peter, *The Electric Stringmobile, 124*
Tilsley, Reg, *301*
Timperley, John, *50*
Titian Records, *270*
Tokarz, Roger, 204
Tommasi, Amedeo:
  Carnet Turistico, 216
  Flash Internazionale - Servizi Speciali, 215
  Il Mondo dei Bambini, 231
Torossi, Stefano, 231, *294*
  Beat in Ampex, 257
  Feelings, 231, *231*
  Il Mondo dei Bambini, 231
Towren, Eric, *301*
Translation (album), *179*
Tregger, Yan (Ted Scotto), 173, 196–201
  Bubble Bubble b/w Sea Love Trumpet, 201
  "Bubble Bubble" b/w "Sea Love Trumpet," 196, 199, 201
  Pictures (Pop Sound), 197, 199, *199*
  The Pop World of Yan Tregger, 196, 199, *202*
  Rhythmiques Statiques, 199
  Stories, 195, *199*
Tremblay, Dominique, *India West - Indies and Quebec, 223*
Trixi Studio, 37, 150
Trombey, Jack, *297*
  "Eye Level," 114, *289*
  Spinechiller, 114
"Tubular Bells" (song), 15
Tusco, *see* Umiliani, Piero

UBM Records, *169*
Umiliani, Piero, 7, 216, 237, *237,* 239, *290, 307*
  Angeli Bianchi... Angeli Meri, 239
  Atmospheres, 241
  Chitarra Classica, 242
  Double Face, 244
  Fascismo e Dintorni, 244
  Guerre et Destruction 1, 246
  Guerre et Destruction 2, 246
  L'Uomo e La Città, 244
  L'Uomo Nello Spazio, 239
  "Mah Nà Mah Nà," *290*
  Motivi Allegri e Distensivi, 243
  News! News! News!, 242

Paesaggi, 244
Paesi Balcanici, 240
Panorama Italiano, 240
Piano Fender Blues, 240
Storia e Preistoria, 240
Suspence Elettronica, 244
Sweden: Heaven and Hell (Original Motion Picture Soundtrack), *246*
Tensions, 243
Tra Scienza e Fantascienza, 240
Unit Eight, *Glass Head, 116*
Universal, 20, 29
Usignolo, 249

Valentino, Thomas and Frank, 7
Vandroogenbroeck, Joel, 24, 159
Biomechanoïd, 156, *158*
Birth of Earth, 159
L'Immagine del Suono, 218
Lost Continents, 160
Meditations Vol. 2, 161
Mesopotamia Egypt, 160
Video Games & Data Movements, 161
Vann, Eric, *see* Vandroogenbroeck, Joel
VDB Joel, *see* Vandroogenbroeck, Joel
Video Moods, 278
Videovoice, 239, *244*
Viger, Robert, 206
Vinciguerra, Franco, *Quips and Cranks, 226*
Voraus, David, 100
Electrosonic, 100
Voyage, 204

Wadsworth, Derek, *302*
Wale, Reginald G., *Go-Go-Go!/Rhythm-Rhythm-Rhythm!, 124*
Walker, Graham, 26, 107
Wang, Eddie, *297, 301*
Warner, Eddie, 23, 133, 199, 202
100% Electronic, 202
"Warning, A" (song), 12
Wary, Cecil, *Scoop, 141*
Waters, Roger, 94
Watkins, Derek, 37, 53
Watts, Jon, *New Blood, 103*
Weinberger, Josef, 124
Weiss, Klaus, 156, 163
Open Space Motion, 163
Sound Inventions, 20
Sound Music Album 28, 169
Time Signals, 20, *165*
Trailers Spots Signatures, 163
Westway Studio Orchestra, *Industry (Light), Industry Heavy, 122*
White, Barry, 197
White, Claudine, *Folklore, 179*
White, Daniel J.:
Folklore, 179
Vin, bière et carnaval, 177
White Noise, 100
An Electric Storm, 100
"Whole Lotta Love" (song), 86
Wiffin, Lawrence, *Thèmes Médicaux, 223*
Wonder, Stevie, 86, 282
Wong, Taylor, *301*
Wood, Doug, 278

Xenakis, Iannis, 208

Yan Tregger Group, 199, 202
  The Pop World of Van Tregger, 196, 199, *202*
Young, Victor, 14

Zalla, *see* Umiliani, Piero
Zanagoria, *Insight Modulation, 250*
"Zarathustra" (song), 15
Zerand, King, *Improvvisi Musicale, 272*
Zivkovic, Branislav, *Moods for Flute, 156*
Zoffoli, Carlo, *Natura e Musica N. 7, 258*

First published in the United States of
America in 2018 by Anthology Editions, LLC

87 Guernsey Street
Brooklyn, NY 11222

anthologyeditions.com

Creative Directors: Keith Abrahamsson and
Johan Kugelberg
Art Director: Bryan Cipolla
Design: Nicholas Law
Cover and section headings designed by
Robert Beatty

Proofreader: Chris Peterson
Index: Cohen Carruth, Inc.

Photography and artwork: Collection of
David Hollander

Additional images courtesy of: APM Music (pp.
102-106, 109-11, 118 top), BBC Photo Library
(p. 101), Bruton/APM (pp. 60-65, 77, 82,
84-85, 87-90, 92 bottom, 120-23), John Cameron
(p. 86), Peter Cox (p. 57), De Wolfe Music
(pp. 112-15), Romano di Bari (pp. 213-14,
217-19), Everett Collection (p. 9), Flipper
SRL (p. 218 bottom), Chris Gibbons (pp. 36, 44
top, 47, 62-63, 116, 120, 122, 123, 127, 132
top, 133, 138, 156, 164 top row, 166, 194-95,
202-203, 207, 229 bottom right, 235, 238-39,
240 bottom right, 242 top, 249, 256-59,
262-65, 267-69, 270 top, 271-73, 274 bottom),
Gerhard Narholz (pp. 137, 149, 152, 155), Paul
Sandell (pp. 39-40, 43, 48, 51, 54, 59, 61,
69, 76, 78), Sonoton Music International (pp.
139-41, 142 top row, 144, 147 top, 148, 153
top), Elisabetta Umiliani (236-37), Universal
Production Music (130-31, 183-89, 202-203)

First Edition
ARC 048
Printed in China

ISBN: 978-1-944860-12-7
Library of Congress Control Number: 2018933443